DATE DUE

ATLANTIC CONVOYS
· AND ·
NAZI RAIDERS

ATLANTIC CONVOYS
· AND ·
NAZI RAIDERS

The Deadly Voyage of HMS *Jervis Bay*

BRUCE ALLEN WATSON

 PRAEGER

Westport, Connecticut
London

Library of Congress Cataloging-in-Publication Data

Watson, Bruce, 1929–
   Atlantic convoys and Nazi raiders : the deadly voyage of HMS Jervis Bay /
Bruce Allen Watson.
      p. cm.
   Includes bibliographical references and index.
   ISBN 0–275–98827–9 (alk. paper)
   1. Jervis Bay (Ship)   2. Admiral Scheer (Cruiser)   3. World War, 1939–1945—
Naval operations, British.   4. World War, 1939–1945—Naval operations, German.   5.
Naval convoys—History—20th century.   6. World War, 1939–1945—Atlantic Ocean.
I. Title.
   D772.J4W37 2006
   940.54'293—dc22   2005019271

British Library Cataloguing in Publication Data is available.

Library of Congress Catalog Card Number: 2005019271
ISBN: 0–275–98827–9

First published in 2006

Praeger Publishers, 88 Post Road West, Westport, CT 06881
An imprint of Greenwood Publishing Group, Inc.
www.praeger.com

Printed in the United States of America

The paper used in this book complies with the
Permanent Paper Standard issued by the National
Information Standards Organization (Z39.48–1984).

10 9 8 7 6 5 4 3 2 1

Copyright Acknowledgment

Photograph 4, attributed to the book *Pocket Battleship: The Story of the Admiral Scheer*, by
Theodor Krancke and H. J. Brennecke, originally published by William Kimber, London,
was reproduced for use in this study. A good faith search has been made for the copyright holders but to no avail. If the holder is eventually found, credit will be given in any
future edition of this book.

CONTENTS

CONTENTS

Photo sections follow page 30 and page 99.

PREFACE

In November 1940, the British Armed Merchant Cruiser HMS *Jervis Bay*, escorting a convoy from Halifax, Nova Scotia, was blownout of the water by the German pocket battleship *Admiral Scheer*. At that time, I was eleven years old, living in San Francisco a few blocks from the bay—about as far removed from the action as one can imagine. Despite the enormity of World War II, which shaped the psyches of so many of us who lived during those years, that single naval action is one I have always remembered.

The reasons for that persistence of memory are simple enough. A few of my friends and I were consumed by what was happening in Europe. In 1938, we posted a large map of Spain on a basement wall, pretending we understood the ever-changing Spanish civil war battlefronts. In 1939, we were horrified when the Nazis invaded Poland and cheered when Britain entered the war. We wanted to join the Royal Air Force and fight the Nazi horde. Age notwithstanding, that was no more than a romantic fantasy because we knew nothing about war much less what was really happening to the RAF Hurricane and Spitfire fighter pilots during the Battle of Britain. We did know that times were dangerous and filled with noble deeds.

Then the news broke about *Jervis Bay*. My friends viewed the battle as heroic but inconsequential. I was riveted by the story; it stirred some personal idealizations, no little imagination, and some family history. I grew up in San Francisco enjoying the sights and sounds of the Embarcadero, experiences reinforced by the sea novels of Howard Pease, the stories I read in one of my father's books about Sir Francis Drake and Horatio Nelson, and

Lowell Thomas's biography of Count Felix von Luckner, the German sea raider of World War I. I loved the smells and bustle of Fisherman's Wharf as it was then, counterpointed by the stately elegance of the Marina Yacht Harbor. When the United States entered the war I would walk the few blocks from our apartment to the little beach between the yacht club and the Presidio to watch the constant parade of warships and cargo vessels passing through the Golden Gate. A friend who often accompanied me once remarked, "Every time we come here you look like you wish you were on one of those ships." He was right.

In 1944, at age fifteen, the desire to "ship out," to join the Merchant Marine, nearly overwhelmed me (but not my mother). Had I gone, I would have stepped into some rather large shoes. In the 1880s my grandfather left Scotland to spend his working life as a ship's steward, sailing from Liverpool for Cunard and White Star lines. My father followed him to sea in about 1906 but left in 1914, becoming a cavalry officer in Britain's New Army. I never knew much about their actual careers but an active imagination filled the gaps. More recently, upon my marriage, I met other men who made their living on the sea. One of them, my late father-in-law Gremur Eggertsson, an Icelander, captained rust bucket Boston fishing trawlers into the North Atlantic. The constant dangers he and his friends faced quickly gained my respect and admiration.

I must confess that heavy seas have never pounded my body. Never have I stood on a burning deck. No one has ever shot at me or sent a torpedo in my direction. My time on the water is limited to occasional boyhood forays into San Francisco Bay, to some crossings of the English Channel, and a mild trip to Norway across the North Sea. Thus, my connection to the oceanic life and more particularly to HMS *Jervis Bay* is based on sympathetic understanding, tenuous but quite genuine.

So what can be made of a fairly minor naval action that lasted only twenty-two minutes? Except for George Pollock's *The Jervis Bay*, based on survivor interviews, the memoir by Captain Theodor Krancke, commander of the *Admiral Scheer*, both published in the late 1950s, and Kenneth Poolman's 1985 survey *Armed Merchant Cruisers*, historians of the Battle of the Atlantic usually offer only brief descriptions of the attack by *Jervis Bay* against the pocket battleship—a few lines, a paragraph, perhaps a few pages (published too late for use here is *If the Gods Are Good: The Epic Sacrifice of the HMS Jervis Bay*, by Ralph Segman and Gerald Duskin, Annapolis, MD: Naval Institute Press, 2004). Brevity notwithstanding, the action has been anointed as legendary.

This study takes a different approach to the narrative. It begins with a synoptic history of armed merchant ships, reaching back to the days of privateering and coming forward to World War I, which gives a broad context for the topic of armed merchant cruisers. Further context is developed by the political and military events of the interwar years and the opening phases of World War II. This may be familiar territory to many readers but the presentation is shaped to give a better understanding of how and why the British used armed merchant cruisers at all and, within that frame work, provides a particular setting for the battle between the *Jervis Bay* and the *Admiral Scheer*. The challenge to British shipping by German surface raiders is discussed, and the role of armed merchant cruisers during the battle of the Atlantic is evaluated. The book ends with a memorial note to *Jervis Bay*.

Much of the material about the battle and the *Scheer's* subsequent chase of scattering merchant ships is based on archival material that has not been previously published. This includes sketch maps of the battle made by an American naval officer, eyewitness accounts of the sinking of *Jervis Bay*, and the *Scheer's* sinking of various merchant ships from the convoy. All this is supplemented by photos, many of which also have never been published. These add a note of reality to the history.

ACKNOWLEDGMENTS

The core of this book, the battle between the *Jervis Bay* and the *Scheer*, together with narratives about other armed merchant cruisers, owes much to archivists. For help with that material I owe thanks to Berit Pistoria of the Bundesarchive/Militärarchiv, Koblenz, the Bundesarchive, Freiburg, and the staff of Public Records Office, Kew, Richmond. The project might not have surfaced at all without the staff of the U.S. National Archives who found the U.S. Navy Intelligence Report about the battle. Most especially, I am indebted to Michael MacDonald, Research Archivist, Canadian National Archives, Ottawa. He met my several requests with great efficiency, providing illuminating documents and considerable advice. Although the photo sources are cited I think they deserve special notice because they met my continued inquiries with patience and cooperation, and provided some rare pictures. They include the U.S. National Archives Still Photo Center, the U.S. Naval Historical Center at the Washington Navy Yard, the Canadian Joint Forces Imagery Centre, Ottawa, the Haupstaatsarchiv, Stuttgart, the National Museum of American History of the Smithsonian Institute, and Chris Plant, Curator, Photo Archive of the Imperial War Museum, London.

At a more personal level, Joe Marriott of New Brunswick Community College connected me to an e-mail family related to *Jervis Bay*. Thus, I am much indebted to Michael Chappell Kent, England. Our small conversations, his advice and enthusiasm, his review and corrections of portions of the manuscript, his continuing investigation of the exact size of Jervis Bay's crew, and the photos and other materials he supplied have been invaluable. Harold

ACKNOWLEDGMENTS

Wright of St. John Heritage has been helpful as well with photos and his regional connections. As with Mike, he embraced the project with enthusiasm.

My son Brian contributed by making maps from my sketch drawings and doing things with his computer that are beyond my understanding. My son John listened patiently, read portions of the manuscript, and offered sound advice. As always, my wife Marilyn bore the brunt of my writing, reading the manuscript again and again, spreading red ink over my paragraphs as she went. I could not have persevered for seven years without her support.

And I need to thank my daughter-in-law Quetta Garrison Watson for retyping the manuscript and transferring it to a disk.

CHAPTER 1

ARMED MERCHANT SHIPS: A BACKGROUND

TOWARD A CONTEXT

The German pocket battleship *Admiral Scheer* sank the British armed merchant cruiser HMS *Jervis Bay* in November 1940. This book is the story of that sinking—the tale of a converted passenger liner fighting one of the Nazi's most powerful ships, of old 6-inch guns versus new 11-inch guns, of a solitary escort vessel protecting a convoy against a deadly surface raider. Obviously, *Jervis Bay* did not stand a chance of surviving the battle; her crew's fatalistic bravery created awe among all those who witnessed the fight. Even a vivid imagination finds difficulty grasping the horror of it all. No wonder, then, that the battle is a great Royal Navy legend.

That the unlikely opponents met mid-Atlantic seems understandable, however tragic the outcome. *Jervis Bay* was squiring a convoy and the *Admiral Scheer* was hunting convoys, a simple enough equation as usually presented in most histories. But one thesis of this study is that the story is more complicated than that.

Both the necessity of arming a passenger liner and pretending it was a warship, and the building of the *Admiral Scheer* and her sister ships for the express purpose of commerce raiding, find their roots in the events, political decisions, rearmament policies, war plans, naval traditions, assumptions, and blunders that were abroad in prewar Britain and Germany. These events and mind-sets must be explored, however familiar some of the territory, to give historical context not only as a means of understanding how the two unequal ships met in battle, but why they did.

were the third group of English seamen, behind Sir Francis Drake and Thomas Cavendish, to circumnavigate the globe.

The expedition's overall prize value has been estimated at a million pounds sterling. But the East India Company filed suit, claiming ownership and the prize money was adjudicated by the courts. One of the crew was Alexander Selkirk, who, some years earlier and after a sharp disagreement with his ship's captain, had been voluntarily abandoned on the Juan Fernandez Islands off Peru. Woodes Rogers rescued Selkirk and made the castaway's tale a part of his own memoir. Thus was born an inspiration for Daniel Defoe's novel, *Robinson Crusoe*.

Britain again went to war with Spain and then with France between 1736 and 1748. Britain enlisted privateers to interdict her enemy's commerce on the Atlantic and in the West Indies. Although many privateers were commissioned in Britain, the assistance of her North American colonies was eagerly sought. On both sides of the Atlantic, the British commissioned 2,598 privateers.[3]

Sloops, single-masted with fore-and-aft rigging, or a ship carrying fewer than twenty-four guns on a single deck, were a favorite privateering vessel in the colonies. Available in considerable numbers, they were fast, did not require large crews, and drifted little from their heading in narrow waters—a great advantage when overtaking another ship. Their size varied from 20 to 40 tons, but larger sloops from 50 to 80 tons were preferred because they could sail deep water without pitching and wallowing. The sloops, among all types of British colonial privateers, accounted for 20 percent of the prizes captured.[4]

The cost to the investors of purchasing a sloop, equipping, manning, and then sending it out on a seven-month cruise was about £1,000 sterling. A successful voyage could yield a financial return of over 130 percent. However, 25 percent of colonial privateers failed to take any prizes. The backers lost their investment. Sometimes the investment was put in outright danger when, in a spate of patriotism, the British colonial privateer attacked a Spanish or French privateer. There was small profit if victorious and absolute disaster if vanquished.[5]

The French Revolution of 1789 spurred further privateering. Britain, along with other European nations, went to war against the revolutionary government. The British saw possibilities of wealth, possessions, and defeat of the enemy in the Caribbean. French colonies were in upheaval, trying to decide whether it would be more prudent to remain loyal to the monarchy or openly support the revolution. The Royal Navy, its own ships blockading French ports, relied on privateers in the West Indies. The French, their regular navy in revolutionary disarray because so many of their officers were royalists, encouraged privateering to counter the British vessels. Their primary base was not one of their Caribbean possessions; rather, it was Charleston, South Carolina.[6]

Despite President George Washington's efforts to keep the United States neutral, South Carolina felt some sympathy toward the French because of strong Gallic roots in their colonial heritage. Thus, French agents granted letters of marque and reprisal from Charleston. Small vessels, such as the sloop *Mediator*, formed the bulk of the first privateers because they were inexpensive to convert and could operate inshore among the Caribbean Islands. As the war lengthened, larger ships, such as the barque *Recovery*, mounting eighteen guns, went hunting in deeper water. The assaults against merchant shipping became fairly standardized: overtake the slower cargo ship, fire a few canon shot as warning, send aboard a prize crew, and sail the captured vessel to Charleston and the prize courts. The Charleston privateers reached their zenith in 1796. After that, profits diminished as the United States federal courts increasingly made their presence felt, much to the disfavor of the privateers.

Privateering in American continental waters reached a high point when the United States and Britain fought the War of 1812.[7] The U.S. Navy, with but sixteen ships and only seven of them frigates, seemed to stand little chance against the Royal Navy's awesome power. Much as the British did in both world wars, the U.S. Navy augmented their fleet by commissioning armed merchant vessels—only these were privateers, some 526 of them by war's end, carrying letters of marque and reprisal.[8]

Schooner-rigged vessels were again the favorite vessel used, comprising two-thirds of the ships commissioned because they were fast and maneuverable, or, as a seaman might say, they were quick to answer the helm. These tenacious privateers upset British shipping. By the end of the war they took 1,300 British ships as prizes. At one point, during a seven-month period prior to March 1813, 500 British ships were seized, causing an outcry in England.[9] Schooners, such as the *Rossie*, *Comet*, *Providence*, and *George Washington*, created havoc as they cruised the Atlantic and Caribbean.

Unfortunately, a dark side lurked behind all the victories. Privateers typically selected their victims with care. Ships containing cargoes of high commercial value were prized over those carrying military stores, for money was more important to many privateers than what damage they might inflict on the British war effort. That could have been significant, for Britain was not only fighting the Americans but was in a desperate war on the Iberian Peninsula. Unwilling to be on the losing side of a fight, privateers let pass ships that looked more heavily gunned than their own or whose crews seemed determined to do battle. Thus, for all the flag-waving and martial music that accompanied departure from their home ports, privateers on the high seas made the early decision to be pragmatic businessmen.

George Little, who had sailed on six privateering expeditions, found himself on his seventh voyage first lieutenant aboard the schooner *George Washington*. Finally, sickened by the life, he determined it would be his last voyage. He wrote despondently, "I behold a band of ruthless desperadoes, for such I must call our crew, robbing and plundering a few defenseless beings who were pursuing both a lawful and peaceful calling. It induced me . . . to relinquish . . . an unjustifiable and outrageous pursuit. . . . No man of conscience could be engaged in privateering."[10]

By the mid-nineteenth century, Europe had enough of this gray area of naval warfare. Privateering was abolished by most nations under the 1856 Declaration of Paris. But some ambiguities remained. The Second Hague Convention in 1907 erased much confusion by clarifying definitions. Thus a merchant ship cannot be a warship unless under the direct command and authority of the commissioning nation, and its crew must be subject to military discipline. The ship must also exhibit external markings common to regular warships—such as a bow number—and it must be listed as part of the commissioning nation's navy.

On the face of it, the grand and romantic days of high adventure seemed over. But World War I demonstrated that new developments remained possible.

WORLD WAR I: ARMED MERCHANT CRUISERS AND THE BRITISH BLOCKADE

Much of our understanding of World War I is conditioned by the land war in Europe. The human cost was appalling. An average of 5,600 soldiers were killed each day—the total over four years was 8,500,000. Trench warfare, a seemingly unending claustrophobic vertical existence, killed most of them. Hemmed by dirt walls, the soldiers saw little but the sky above. Exposure meant death. The major offensives, attack over open ground against artillery and machine-gun fire, devastated a generation. Edmund Taylor concluded that "the trench warfare of 1914–1918 was perhaps the cruelest large-scale ordeal that the flesh and spirit of man have endured since the Ice Age."[11] The war at sea took on different dimensions. The ocean was horizontal, featureless. Another ship, much less an enemy vessel, might not be seen for days or weeks or, in some cases, not ever. The sea battles of World War I— Jutland, Dogger Bank, Helgoland Bight, Coronel, and the Falklands—each killed a few thousand men. But most sea fights were between individual ships. No sea battle ever produced 20,000 British dead in a few hours as did the

Somme offensive of 1916. Thus, as Martin Gilbert notes, the "death toll [at sea] was not determined by the intensity of the fighting, but by the size of the ship and how quickly it sank."[12]

The centerpiece of Britain's naval war was their North Sea blockade, established 12 August 1914, to prevent merchant ships carrying war-related goods and food from reaching German ports. The blockade necessitated patrolling a vast expanse of ocean (Map 1). The tightest blockade closed the Skagerrak, the waters between Denmark's most northern tip and Norway. Patrols also extended across the northern entrance to the English Channel, to the Norwegian Sea—the area between Norway and Iceland—and into the Denmark Strait between Iceland and Greenland. Royal Navy ships also patrolled as far south as the Falkland Islands that covered Cape Horn (the Panama Canal was not yet open).

The Royal Navy enjoyed a numerical superiority of thirty-four cruisers to the Germans' eight. Nevertheless, Britain's cruiser forces, the backbone of the far-reaching patrols, was stretched thin from Gibraltar to Suez to South Africa, on to India, Hong Kong, Singapore, Australia, and New Zealand, and across the Pacific's vast reaches where the Germans claimed several islands. Royal Navy cruisers were deployed virtually around the world. The British found two ways of filling the gaps.

One method was laying mines in the North Sea. This forced many Germany-bound merchant ships into British ports for inspection of their crew's papers, cargo manifests, and the cargoes themselves. Contraband was confiscated and, in some instances, so were the ships.

A second method of compensating for the cruiser shortage was commandeering passenger liners and arming them, creating a class of ships called armed merchant cruisers (AMCs). By April 1915, twenty-nine such ships were organized into the Tenth Cruiser Squadron that operated as the blockade's outer screen from the Denmark Straits to zones north and south of Iceland and around to Scotland. The converted ships were usually fast enough at about 15 knots to overtake any freighter or, for that matter, most existing German submarines operating on the surface. Mounting from six to ten 6-inch guns, with an occasional 12-pounder and some smaller caliber guns such as 6-pounders, 2-pounders, and machine guns and rifles, the AMCs appeared to be adequate replacements for regular cruisers. After all, they were never considered "real" warships that would have to fight major engagements. Alas high, even modest, expectations soon were dashed at four levels.

First, whatever speed the merchant cruisers generated was lost to unwieldiness in combat situations. True, they seldom confronted German warships, but chasing a merchant ship or trying to outwit a surfaced U-boat necessitated a measure of maneuverability. Liners were designed for the

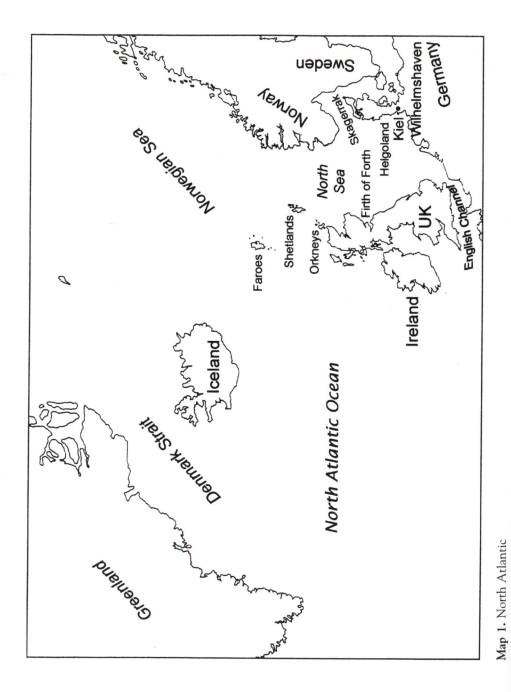

Map 1. North Atlantic

straight-ahead dash. The AMCs were like so many racehorses suddenly expected to meet the stop-and-go abilities of a cowboy's quarter horse. The liners did not comfortably fit their new assignment. Second, the liners were usually big and bulky, conspicuous in profile, easily avoided by German U-boats and surface raiders, or easily dominated by a faster, more heavily armed and armored enemy warship. Third, the liners consumed huge amounts of coal, a matter of grave concern to Admiralty at a time when conversion to oil-burning engines was still in its infancy. And fourth, the AMCs, being conspicuous, were vulnerable to submerged submarine torpedo attacks, partially explaining what happened to the 32,000-ton Cunard liner, *Lusitania*.

For the *Lusitania* was built in 1907 with the provision that she could be converted to an AMC if war erupted. In August 1914, the liner was put on the official list of AMCs, and 6-inch gun mounts were positioned on her decks. Then the Admiralty changed their mind, deciding not to use the ship as a merchant cruiser. Although no guns had been installed, the gun mounts were left in place, and the Admiralty made the fatal mistake of leaving the ship on the AMC list. The Germans technically had few reasons to consider the *Lusitania* anything but an AMC. She was torpedoed on 7 May 1915 by the U-20. Nearly 1,200 people lost their lives.

GERMAN WARSHIP RAIDERS: THE VOYAGE OF THE *EMDEN*

The British blockade slowly but steadily strangled Germany. As Martin Gilbert states in *The First World War*, the 1915 blockade caused 88,232 deaths. The next year 121,114 died. Food riots erupted in over thirty German cities.[13]

The German Navy retaliated. They bombarded a few British seacoast towns, such as Scarborough in North Yorkshire, and they dropped mines in the sea-lanes around various channel ports. The Germans also sent out surface raiders to effect their own stranglehold on Britain, an island nation that had to import everything from food for its people to raw materials for its industries.

An early and legendary example of German surface raiders by a regular warship was the light cruiser *Emden*. Launched in 1908, she was another of the Kaiser's entries into the catch-up race against the Royal Navy. Unfortunately for the Kaiser, she was obsolete before leaving the drawing boards. To be sure, at 3,600 tons and 387 feet long, *Emden* was a sleek ship. Yet her piston engines were out of date; in fact, she was the last German warship of her kind. She burned coal, giving her limited range (because of the necessity of refueling) and speed of (24 knots). Dan van der Vat points out in

Gentlemen of War that the bridge was more like a conning tower, lacking space and room for any of the newer sophisticated equipment.[14] The deck amidships was protected by only 2-inch armor. Her main armament was ten 4.1-inch guns. That was a formidable number but six of these—three on each side—were mounted in the hull, limiting their effectiveness to broadsides only. British cruisers, in contrast, were larger and as much as 5 knots faster. Expected to go anywhere in the world, they carried large amounts of fuel and many were oil burners. Also, British light cruisers were armed with 6-inch guns in revolving turrets. Heavy cruisers mounted 8-inch guns. The *Emden* could be considered little more than an obsolete heavy destroyer.

Despite the drawbacks, the *Emden* began its career as a serendipitous ship. In 1914, her captain was Karl von Müller, a humane, if aloof, skilled professional, and her crew was well-trained, loyal, and steadfast. Given her role as a raider, *Emden* was fortunate to be stationed in August of 1914 at Tsingtao, China, a German colonial port, as part of the Far East Squadron. On 13 August, squadron commander Rear Admiral Maximillian von Spee, after consulting his captains, ordered Müller to commence raiding in the Indian Ocean. Spee reckoned there would be ample shipping to sink. Moreover, the raider would cause considerable dislocation of British naval forces as they searched for the lone ship. Indeed, the decision bore fruit. The next morning, as Spee led the Far East Squadron into the Pacific, the *Emden* received the admiral's signal "Detached. Wish you luck." Müller steered south to Yap Island, through the Molucca Sea, looped south around the East Indies, reaching the Indian Ocean on 5 September. *Emden* made her presence felt five days later, on 10 September, when Müller sighted the British steamer *Indus* bound for Bombay to load troops and horses. He ordered a shot across her bow and signaled an order that she not send a help message but prepare for boarders. *Indus* immediately stopped as her officers destroyed the code books and secret orders. The German boarding party searched the ship carefully, taking equipment and supplies including soap, candy, cigarettes, food, utensils, charts, chronometers, and the ship's transmitter. The *Indus*'s crew was later transferred to a German supply ship. The Germans sank the *Indus* by opening the seacocks and sending some well-aimed shots into her hull. By this action, Müller established his basic tactics.

By early November 1914, *Emden* had sailed 30,000 miles, sinking 16 merchant ships and seizing five others to use as collier and to carry prisoners who were eventually sent to friendly ports. Müller also bombarded the ports at Madras, India, and Penang, an island of Malaysia, where he also sank a Russian cruiser and a French destroyer.

On 9 November 1914, overtaken by the 6-inch-gunned Australian cruiser HMAS *Sydney*, the *Emden*, severely damaged in the fighting and with 134 of the crew killed, ran aground on North Keeling Island of the Cocos group. This end to the voyage was probably inevitable. Four navies dedicated some seventy ships to hunt the *Emden* over the 28 million square miles of the Indian Ocean. The British alone sent over thirty warships. That impact was not forgotten in later years as the German Admiralty planned for another war. Unfortunately, the lesson did not register with the British Admiralty.

GERMAN SURFACE RAIDERS: ARMED MERCHANTMEN

In 1914, the German Admiralty, much like their British counterparts, converted passenger liners to armed merchant cruisers. Among these were *Prinz Friedrich*, *Kronprinz Wilhelm*, and the *Kaiser Wilhelm Grosse*. Although fast and mounting 5.9-inch guns, they all harbored glaring weaknesses. Their great bulk gave them distinctive profiles; they were not quick to answer the helm; they lacked armor; they consumed too much coal; and they were more easily intercepted by the Royal Navy than were regular German warships. The Germans quickly abandoned their AMC program.

The German Admiralty nevertheless reinforced their surface raider force by sending out ships—freighters, packets, trawlers, a whole panoply of vessels—easily disguised as ordinary merchantmen but armed with 6-inch and 4-inch guns supplemented with 6-pounders and 2-pounders, machine-guns, some with torpedo tubes, and some fitted as minelayers.[15] These ships, a reinvention within the German Navy of the privateers of old, became "quite as deadly as an agent of commerce destruction."[16]

The *Möwe* was a 4,790-ton banana boat before the war. Commandeered and armed with four 6-inch guns, a 4.1-inch gun, four torpedo tubes, and carrying 500 mines, she became a dangerous weapon despite her innocent-looking veneer. On two voyages in 1916 and 1917, *Möwe* captured or sank forty-three ships. Another example was the *Wolf*, whose fifteen-month, 64,000-mile voyage was a saga of endurance. She was a 6,000-ton freighter armed with seven 5.9-inch guns, four torpedo tubes, and 463 mines. Leaving Kiel on 30 November 1916, she sailed down the Atlantic, around the Cape of Good Hope, across the Indian Ocean, and on to Australia and New Zealand. She captured or sank fourteen ships before returning home.

The most romanticized German raider was the *Seeadler*, commanded by Count Felix von Luckner.[17] As a boy, Luckner ran away from his strict Prussian home for a life at sea. And he had a full life indeed, sailing mostly in square-rigged vessels and living a life of high adventure. When twenty years old, he returned to Germany, undertook formal seamanship studies, and received a lieutenant's commission in the German Navy. Then he presented

himself to his startled mother and father. Early in the war, Luckner participated in the engagement at Helgoland Bight, and was wounded at Jutland.

The Kaiser and the navy's high command concluded that Luckner was the
obvious pick to command the *Seeadler*. She was a 1,600-ton, steel-hulled,
Scottish-built windjammer, 275 feet in length. Captured by a U-boat, she
was taken to Bremerhaven and converted to a raider. A diesel engine was
cleverly hidden behind false bulkheads. False lifeboats hid two 4.1-inch guns
amidships. In addition to comfortable crews quarters, accommodations were
made for 400 prisoners to be taken from enemy ships.

The *Seeadler*, sailing as a Norwegian timber ship, slipped away from Bremerhaven, headed north along the Norwegian coast, then cut west toward
the Faeroes and Iceland. On Christmas Day 1916, she was stopped by the
AMC HMS *Avenger*. The British boarding party found nothing amiss. Luckner and several of his crew spoke fluent Norwegian and one of the seaman
was even disguised as a young woman pretending to be the captain's wife.
The raider was sent on its way. Fifteen days later the *Seeadler* sank the 3,300-
ton collier *Gladys Royale* near the Azores and the *Lundy Island* was sunk the
next day. A series of other mid-Atlantic sinkings followed, most of them sailing ships. No doubt Luckner, having spent his youth on such ships, was much
saddened by these losses. In the age of steel and steam, sailing ships would
never be replaced. On 21 March 1917, after sinking about a dozen ships,
Luckner captured a French barque. He put his prisoners on board and sent
them to Rio de Janeiro, paying them wages for work they willingly did while
on the *Seeadler*.

The *Seeadler* sailed on into the Pacific, sinking an enemy ship on 8 July
1917. That was the last victory for the raider. In August, low on supplies,
Luckner sailed for Mopelia in the Society Islands and anchored outside the
lagoon. Most of the crew and new prisoners went ashore. Soon after, due to
either strong currents or a violent storm—the argument continues—*Seeadler*
was smashed on the reef. The German crew split up, sailing away in different directions. The prisoners, left behind, were later rescued. Luckner and
six of his men left Mopelia in an open launch and sailed 2,250 miles only
to be captured in the Fiji Islands. They were sent to prison camps in New
Zealand. He escaped, was recaptured, and again imprisoned in New Zealand,
this time in a more secure facility.

German surface raiders harried the sea-lanes for the entire war, building
a mystique. The Germans, naturally enough, treated their sailors as genuine
heroes, men cast in the old model of virtue and humanity. Certainly, they
contributed to the war effort by sinking valuable cargo and, probably of
greater significance, they caused large numbers of warships to search for
them, thus dispersing Allied naval forces. The British looked upon the

raiders as an inevitable consequence of war, an enemy to be found and destroyed. But upon the German crews, the British placed a romantic mantle, no less sincere than the one extended by the German people, as if it were an expression of chivalry in a war which, with each passing year, became more brutal. In comparison to the tonnage sunk, the raiders killed few of their opponents and generally gave their captives good treatment (although those in the hold of the *Wolf* contracted scurvy). The prisoners often reciprocated by assisting the raiders in running their ships and, on the *Seeadler*, even taking turns as lookouts. The German surface raiders mostly "played the game" according to the rules of war.

Q-BOATS: THE DISGUSED U-BOAT HUNTERS

A more ominous side to the use of armed merchant ships emerged. These were the Q-ships, better know as Q-boats, that sailed from British ports to battle the growing submarine menace.[18] The idea that a merchant ship, however armed, could fight a submarine was predicated on the international agreement requiring U-boats to challenge merchantmen on the surface and that none of the crew or passengers would be left adrift in lifeboats on the open sea. It seemed reasonable at the time. After all, German surface raiders regularly brought these people onto their own ships or accommodated them on another captured merchant ship. At an appropriate time, the captives were sent to a nearby port. What was lost in the legalisms of the international agreement was the reality that U-boats had no space for such niceties. During the first several months of the war this contradiction was not really an issue because the Germans did not possess many submarines. Unfortunately for the Allies, more were being built. February 1915 was the pivotal month in the U-boat war. The Germans announced a policy of unrestricted submarine warfare against all ships bringing supplies to Britain.

Q-boats sallied forth from British ports to counter the new menace in what might seem a fool's game. No electronic gear existed with which to detect submerged submarines, and depth charges were still rather primitive by later standards. Consequently, the Q-boat captain had to find a surfaced U-boat, convince its commander that he was confronting just another buckety old freighter, and maneuver close enough to the U-boat to drop the Q-boat's disguises and open fire at point-blank range. This tactic of lure rather than chase was indeed hazardous. Nevertheless, time would prove it far more effective than an earlier method by which naval personnel paddled about in harbor entrances looking for a periscope to appear. If one was spotted, the sailors rowed next to it, tied on a gunnysack, and gave the lens a good whack with a hammer.

All sorts of vessels were converted to Q-boats: steam trawlers, tugs, ketches, schooners of various sizes, luggers, barquentines, colliers, freighters, and packets, ranging in size from 5,000 tons down to 32 tons. Each vessel received a Royal Navy Q number, but the ships' names under which they sailed changed frequently to preserve their anonymity. Main armaments varied from 6-inch guns down to 2-pounders. Most also carried Lewis and Hotchkiss machine guns, rifles, and grenades. A few, even among the smallest, carried torpedo tubes. The guns were cleverly hidden from prying eyes, ingeniously covered with false deck housing, collapsible lifeboats, built-up gunwales, and even fake piles of canvas. Most looked like dreary tubs, the flotsam left by too many years at sea. Paint peeled, rust ran down their sides, smoke belched from their stacks, and they chugged along at ridiculously low speeds. All of this subterfuge was meant to entice a U-boat captain to take the over-ripe bait.

An engagement in July 1915, albeit not the first, illustrates the deadly scenario the Q-boats set in motion. The 373-ton converted collier *Prince Charles* set sail from Longhope, near Scapa Flow in the Orkneys, heading toward the Outer Hebrides. The vessel carried two 6-pounders, a 3-pounder, machine guns, and rifles. A dozen Royal Navy personnel, Lieutenant William Mark-Wardlaw commanding, comprised the combat crew. The civilian captain and his ten-man crew insisted on staying aboard.

About ninety miles west of the Orkneys, Mark-Wardlaw sighted a steamer stopped dead in the water, a U-boat along side, and a launch of some sort of heaved-to further west. The U-boat spotted the oncoming collier, swung away from the steamer, and headed toward the newly arrived ship.

Mark-Wardlaw stopped his engines and blew the ship's whistle. The civilian crew ran about the decks in well-rehearsed panic, and swung out of the lifeboats. The naval crew remained absolutely still beside their disguised guns. Even though the collier stopped, the U-boat kept firing its deck gun, shells landing perilously close to the *Prince Charles*. Then the U-boat commander blundered by turning his submarine broadside to the collier at a range of 600 yards. Mark-Wardlaw ordered the gun screens dropped and immediately opened fire. The first two shots missed but another two hit the U-boat's stern, damaging the steering gear. Unable to dive, its rudder stuck, the submarine turned in ever-tightening circles to a range of 300 yards. The British gunners could not miss. The submarine, the U-36, went down by the stern. *Prince Charles* rescued sixteen of the thirty-seven-man crew.

Q-boats often received as much as they gave out in battle. HMS *Penshurst*, a thousand-ton low-slung tramp steamer, quite an ugly little vessel, battled eleven U-boats from November 1915 to Christmas Eve, 1917, establishing a Q-boat record for both number of engagements and length of service. Until

July 1917, she was skippered by Commander F. H. Grenfell, and then by Lieutenant Cedric Naylor, both courageous and innovative seamen.

In January 1916, *Penshurst* endured shelling from a U-boat for over an hour. The men who were among the gun crews had to remain perfectly still lest they give away the surprises awaiting the U-boat. When the right moment arrived, Penshurst returned fire and sank the enemy. In January 1917, U-37 pumped shells into the *Penshurst* for a half hour, killing two men and wounding several others among the undercover gun crews. Again, the wounded men, regardless of their agony, had to keep still. At last, the U-boat swung broadside to the *Penshurst*. The British gunners opened fire, cracked the conning tower, and sent the U-boat to the bottom. In August, *Penshurst* was torpedoed by the U-72. Crippled, she was towed to Plymouth for repairs.

In December, *Penshurst* sighted a U-boat while patrolling the Irish Sea. The Germans struck first with a torpedo that hit between the freighter's engine and boiler room. The British deck crew did their "abandon ship" routine as the *Penshurst* began to settle by the stern. The still submerged U-boat cautiously circled the freighter for an hour, then surfaced and bombarded the ship with her deck gun. The gunners on the *Penshurst*, at a disadvantage because of the upward tilt of their ship, managed a few return shots but could not seriously damage the U-boat. When a British patrol boat hauled into view, the German boat made a fast exit. Around 8:00 P.M., *Penshurst* slipped beneath the waves. All her crew were rescued.

The value of armed merchant ships created a debate, especially in Britain and Germany, both during and after the war. But, in the context of ensuing history, all the argumentation mattered little: twenty-one years after World War I, the same kinds of ships were again commandeered to ostensibly play much the same roles in a new world war. With few questions asked, the merchant ships and their crews would be ordered yet again to fill the gaps in the naval strategy of World War II.

· CHAPTER 2 ·

REBUILDING THE GERMAN NAVY BETWEEN THE WARS

HUMILIATION TO RESURRECTION: THE WEIMAR REPUBLIC

No great battle—guns blazing, ships torn apart, men dying gloriously for the Fatherland—brought about the death of the German High Seas Fleet in 1918. They had fought well at Jutland in June 1916 against the full power of the Royal Navy's Home Fleet. Kaiser Wilhelm II even claimed victory. After all, his navy sank more ships and caused more casualties than did the Royal Navy. Yet, it was the High Seas Fleet that returned to their ports never again to engage the British in a major battle.

In October 1918, Admiral Reinhard Scheer ordered the fleet into battle for the sake of German honor. The sailors did not obey. Scheer repeated his order four more times. The sailors did not obey. The crews knew the war was all but over. The Prussian aristocrats could issue all the orders they wanted. They did little of the dying. It was too late to fight a battle for the sake of honor and naval tradition. Scheer's order ran hollow after the long idle months following Jutland. If the fleet would not, could not fight earlier, why now? Dying in what the crews called Scheer's Death Sortie for empty ideals was stupid and useless. Mutiny was in the air. Revolution would soon follow as many ships contemptuously flew in the red banner of Bolshevism. "*Hock Der Kaiser!*" Indeed, on 10 November, the Kaiser abdicated, mounted his imperial train, and fled toward voluntary exile in Holland, leaving behind the shambles of his army, his navy, and his nation.

On 21 November 1918, a long melancholic marine cortege, following the British cruiser HMS *Cardiff*, steamed from Wilhelmshaven Naval Base to internment at the Firth of Forth in Scotland. The ships—nine battleships, five battlecruisers, seven cruisers, and forty-nine destroyers—were the rusting, run-down core of the High Seas Fleet. As they entered the Firth, they sailed between two rows of British and American ships, 370 in all, whose crews stood at battle stations in the event of German trickery.[1]

Admiral Sir David Beatty, Royal Navy commander in chief, orchestrated the intimidating if not over-stated reception, sending an implied message to Germany, indeed to the world, that the German Navy was washed-up and that Germany was now a second-rate nation against which Britain would never again have to compete. If the reception was humiliating to the Germans, it was supposed to be. Beatty presented Rear Admiral Hugo Mürer, representing the German high command, a list of nonnegotiable demands. Upon signing the next morning, Mürer was nearly overcome by exhaustion and the enormity of the event, for he was literally giving away the German Navy. His hands shook so violently that he twice put his pen down to compose himself.

Although the Armistice Agreement called for the German ships to be interned in neutral ports, their arrival in Scotland put them firmly in British hands—meaning Beatty's. As an added humiliation, and to emphasize who was in charge, Beatty decided the German ships were in the way of commercial shipping, so he unceremoniously sent them to Scapa Flow in the Orkneys. There, under bleak skies, the German fleet swung at their moorings, gradually deteriorating, their crews cut to skeletal size. Ironically, the local fleet commander Rear Admiral von Reuter did not mind the personnel reduction. He sent packing the political activists and mutineers among the crews, and kept those he considered loyal to naval traditions.

By spring 1919, the curtain lifted on Allied intentions never to give the ships back to Germany. German Navy Chief of Staff Vice Admiral Adolph von Trotha sent an angry letter to von Reuter, denouncing Allied duplicity, and claiming the ships were interned, not surrendered; therefore, they were still German property. Von Reuter was in no position to unravel the legalities but he could hatch a plot to salvage German honor: scuttle the ships. He alerted the crews.

Von Reuter saw his opportunity on 21 June when his British watchdogs left the naval base for maneuvers. He sent a signal to his captains: "*ist sofort mit der Sabotage der Schiffin zu beginnen.*" The sabotaging of the ships will begin immediately. And then, "*Kein Aufsehen nach aussen!*" No activity to be visible from the outboard![2] That is, the sabotage was to be hidden from British view. Despite British efforts to intervene after the first ships visibly foundered, some fifty of them went to the bottom. Von Reuter believed the scuttling salvaged the German Navy's honor. So, too, did forty-three-year-old Captain Erich Raeder, who later noted that the destruction of the ships at Scapa Flow lifted the German Navy's morale and laid the foundations for a new fleet.[3] For even the newest of the sunken ships, had they survived and been retained in German hands, soon would be obsolete. Instead, the great event at Scapa Flow swept the sea clean. New visions were in the offing.

The new German Navy, the *Reichsmarine*, was officially established on 16 April 1919 by vote of the national assembly, the *Reichstag*. Voting a navy into being was comparatively easy for the new Weimar Republic's representatives—once they reached agreement. Bringing it into existence was another order of reality. From the start, there were problems and restrictions that impeded progress.

It was no small task to reach consensus among the diverse political factions that existed within postwar Germany. The *Reichstag* was officially formed in January 1919. Civil disorder, approaching outright civil war, created political and economic chaos as extremist groups tried to overthrow the new government. Within the government, there were some ten political parties—social democrats, socialists proper, communists, Catholic centrists, and monarchists among others—each with their own agenda, each caring little for national problems at the expense of satisfying their constituents' often very particular demands. Certainly not all wanted a new navy. The enormous expense involved would inevitably cut into money available for their parochial programs. Then, of course, Germany never before experienced a full-blown democracy. Political behavior often turned erratic, if not operatic, as rhetoric escalated. Moreover, the fledgling democracy struggled for existence in the context of a failing economy impacted by exorbitant reparations payments to the Allies and by the declining worth of the German mark. Its value in relation to the American dollar fell following the war to millions, billions, and even trillions. In 1920, a potato sack filled with marks would not buy a loaf of bread.

In March 1920, Wolfgang Kapp, an ultraconservative and former *Reichstag* member, stepped into the vortex swirling through the young republic. He boldly seized the government's offices and proclaimed himself chancellor. Vice Admiral von Trotha imprudently and naively declared the navy's loyalty to the new head of state. But Kapp's revolt lacked substantial backing and failed in four days. Von Trotha was forced to resign and the 171 officers who supported him were dismissed or retired. Many other officers who had nothing to do with the revolt also resigned because of the dark cloud of suspicion that blanketed the navy. Erich Raeder, disillusioned by the mess, concluded that the Kapp affair strangled the navy's development, reducing it to a minor role in national defense.[4]

The loss of all those experienced officers exacerbated the *Reichsmarine's* manpower problems. The Versailles Treaty mandated that the navy could have a maximum of 1,500 officers and 15,000 enlisted men. Officers would serve for a minimum of twenty-five years and ratings would enlist for twelve years. Shorter terms than those meant that men would have been constantly entering and leaving the service, enabling Germany to create a large reserve force. That the Allies would not countenance. The navy's small size also required that many experienced men be discharged. The impact, especially on such technical departments as engineering and ordinance, was tantamount to emasculation.

But in 1923 a new cabinet put through currency reform and renegotiated reparations payments with Great Britain and France. Moreover, the Germans offset reparations payments by borrowing foreign capital. Thus, from 1924 to 1931, while the government made $2,750,000,000 in payments, German businesses, industry, and local jurisdictions borrowed about $4,500,000,000—more than half of which came from banks in the United States, an anomalous situation if ever there was one. Winston Churchill condemned the dealings as insane.[5]

The consequence to the navy of this emerging governmental stability was that money became available for new ships. Germany, however, was required to rebuild her fleet under the restrictions outlined in the Versailles Treaty. They could retain eight prewar battleships (classes built between 1902 and 1914), eight aging light cruisers, thirty-five destroyers and torpedo boats, and some minesweepers and other auxiliary ships. The German Navy was forbidden a U-boat fleet and a naval air arm. Capital ships could be built but on a limited ratio. Thus, for example, a battleship could be constructed only if an existing battleship was retired and was over twenty years old. Replacements were limited in size to 10,000 tons for battleships and 6,000 tons for cruisers. And the battleships could only mount 11-inch guns. But new British and American battleships exceeded 30,000 tons and cruisers with 8-inch guns commonly displaced 10,000 tons. Thus, the German Navy was purposely relegated—on paper—to a fleet barely sufficient to guard its own coastline and, if necessary, prevent the Russians from breaking out of the Baltic Sea.

In February 1922, the Washington Naval Treaty was signed, a mostly American maneuver to limit the size and number of capital ships among the five leading maritime powers—Great Britain, the United States, Japan, Italy, and France. The purpose was to prevent a naval arms race. With the restrictions placed upon the Germans, this seemed a safe course to take. A ten-year moratorium was placed on the building of capital ships. After that period, no ships were to be built larger than 35,000 tons and no guns could be mounted larger than 16-inchers. Cruisers mounting 8-inch guns were limited to 10,000 tons. As with the limits imposed on Germany, capital ships could be replaced on a one-to-one ratio if the retiring ship was at least twenty years old. The treaty delayed the Royal Navy's capital ship replacement program because of the number and ages of her existing battleships. The British resented this because they now ranked second to the United States. But the ratios developed by the Washington Naval Conference made it quite clear that Germany, adhering to the limitations imposed by the Versailles Treaty, would never again compete in numbers of ships and ship sizes with the major maritime powers. That outcome did satisfy the British. The German Navy began rebuilding.

The light cruiser *Emden*, laid down in 1921 and completed in 1925, was the first major German ship built since the war. She was low in the water and her slim lines were reminiscent of the earlier *Emden*. In fact, the new *Emden* was built from plans on the drawing boards in 1918. But she was obsolete by recent standards (her original engines were coal-fired). She had a declared displacement of 6,000 tons, and her main armament consisted of eight, single-mounted 5.9-inch guns and four 19.7-inch torpedo tubes. Within a year after her commissioning, she was used as a training ship—a failure but a beginning.

Five more cruisers followed—*Königsberg*, *Karlsruhe*, *Köln*, *Nuremberg*, and *Leipzig*—all launched between 1927 and 1934, and all with declared displacements of 6,000 tons. But these were false declarations made to conform with the Versailles Treaty. Actual displacements were around 6,400 tons. These cruisers were much improved over the *Emden*. Their armor was increased, accounting for their concealed weight. They carried nine 5.9-inch guns in three revolving turrets and they were propelled by mixed turbine and diesel engines that extended their cruising range.

In 1927 and 1928, the *Wolf* and *Möwe* classes of torpedo boats were laid down. These ships supposedly displaced no more than the 800-ton limit, but they actually came in at 924 tons. The German designers again engaged in a calculated evasion of the Versailles Treaty to increase armor protection. The boats carried three 4.1-inch guns and six 21-inch torpedo tubes. Unfortunately for the Germans, they proved inadequate for deep-water duty as they pitched and wallowed in heavy seas.

In the mid-1920s, the real development and design coup for the new navy were the *panzerschiffs*—armored ships—as the Germans preferred to classify them. They became much better known as "pocket battleships." There were three ships in the class: *Deutschland* (renamed *Lützow*), 1931; *Admiral Scheer*, 1933; and *Graf Spee*, 1934. The Germans faked their displacement to comply with treaty restrictions. Each of the three ships supposedly displaced

10,000 tons. The announced tonnage was readily believed because they were welded construction rather than riveted and so looked lighter than they were. In fact, they displaced over 12,000 tons. Each ship mounted six 11-inch guns in two turrets, eight 5.9-inch guns in single turrets, and, for anti-aircraft defense, they mounted six 4.1-inch guns and eight 3-pounders. Each ship also carried eight 21-inch torpedo tubes in quadruple parallel banks on the afterdeck. Diesel engines gave them a speed of 26 knots and a range of 20,000 miles. Pocket battleships were not designed for coastal defense or for blockading the Baltic Sea, but were commerce raiders whose only battle area could be the Atlantic Ocean. The British and French were stunned. No other ship of their size combined such speed with such powerful armaments.

The lie about the pocket battleships' displacement nonetheless seems rather minor when set against another and more sinister German naval re-armament development. In October 1918, a young U-boat commander named Karl Dönitz was captured and sent to a prisoner-of-war camp after his submarine was attacked and sunk. When he returned to Germany in 1919, he reported to the director of naval personnel at Kiel. Dönitz was asked if he would like to stay in the navy. He responded: "Do you think we shall soon have U-boats again?" The director said, "I am sure we shall . . . within a couple of years or so."[6] Dönitz stayed.

Because German submarines were expressly forbidden under the Treaty of Versailles, that answer must have seemed cryptic. Yet, within three years, the navy was building clandestine U-boats. The German Navy established a phony business in the Hague, Holland, under the name *Igenieurskantoor voor Scheepsbouw*, to design submarines for foreign navies. But the submarines they developed were prototypes of future German U-boats. They were built in Spain, Holland, and Finland. Some boats, prefabricated, were crated and stored at Kiel. When in 1936 one of the Finnish-built submarines when out for sea trials, all but four of the crew were German Navy officers. Thus, cycles of selected German officers spent about six months each year for several years training on Finnish submarines. They were the cadre of a new and secret U-boat service.

The navy was allowed antiaircraft guns. In 1928, General Wilhelm Gröner, minister of defense, purchased a few seaplanes to supposedly tow targets. Erich Raeder described the subsequent subterfuge with the planes, for he had grander plans than target towing. His staff created a dummy business called Air Service, Incorporated, and hired a group of veteran flyers from the war. These pilots helped train carefully screened cadets in the seaplanes at secret locations. They were later commissioned in the navy as the nucleus of a fleet combat air arm.[7]

As the naval historian Edwyn Gray points out in his study *Hitler's Battle-*

ships, all this sleight of hand, all these purposeful violations of the Versailles Treaty, occurred in the Weimar Republic before Adolf Hitler came to power.[8] The navy's conventional rationale for all these purposeful violations was that the treaty was manifestly unfair to Germany; therefore, any breech was considered justified.

In 1922, Admiral Hans Zenker became the navy's commander in chief. His reputation as a disciplinarian, firm but fair, as a superb tactician, and as one who believed in solid training, brought him the loyalty and dedication of senior officers.

Under Zenker's leadership, Erich Raeder was promoted to rear admiral and appointed inspector of naval education. He established a new system based on the beliefs that "firm but friendly" discipline was the path to high levels of efficiency among ships' crews, and that the "prerequisite for such a state of discipline" was well-disciplined officers and petty officers who must also possess a modest pride and self-respect.

Raeder believed that all naval officers should stand aloof from every form of political activity and, as he stated in his autobiography, must give "unconditional loyalty to the State and to the government chosen by its people."[9] Karl Dönitz, who was to later command the U-boat fleet, expressed the same belief in his memoirs: post–World War I officers had to remain politically neutral "for only thus could we fulfill out duty to our people . . . and to the state which they created."[10] Both Raeder and Dönitz wrote their respective autobiographies after World War II. From that perspective, their noninvolvement stance in Germany's politics may be ex post facto explanations, more likely rationalizations, for their tacit approval of the navy's subordination of the Versailles Treaty during the Weimar Republic and their later willingness to serve Adolf Hitler and the Nazi cause. Yet, in the late 1920s, such matters of conscience were easily surrendered to the more immediate issue of the navy's survival because the Weimar Republic's very existence was again challenged as the Great Depression gripped the nation.

Although the armed forces remained generally but superficially loyal to the republic, the higher echelons of the military were distrustful of the young democracy and longed for the respectability they enjoyed under the Kaiser. The *Reichstag's* debates on military spending, always quarrelsome and demeaning to the military, often resulted in close-run votes. The margin of victory was given on more than one occasion by a new party that gathered momentum as the decade of the 1920s drew to a close.

The National Socialist German Worker's Party—the Nazis—had twelve members in the *Reichstag*, just enough to tip the scales away from the ultra-left-wing political parties and toward larger military budgets. The admirals and generals would not forget.

REBUILDING UNDER THE HITLER REGIME

On 30 January 1933, Adolf Hitler, head of the surging Nazi party, was appointed chancellor of Germany by the ailing president Field Marshal Paul von Hindenberg. Three days later Hitler met with the nation's leading admirals and generals. He assured them that rearmament would move ahead without the distractions of civil disorder. Their assistance in quelling domestic violence was no longer needed. There would not be a civil war. Then, in April 1934, Hitler again called the admirals and generals together in the salon of the new pocket battleship *Deutschland*. He told them that Hindenberg was seriously ill. He wanted their support to succeed the old man. If they agreed, the military would experience an unparalleled expansion and be well-equipped for war against Germany's external enemies. The military establishment, including Erich Raeder, gave Hitler their support.

The Prussian generals in particular wanted Hitler to do something for them in return for their backing. They required suppression of the Brownshirts, the *Sturmabteilung*, the S.A.[11] Originally organized from street toughs, criminals, and the urban dispossessed, they had grown under their leader Ernst Rohm into the Nazi party's 2-million-man private army. Rohm saw a grandiose future for the S.A. Under him, they were to become the core of a revolutionary people's army in which all the old military traditions and class hierarchies were tossed aside. The Prussians bristled. Hitler, the quintessential political pragmatist, knew he no longer needed the Brownshirts. But he did need the Prussians and the *Wehrmacht*—the regular army—and the legitimacy they gave to his dream of a Third Reich.

Hitler promised to reduce the S.A. by two-thirds. On 30 June 1934, he unleashed a bloody purge. Rohm was among the first shot, accused of moral deviancy and of plotting the government's overthrow. Over 100 S.A. were slaughtered, some as their wives and children looked on. Perhaps a thousand died. No one is certain.

Although the generals cheered Hitler's move against their great rival, they did not want to appear involved in political action. General Werner von Blomberg, minister of defense, covered them by issuing a proclamation stating that the army stood above politics and that its sole purpose was to defend Germany against all foreign enemies. Meanwhile, President Hindenberg thanked Hitler for rescuing Germany from revolution. The German people could go to bed reassured that all was well.

Admiral Raeder later concluded that the events of 30 June were both "morally unjustified and highly illegal."[12] Make no mistake. Raeder was glad to see the S.A.'s power broken. The violence by which that took place only served to reinforce his position that the navy must stand apart from what he called "all political squabbles."[13] The murder of over 100 people was hardly a squabble. But, by trivializing the purge, Raeder could continue building his fleet without the burden of conscience. He had put on political blinders and did not take them off, even to his last breath.

Hindenberg died in August 1934. Predictably, Hitler succeeded him as the Weimar Republic's president. Raeder and his fellow officers then signed an oath of personal allegiance to Adolf Hitler. This was a fateful act. In most Western democracies oaths of allegiance are usually given to the nation or the constitution, not to an individual. Germany's admirals and generals apparently did not appreciate the distinction. They previously served under the Kaiser to whom they gave their oath. They were fed up with German democracy. Better to be on the side of a jumped-up former corporal whom they believed they could control. Little did they realize how inextricably bound they were to Hitler. Nor could any imagine how deeply stained their beloved sense of honor would become.

In 1935, Hitler kept his promise to expand the navy. He approved two new capital ships, the battlecruisers *Scharnhorst* and *Gneisenau* which, at 32,000 tons, were not even close to Versailles Treaty limit of 10,000 tons. Diesel powered, capable of 31 knots speed, and over 750 feet long, these ships were a major development over the earlier pocket battleships. Both mounted nine 11-inch guns in three turrets. The ships each also mounted twelve 5.9-inch guns and, for antiaircraft defense, fourteen 4.1-inch and sixteen 37-mm guns. They additionally carried six 21-inch torpedo tubes.

Hitler told Raeder that these new ships did not mean he wanted a war with Britain.[14] But he stopped short of designating which nations might be future enemies. Raeder was relieved. Hitler obviously would not repeat the mistakes of Kaiser Wilhelm II when, in the pre–World War I era, he attempted to challenge Britain's naval supremacy. Hitler even suggested an Anglo-German naval treaty that fixed the relative strengths of the two fleets, thus giving Britain assurance that war between the two nations was unthinkable. Yet, at the same time, he changed the navy's name from the *Reichsmarine* to the *Kriegsmarine* (war navy). Of course, nothing sinister was to be read into that fine tuning—not yet.

On 16 March 1935, Hitler, appearing before the *Reichstag*, publicly renounced the Treaty of Versailles, asserting Germany's rights as a sovereign nation. As the London *Times* Berlin correspondent explained to his British readers two days later, the German government—Hitler—declared that since all the provisions of the Versailles Treaty had been met, even to the stripping of its armed forces, Germany was fully discharged from any further obligations. Therefore, Hitler stated, "The German government, as guardian of the honor and interests of the nation, desires to make sure that Germany possesses sufficient instruments of power not only to maintain the integrity of the German *Reich* but also to command international respect and value as co-guarantor of peace." Thus, he revealed the existence of a heretofore secret air force, the *Luftwaffe*. He also announced his plan to conscript a half million men into the military. The *Times* correspondent reported that Konstantin von Neurath, the foreign minister, and Hermann Göring, reichmarshal and commandant of the *Luftwaffe*, jumped from their chairs and cheered "*Heil! Heil! Heil!*" Three hours later, as the news of Hitler's pronouncements reached the streets, Berlin's citizens cheered and sang, crowds swirling down the avenues as if released from purgatory.

Hitler was not through with his surprises. On 21 May, he announced that he was willing to hold Germany's fleet size to 35 percent of the Royal Navy. The British press greeted the proposal with enthusiasm. The London *Times*, on 19 June, thought the idea sincere, well-considered, and a pathway to further negotiations on arms limitations. But Joachim von Ribbentrop, ambassador to Britain, arrogantly stated that the proposal was nonnegotiable. The British accepted. They did so unilaterally, not informing the League of Nations, including their French and Italian friends, of their intentions. They even refused to tell the French what kinds of ships and what tonnages were involved.[15]

Thus, as Karl Dönitz pointed out, Germany was allowed to build up to 35 percent of British warship tonnage, "a condition which applied to each class of ship individually."[16] Germany could build, for instance, 184,000 tons of battleships and 51,000 tons of cruisers. They could also build 24,000 tons of submarines, a special 45 percent of British tonnage. There was, however, a codicil that if "exceptional circumstances" arose the Germans could build to a full 100 percent of British submarine strength following appropriate consultation.

The treaty gave Hitler a major diplomatic coup for, in one stroke, he shredded what little remained of the Versailles Treaty. As William L. Shirer pointed out in *The Rise and Fall of the Third Reich*, the new treaty did not restrict Germany's naval rearmament but gave "Hitler rein to build up a navy as fast as was physically possible. . . . It was not a limitation of German rearmament but an encouragement to expand it."[17] Winston Churchill was horrified. As he stated in *The Gathering Storm*, Germany could build its navy as rapidly as they wished, and the British acceptance of the submarine ratio was the "acme of gullibility."[18] Admiral Raeder, however, consumed by feelings of camaraderie toward Britain, asserted that the treaty offered good reason "to look forward to the future with confidence" because Hitler emphatically declared over and over that war with Britain was unthinkable.[19]

Further faith in Hitler's apparently diplomatic and peaceful intentions resided in the so-called London Submarine Protocol of September 1936. Because the Washington Naval Treaty was nearing its expiration date, the United States, Britain, France, Italy, and Japan decided to meet again and, in light of the Anglo-German Naval Treaty, to invite German representatives.

The key provision of the new document was the regulation of submarine warfare. Thus, a submarine was required to approach a targeted merchant ship on the surface. The crew and any passengers were allowed to take to the lifeboats or be taken aboard the submarine. If there were too few lifeboats to accommodate the passengers and crew, if the submarine could not hold all of them, or if the sea was too rough, then the ship was not to be sunk. The Germans signed the protocol. Churchill's reaction to the German concession contained a bitter logic: "Who could suppose," he wrote, "that the Germans, possessing a great fleet of U-boats and watching their women and children being starved by a British blockade, would abstain from the fullest use of that arm?"[20] Certainly, when faced with what he called Germany's recent "brazen and fraudulent" treaty violations in the laying down of the *Scharnhorst* and *Gneisenau*, Churchill found no reason to believe Hitler's promises about naval strength or purposes.

Despite Raeder's optimism, Karl Dönitz was not a happy man. Although he was appointed commander of the *Kriegsmarine* U-boat fleet in July 1935, he felt slighted. His fleet crawled rather than leaped into existence. Six boats, in the 250-ton class, clandestinely prefabricated in Spain, Holland, and Finland, and shipped in pieces to the Kiel navy yard were assembled during the Anglo-German talks. The first hit the waves the day after the treaty was signed. Three more boats were added in September 1935, and another nine were assembled over the next few months. Given the secrecy under which they were designed and constructed, a baker's dozen was a remarkable number. But Dönitz believed his service was strangled by the conditions of the Anglo-German Treaty. Britain's historical concern was defense of her trade routes and outposts of empire. Submarines, in contrast, were offensive weapons. Consequently, they never loomed large in British naval planning. Even though the 45 percent tonnage ratio of German to British boats was the largest allowed by the treaty, this figure did not translate into the number of U-boats that Dönitz thought necessary to wage a full-scale war. He believed the submarine service was relegated to a minor role in German rearmament. He stated that the 1936 Submarine Protocol, requiring U-boats to act on the surface, "further reduced their operational value," and, with some justification, concluded that there existed in the German hierarchy "considerable doubts about the real value of the new U-boats."[21]

In May 1937, Raeder was called to the chancellory and told by Hitler that he should consider Britain to be Germany's future enemy but that a battle fleet would not be needed before 1946. Raeder was ordered to create a plan for intensive naval rearmament. Actual planning fell into the lap of Commander Helmuth Heye, a young staff officer. Various plans were created but rejected by a senior naval staff review committee. Finally, after months of argumentation, Heye produced two plans, both dubbed Plan Z.[22]

One plan called for a large number of U-boats operating in conjunction with pocket battleships, cruisers, and disguised commerce raiders against British shipping. All these vessels could be cheaply and quickly built. The second plan visualized a fleet of battleships, aircraft carriers, cruisers, and big destroyers capable of not only hard-hitting operations against British shipping but of taking on and vanquishing the Royal Navy's best and biggest ships. The Kriegsmarine would naturally win because its ships would be newer, more heavily armed and armored, and faster than anything possessed by the British.

Raeder presented the two plans to Hitler on 31 October 1938. The Führer, already impressed with the power of the pocket battleships and undoubtedly thinking of the prestige and glory to be garnered from big guns on big ships, chose the second Plan Z.

Two battleships already under construction, Bismarck and the Tirpitz, officially displaced about 42,000 tons each and carried eight 15-inch guns. Plan Z called for an additional six super battleships, as Raeder called them, each mounting 16-inch guns and displacing 50,000 tons. The existing Scharnhorst and Gneisenau were to be upgraded from 11-inch guns to 15-inch guns. One aircraft carrier, the Graf Zeppelin, was under construction and two more would be built. These heavy ships would be supplemented principally by five heavy cruisers of 10,000 tons each, sixteen light cruisers of 8,000 tons each, and an entirely new Z-23 class of sixteen super destroyers. The usual armament 4.7-inch or 5-inch guns for destroyers was discarded. The Z-23s would carry four 6-inch guns, eight 21-inch torpedo tubes, carry up to sixty mines, and have a speed of 38 knots. Dönitz would get 233 U-boats.

A grand strategy lurked behind this heavier, more powerful version of Plan Z. Its first target was British shipping. Thus, merchant ships, singly and in convoy, would be attacked by battlecruisers, cruisers, disguised commerce raiders, and U-boats, all working in concert. Surface raiders would force the Royal Navy to guard their convoys with capital ships. But these "lumbering British battleships," as Raeder called them,[23] could not catch the faster, sleeker German battlecruisers and cruisers. The new German battleships with speeds over 30 knots and with great cruising range could support the convoy raiders, attack convoys when the opportunities arose, and even engage the British escorting battleships.[24] The Royal Navy would be forced to spread their forces over 31 million square miles of the Atlantic, uncertain when and where the Germans would strike. The Germans would relish the confusion they created just as they had in World War I.

Raeder, for all the grandiose planning and strategy, retained some sense of reality. Wanting the ships was one thing. Producing them was another. He told Hitler that the navy would not be ready for a naval war with Britain for at least six years and perhaps eight. The Führer appeared to agree.[25]

Dönitz knew full well a war with Britain was a reality and that the German Navy was not ready. Any hope he harbored of getting the 233 U-boats promised under Plan Z, any expectation he had that he would see an accelerated submarine building program soon crumbled. Only nine boats joined the fleet in 1938, and another eighteen in early 1939, few of them of the long-range ocean-going type. One new class suggested under the plan was a response to the Submarine Protocol's requirement that U-boats make surfaced approaches to targeted merchant ships. These new submarines would displace between 1,400 and 2,000 tons and carry 6-inch guns. Indeed, they would hold their own on the surface. But they remained just a planner's dream. In fact Hitler overrode Dönitz's Plan Z allotment, putting all U-boat development at a low priority. He believed, or said he believed, that at this time he could bring Britain and France to the peace table; therefore, U-boats would not be needed.

Admiral Friedrich Ruge concluded that if all German shipyards concentrated on building all the U-boats Dönitz wanted, they still could not have been built in a reasonable time.[26] The industrial capacity was simply not there. Hitler certainly did not mind. He stressed the need for battleships. As Ruge observed, "The big ships seem to fascinate him."[27]

But Ruge was right in his assessment, for Plan Z put forth generally unreachable goals. The German steel industry was not yet up to wartime production. What steel did roll from the mills had to be shared because the *Wehrmacht*—the army—needed steel for its guns, tanks, and trucks. Even then, the army faired no better than the navy. When, in 1940, the Germans poured through France, the *panzer* divisions received all the publicity: *blitzkrieg*, lightning warfare—tanks, mobility, speed. The German Army seemed unstoppable as it knifed through the Ardennes and roared to the English Channel coast. Yet, for all the notoriety accorded the ten *panzer* divisions fighting in France, there was another side to the invasion. As John Keegan pointed out in *The Second World War*, 120 German divisions walked to war because they lacked trucks.[28] What additional mobility they possessed came from horses and carts.

Inadequate resources notwithstanding, the navy's root problem was that

Hitler purposely did not clearly define Britain as the enemy until 1938. And his stated completion date for Plan Z of 1945, perhaps 1946, was so much dissembling if not outright deceit. Thus, on 28 April 1939, when Hitler spoke to the *Reichstag*, a speech heard around the world,[29] he expressed his admiration and wish for friendship with Britain but was angered by their mistrust of him. In the next breath, he renounced the Anglo-German Naval treaty, because the "basis for it has been removed."[30]

The German navy eventually paid a heavy price for their Führer's chicanery as he plunged blindly ahead into an unthinking competition with the British, repeating after all the mistakes made in the pre–World War I era. One might logically believe that Admiral Raeder could not help but see an inevitable war with Britain. He did not. He possessed two characteristics fatal to a commander in chief, especially one tied to Hitler. He was politically naive and had tunnel vision. Thus, he believed Hitler's promises with amazing consistency, and he perceived his navy to be above the world's vexations. By wishing it so, he made it so. He was going to be disappointed.

HMS *Polycanthus* (K-47), a Flower Class corvette. These small antisubmarine escort ships were the main protectors of the Atlantic convoys. *Polycanthus* was torpedoed and sunk in September 1944. Reproduced by courtesy of the U.S. National Archives, Washington, DC.

Light cruiser HMS *Ajax*, Commodore Harwood's flagship during his hunter group's battle with *Graf Spee*. Reproduced by courtesy of the U.S. Naval Historical Center, Washington, DC.

The German pocket battleship *Admiral Scheer* at Wilhelmshaven Navy Yard on the ship's commissioning day, 12 November 1934. Reproduced by courtesy of the U.S. Naval Historical Center, Washington, DC.

Admiral Erich Raeder (*foreground*) and Captain Theodor Krancke inspecting the *Admiral Scheer*. From Theodor Krancke and H. J. Brennecke, *Pocket Battleship: The Story of the Admiral Scheer*. London: Kimber, 1958.

Model (by Glossop) of HMS *Jervis Bay* as an armed merchant cruiser. The placement of the 6-inch guns was typical. Compare with HMS *Alcantara*. Reproduced by permission of the Trustees of the Imperial War Museum, London.

Captain Edward Stephen Fogarty Fegen, commander of the HMS *Jervis Bay*. He was posthumously awarded the Victoria Cross for the battle against the *Admiral Scheer*. Reproduced by permission of the Trustees of the Imperial War Museum, London.

Seven Canadian sailors in Halifax, survivors of the battle, give the thumbs up. *Back row, left* is Stoker First Class George Beaman, who was subsequently awarded the Distinguished Service Medal. Reproduced by permission of the National Archives of Canada/PA-1440484.

The German battleship *Bismarck* was the most powerful ship to enter the Atlantic raiding. However, Admiral Lütjens, commanding the sortie, made errors that doomed the ship and her crew. Reproduced by courtesy of the U.S. Naval Historical Center, Washington, DC.

CHAPTER 3

THE ROYAL NAVY BETWEEN THE WARS

THE 1920s: TREATIES, COMMITTEES, DEBATES

On 11 November 1918, Britons flooded onto the streets and into the squares of cities and villages, venting a joyous clamor. Church bells rang across the nation, ceremonial cannon thundered, and fireworks vaulted into the skies. The Great War, the War to End All Wars, as H. G. Wells called it in 1914, had finally ended. The savage Huns, who ravaged Western Europe and brought agony to the rest of the world, were ground to dust. The war's terrible grip loosened, a release from constant dread—the official notice of a father, another son, a brother killed or wounded; or the chilling sounds of heavy artillery announcing another offensive, their thunder reverberating from the front across the English Channel as far as St. James's Park in London; or the disguised fears about what new and lethal surprises the Germans might unleash upon the British troops; or that the killing might go on for yet another year.

Despite the euphoria, the realization of what the war did to Britain and its people inexorably wound its way into the nation's life. There was much to remember. The war monuments came soon enough, from the quiet magnificence of the Scottish National War Memorial, where a single casket contains the names of all the Scots killed, to the bronze statue of the young infantryman in London's Paddington Station from which so many like him went to war, to the little weed-choked roadside stone near Dunvegan, Isle of Skye, containing names of some local lads who died with the Cameroni-ans. More poignant still, evoking pity, wonder, guilt, awe, were the living memorials: the 50,000 men with permanently shattered minds, some eter-nally staring into their private hells, mumbling into their tea cups; or the men with shattered bodies, their crude prostheses—wood, leather, buckles, straps, and ties holding them together. There were so many visual recitations of continuing agony. Indeed, there was much to remember.

Correlli Barnett cogently argues in his *The Collapse of British Power* that the war's psychological impact was greater than the physical.[1] Thus was born a myth that Britain was savaged by the war, a whole generation lost to it. Vitality spent, the lion metamorphosed into a paper tiger. Barnett's thesis can be debated but, correct or not, myth can be transformed into a potent reality, shaping the perceptions a nation makes of itself and its future. And so it was that the British people, repelled by the war's horror, willingly com-promised the safety of their island in the name of peace.

But real peace could only be attained after the Germans, perpetrators of the war, received the punishment due them. The Germans denied guilt and demanded an investigation into the question. The Allies, scoffing at the cries of innocence, fixed blame squarely on Germany and cast little doubt on the Versailles Treaty's intent to punish them for the war's depredations. The vanquished Hun should pay overwhelming reparations, lose territory, and have their army and navy denuded. Let the consequences of these harsh treaty articles fall where they may. The German nation earned them. The victors would have their justice however it came to them.

But time passed, passionate fires were banked and memories turned gray. The taste for blatant revenge altered to a more rational, even optimistic, tone during the decade of the 1920s. Gilbert Murray, an Oxford University professor and a strong supporter of the League of Nations, developed such an approach. In 1928, he lectured that the League of Nations was success-ful, flexible, and comprehensive, "and exactly directed to the main evil which it was intended to cure. It does aim straight at the heart of interna-tional anarchy," the pressure of public opinion its greatest sanction.[2] The British widely shared his convictions. Thus, any move toward new arma-ments was met with much wariness and accusations of war mongering. Who needed to rearm? Had not Germany become a member of the League of Na-tions in 1926, demonstrating to all a rejection of war as a means of solving problems? Obviously, they had learned their lesson.

But, in the meantime, the roof fell in on Britain's economy during 1921. Her two greatest prewar markets had been Germany and Russia. Devastated by the war, Germany experienced economic collapse, and Russia was in the throes of the Soviet revolution. As Correlli Barnett noted,[3] Britain's debts weighed heavily, portending a grim future after all. Thus, in 1914 the national debt was £650 million but in 1919 the debt stood at over £7 billion. The United States added to the decline. Caught in an isolationist tide, and more interested in selling than buying, America increased tariff rates at the moment Britain desperately needed big foreign markets. This was further complicated because British heavy industry, which included coal, steel, shipbuilding, and textiles—long-standing victims of technological obsolescence—lost out to modernized competitors such as the United States and Japan.

Falling revenues forced Parliament to swallow a dose of frugality. With the war over and with no enemies lurking about, why not cut armed forces spending? A simple rule was adapted for calculating armed services budget estimates: assume there would not be a major war for ten years—thereafter known as the Ten Year Rule.[4] The Royal Navy's budget fell from £344 million in 1919 to £76 million in 1921 and to £60 million in 1922.[5]

Sir David Beatty, now first sea lord, the Royal Navy's commander in chief, insisted that all future naval estimates must include battleships, for he fervently believed the fleet's power resided in the big ships. The Battle of Jutland proved that—and he had been there! His belief found support in a report issued 19 December 1919 by the Post-War Questions Committee organized to help shape the Royal Navy's direction over the next decade. The report concluded, "The duel between the gun and armor . . . will doubtless continue."[6] Although Britain finished the war with sixty-one battleships, most were prewar dreadnought models, and the war made obsolete many others of later vintage. The Battle of Jutland, which conditioned so much postwar naval thought, clearly revealed the superiority of German fire control systems, armor, and ammunition. They had sunk fourteen British ships compared to a loss of ten of their own. Equally demonstrated was the inferiority of British shells that often failed to penetrate German armor, inadequate armor on British ships, and faulty lower-deck construction, especially around ships' munitions magazines. British naval supremacy could only be maintained by new ships of modern design.

Then along came the cheeky Americans. They possessed thirty-nine battleships during the war and had plans to build six more plus six battlecruisers and a hundred other vessels. The plan, developed in 1916, was put aside the next year because of the wartime need for escort ships and submarine chasers. The United States Congress revived it in 1918. Admiral Beatty viewed this development as a direct challenge to British sea power. Winston Churchill sided with Beatty, declaring that four battleships must be built every year for four years. Stephen Roskill, the British naval historian, commented that Churchill's thinking, considering the reality of Britain's economic situation, was "little short of fiscal lunacy."[7] Lunacy? Perhaps. More likely paranoia. An uneasy belief was surfacing in the Royal Navy's higher echelons that the United States might somehow become Britain's next enemy.[8] Strangely, no one bothered to explain just how a war between Britain and the United States would happen. It is much easier to carry about assumptions than demonstrate realities.

Assertive naval planning by the United States was disconcerting enough. Japan grew more troublesome, a nation whose Asian intrigues were noted as early as 1915. During that year, Japan moved to control aspects of China's internal affairs: insisting on Japan's right to economically exploit Manchuria; demanding that Japan take over the German concession in Shantung Province; and demanding Japanese advisers be placed on Chinese military councils. Then, in 1920, under the Treaty of Versailles, Japan took possession of Germany's former Pacific island colonies. Although several Japanese battleships and battlecruisers were already under construction, Japan declared the need for a still-larger fleet to protect their growing interests and establish a place in international circles.

The British Admiralty, seeing Japan as a potential threat to British interests in Asia, established an advisory commission on imperial defense.[9] Admiral of the Fleet Sir John Jellicoe, commander at Jutland, led the commission. His findings were wide-ranging and insightful. Japan, he concluded, might create turmoil, if not outright war, in the future. If war did erupt, he was confident the United States would do nothing. Britain would be alone. Based on that gloomy finding, he made three tragically accurate predictions. First, the Royal Navy was spread so thin around the world that they could not send a strong force to the Pacific against Japanese aggression. Second, the Japanese would move against New Guinea and the Dutch East Indies (now Indonesia) as a prelude to invading Australia. Third, the Japanese could take Singapore with a fully equipped army of 100,000 men. As Stephen Roskill stated, Jellicoe's conclusions regarding Japan's strategic goals portrayed exactly the events of 1941 and early 1942.[10] Jellicoe urged the creation of a Far Eastern fleet centered around eight battleships and eight battlecruisers to deter the Japanese.

Alas, the report met official apathy for a number of reasons that are aside from this study. Suffice to say that the government, regardless of party, bowing to the constant call for disarmament and the need to cut budgets, remained unconvinced that Japan was a potential enemy. Even Churchill scoffed, "But why should there be a war with Japan? I do not believe there is the slightest chance of it in our lifetime."[11] Sir Austen Chamberlain, the future foreign secretary, supported Churchill's position, stating that war with Japan was improbable.[12] With indecision reigning, the government chose to do little or nothing about imperial defense. Thus, British naval supremacy drifted toward extinction in the corridors of power.

Then, much like a cowboy on a white horse, the Americans galloped into the vexatious international situation. Responding to a strong domestic disarmament sentiment, buttressed by calls for fiscal frugality, the United States government made two conciliatory moves. First, in early 1921, the Senate recessed without approving the most recent and expansive naval budget. When the Senate reconvened a month later, they unanimously passed a naval disarmament resolution. President Warren Harding would invite selected maritime nations to a conference in Washington, DC, on 1 November 1921. The invited nations incuded Britain, France, Holland, Belgium, Italy, Portugal, Japan, and China.

The Washington Naval Conference produced a series of agreements and pacts, two of which were, arguably, the most important.[13]

First, many existing capital ships went to the scrap yard and, at America's insistence, no new ones could be built for ten years. Royal Navy advisers exhorted their delegates not to approve the proposals, but to no avail. The British delegation surrendered to American pressure. A battleship tonnage ratio determined allowable existing strengths. The United States and Britain could each retain 500,000 tons and Japan 300,000 tons. This was known as the 5:5:3 formula. These tonnages translated to fifteen battleships each for the United States and Britain, nine for Japan, and the French and Italians might have five each. The formula resulted in the British scrapping twenty-two old dreadnoughts and four battlecruisers that were under construction. After the ten-year hiatus, new battleships could displace no more than 35,000 tons and mount nothing larger than 16-inch guns.

The Japanese delegation, much criticized at home by ultranationalists, wrapped themselves in righteous indignation, and let it be known that the 5:5:3 ratio was an insult, even a betrayal of trust, after the loyalty to the Allied cause they demonstrated during the war. They felt shunted aside. Yet, the Japanese offered a way to save face for themselves and quell any fears rising from their two former allies. Japan would accept the 5:5:3 ratio provided the United States, Britain, and France sign a Four Powers Pact with them. The pact required a British promise not to strengthen existing fortifications or construct new ones north of Singapore. The United States must promise not to fortify Guam and the Philippines. In return the Japanese promised to respect the sovereignty of France over Indo-China, the British over the Malay States and Hong Kong, and the Americans over the Philippines. The Western nations signed.

An unsettling undercurrent nevertheless persisted for the British. Although the Admiralty accepted the naval conference's ratios as an inevitable consequence of their nation's inability to compete with the United States in monetary wealth and natural resources, the realization that the Royal Navy was no longer preeminent on the world's oceans did not settle comfortably. More was to come. Having effectively reduced British naval power, the Americans quickly pressured Britain to abrogate an alliance with Japan that had been in place since 1902 and which made naval cooperation possible during the war. Britain, as their way of stemming Japan's increasing demands, was considering renewal. But the Americans, also looking for a way to slow the Japanese, viewed with disfavor British intentions. The British delegates once again acquiesced to the Americans.

The Washington Naval Conference was heralded as a peacemaker in the spirit of the League of Nations, a potent movement against an arms race, an accord among responsible nations. The United States, Britain, France, Italy, and Japan had been allies in the Great War. They had remained friends since the war. Friends do not go to war with friends. How rational it all seemed. But Japan bristled at their treatment by the British.

In 1924, the conservative Stanley Baldwin became prime minister and promptly brought Churchill into his cabinet as chancellor of the exchequer—secretary of the treasury. From that august position Churchill used his considerable energy and political acumen to oppose the very positions he supported a few years before. He made permanent the Ten Year Rule for armed forces budgeting, successfully arguing that the rule should be self-perpetuating. Henceforth, the decade would be calculated from each successive calendar day. Churchill's innovative interpretation of the rule strangled the Royal Navy from 1924 to 1929. Every proposal for new equipment was denied because the Treasury deemed they violated the Ten Year Rule.[14]

Within this tempestuous atmosphere—the Admiralty's insistence on new ships and the Parliamentarians' quest for budget cuts—emerged the debate over a naval base at Singapore. The base was pivotal to the Admiralty because of its geographical location, the half-way point between Britain's empire in the Pacific and its major holdings to the west in India, Africa, and the Mediterranean. The base was also important because whether or not it existed strongly influenced the deployment of the entire Royal Navy. Although approved in principle in 1922, the same year that the Anglo-Japanese alliance was terminated and replaced by the Four Powers Pact, both Conservative and Labor governments viewed the Singapore base with skepticism. Conservatives thought it would drain Britain's monetary resources, and Laborites thought it despoiled faith in the League of Nations. Both parties believed the base was the Admiralty's excuse for a larger fleet that would encourage warmongering and an arms race. Consequently, and to no one's satisfaction, Singapore was an on-again, off-again proposition during the 1920s. Despite Admiral Beatty's continuing support for the base (he wanted it completed by 1925) the British government fumbled along not knowing quite what to do. Toward the decade's end, the chiefs of staff recommended delaying construction in order to solve constructional and tactical issues. Then the Committee on Imperial Defense requested that the installation of the shore batteries, key to the base's defense, be delayed. The Conservative government willingly complied. As the decade ended, the new Labor government redundantly ordered all work on the base stopped. Meanwhile, the Admiralty wondered what expectations would be made of them if war did erupt.

More white doves took wing in 1925 with the signing of the Treaty of Locarno. Germany, struggling to join the European community as a responsible nation, together with France and Belgium, agreed to recognize the integrity of their mutual boundaries and of the demilitarized Rhineland. They pledged not to war upon each other. Britain and Italy, as the treaty's guarantors, would immediately intervene against the nation that violated the agreement. But how Britain, with a limited armed services budget and a national climate of opinion suspicious of any maneuver anticipating armed conflict, could intervene was a question never asked. Perhaps spurred by optimists such as Gilbert Murray, few believed the need would arise.

A London Naval Conference was held in 1930 to adjust the original Washington accords. The British walked into a disaster. Outmuscled by the Americans and Japanese, they agreed to cut their cruiser force to fifty ships with an aggregate displacement of 328,000 tons. In order to see any increase in new ships, that tonnage limit meant the building of light cruiser mounting 6-inch guns rather than heavy cruisers mounting 8-inch guns.[15] The economy seemed logical enough at the time, at least to Parliament.

The Admiralty was appalled. For all the rhetoric about big guns on big ships, the cruiser force tied the empire together, protecting sea-lanes vital to the British Isles. With high speed and ranges up to 10,000 miles, cruisers projected British force across the world's oceans. The cruiser reductions, approved by the Labor government, blunted the Royal Navy's power at its point. The eventual scramble to rebuild the cruiser force proved inadequate in 1939. Substitutes would have to be found, opening the door to the commissioning of armed merchant cruisers.

The 1930s was a new and troublesome period for the Royal Navy. The British government continually entered contradictory agreements that, on one hand, committed Britain to intervene against aggressor nations and, on the other hand, cut away the means to fulfill those obligations. At the same time, the Royal Navy was also committed to imperial defense. The dominions of the empire could not defend themselves. They had neither the financial nor material resources to do so. As Barnett points out, the Royal Navy was trapped in "one of the most outstanding examples of strategic over-extension in history."[16] He gloomily concluded that in the early 1930s, the Royal Navy, its size reduced, its technology obsolete, became a "kind of fashionable yacht club more apt for elegant displays of ship handling and royal tours of the Empire than for battle."[17]

THE 1930s: THE STRUGGLE TOWARD REARMAMENT

Any existing enthusiasm for the Singapore base deflated during the early 1930s. Few in government saw the big picture. Myriad committees, sub-committees of committees, the Treasury, and Parliament debated to uncertain conclusions. Money was budgeted for the base; work stopped; work started. The continuing indecision caused horrendous damage. There were no ships for a Far East fleet. There was no money for a Far East squadron or even a flotilla. There never would be a major ship permanently based at Singapore. Yet, building the base somehow lurched on, driven by some mad dream that its mere existence would curtail aggression.

The Royal Navy had been grievously wounded by its own government for over a decade. Battleships remained limited by the Washington Naval Conference, allowing Britain to still retain fifteen of them. But by 1930, seven remained virtually untouched since their days of service during World War I, and five were out of commission in dry dock for antitorpedo armor and bridge reconstruction. The battle cruiser HMS *Hood*, commissioned in 1920, the "pride of the fleet," slid down the ways into immediate obsolescence, for its deck armor was too thin and its lower-deck design faulty. The battleships *Nelson* and *Rodney*, commissioned in 1927, displaced almost 34,000 tons. Each carried nine 16-inch guns, twelve 6-inch guns, and numerous antiaircraft guns. The problem with the two ships was that all nine big guns were forward of the superstructure, making oblique firing rather dangerous. The turrets and gun decks carried most of the armor, concentrating great weight forward of the bridge. That made the battleships difficult to handle. Additionally, they could generate only 23 knots, far too slow for modern naval warfare.

The 1930 London Naval Conference not only stripped down the cruiser force but allowed the Royal Navy only 120 destroyers, half of which would be over-age by mid-decade.[18] The conference allowed six aircraft carriers but that favorable number was compromised by the big gun admirals.[19] Rather than being viewed as floating bases for offensive operations, the carriers were looked upon as useful for artillery spotting, reconnaissance, and fleet defense. A long and sometimes-vicious argument began in 1918 when the Royal Flying Corps and the Royal Naval Air Service were combined into the Royal Air Force as an independent service. Trying to establish an identity distinct from the older services, they did not want the navy taking control of any aircraft. Naval planes, those new weapons rife with strategic possibilities, languished. One poor design after another came off the drawing boards. The few from the early 1930s that did work would have to make do late in the decade.

In April 1931, the incumbent First Sea Lord, Admiral of the Fleet Sir Frederick Field issued a report in which he blasted the Ten Year Plan for diminishing the Royal Navy's strength to the point where it could not be relied upon to efficiently protect British overseas trade. He wrote that battleship and battlecruiser reductions had reached such a critical level that transferring any of them to the Far East would endanger British shipping in European waters and the very security of the British Isles.[20] The chiefs of staff came to a similar conclusion in 1932 when they wrote the Cabinet that the Royal Navy could not respond adequately to aggression in the Far East because the forces stationed there were inadequate and the bases at Singapore and Hong Kong were in poor defensive condition.[21]

The alarms sounded by the British military became a reality when the Japanese marched into Chinese-held Manchuria in September 1931. In February 1933, the League of Nations issued a proclamation calling for Japan to restore Manchuria to China. The Japanese envoy responded in an angry speech that his nation would not comply. Instead, Japan would quit the League of Nations. With that, the entire Japanese delegation walked out of the assembly. There would not be rational discussions. There certainly would not be negotiations between friends. There would be another war.

But the year was not over. Hitler assumed power in Germany. Once again, Britain's chiefs of staff sent a warning to the Cabinet stating that Germany was rearming and within a few years would be "a formidable military power."[22] Certainly the abandonment of Versailles Treaty restrictions in favor of the unilateral Anglo-German Naval agreement did nothing but increase the British chiefs' alarm. Restraints on German naval development no longer existed. Despite his rearmament plans, Hitler used the agreement to demonstrate to a European audience willing, indeed needing, to believe his every word, that Germany had only peaceful intentions.

Yet another danger erupted in the mid-1930s. Ever since 1918, Britain assumed Italy would remain a steadfast ally. But Italy in the 1920s and 1930s was not Italy of World War I. Benito Mussolini's fascism took hold, driven by his dreams to restore the might of the Roman Empire. First he beat down the Libyans in an early example of ethnic cleansing. Then he turned his imperial ambitions to connecting Libya with Italian Somaliland on the Red Sea, but Abyssinia (Ethiopia) stood in the way. The Italians invaded Abyssinia in October 1935. The British government, echoing public opinion, condemned the aggression. The new First Sea Lord Admiral of the Fleet Sir Ernest Chatfield believed the government's move a disaster in the making. He wanted Italy to be Britain's best friend in the Mediterranean. Calling the League of Nations' policy of collective security a "miserable business," he believed Britain now faced the impossible situation of having to fight "any nation in the world at any time."[23]

The Abyssinian crisis turned into a nightmare for the British. Liberal voices in Britain clamored for the government to do something. But what? More speeches in the League of Nations further estranged the Italians. Chatfield was concerned that armed intervention would lead to the sinking of valuable British naval ships. Thus, to avoid any accidental engagements, the Royal Navy stayed in Alexandria harbor and at Gibraltar. Meanwhile, the Suez Canal remained open to Italian troopships and supply vessels for fear that Mussolini might retaliate were the passage closed.

In June 1936 the Abyssinian crisis ended as King Halie Salassie fled to England. Nothing could alter Mussolini's despicable victory, least of all the speeches in the League of Nations. The Italian dictator focused his venom on Britain who, among the League of Nations' members, was most vociferous in its opposition to the invasion. Mussolini would neither forgive nor forget. Just as Chatfield predicted, Britain created another enemy—Italy—but without firing a shot, much less lifting an anchor, an enemy dominating the Central Mediterranean, the major sea passage between the British Isles and her Far East possessions. A worse strategic position is difficult to imagine. Belatedly, reluctantly, the government slowly moved to rectify the naval situation. The Ten Year Rule was abolished. Then, under the accumulative impact of world events—the Japanese invasion of Manchuria, the Italians in Libya and Abyssinia, Hitler's public renunciation of the Versailles Treaty and his reinstitution of military conscription and revelation of the *Luftwaffe*'s existence—the Cabinet approved a budget increase for building warships. The goal was a navy comprised of fifteen battleships and battlecruisers, eight carriers, seventy cruisers, 144 destroyers, and fifty-five submarines. The important factor in the rearmament program was a twenty-ship increase in the cruiser force. Five were to be laid down every year for four years. Thus, by 1940, the date for completion of the program, the Royal Navy would have seventy cruisers, the same size force they had in the 1920s.[24]

The King George V class of vessels was the major thrust of the battleship program. In addition to *George V* were *Prince of Wales*, the *Anson*, the *Howe*, and *Duke of York*. *Prince of Wales* was finished in late 1939, and *George V* was completed in December 1940. The other ships were completed in 1941 and 1942. They displaced a standard 35,000 tons, were 740 feet long, and had a top speed of 28 knots. They each mounted ten 14-inch guns grouped in three turrets, one each fore and aft of the superstructure containing four guns, and one surmounting the forward turret having two guns. These guns, as *Jane's Fighting Ships of World War II* noted, were a new model with a greater range and penetrating power than the *Hood's* 15-inch guns. The new battleships also mounted sixteen 5.25-inch guns in eight twin turrets, plus numerous pompom and Bofors guns, and up to thirty-eight 20-mm guns.

The so-called Town Class cruisers—*Newcastle*, *Birmingham*, *Belfast*, *Liverpool*, *Sheffield*, and *Glasgow*—were laid down between 1934 and 1936 and completed over 1937 and 1938. These sturdy ships mounted twelve 6-inch guns in four triple turrets, eight 4-inch guns in twin turrets, and numerous smaller antiaircraft guns. They also carried six 21-inch torpedo tubes in triple mounts. At 9,100 tons, they could make 32 knots. The Fiji Class cruisers, a six-ship group, were begun in 1937. Their armaments and performance matched those of the Town Class. Seven Dido Class cruisers, ordered in 1937 (another three were ordered the next year), displaced a standard 5,450 tons and made 33 knots. Their main armament was ten 5.25-inch guns in five turrets, three forward, two aft. They also carried six 21-inch torpedo tubes and numerous 40-mm and 20-mm antiaircraft guns. Ostensibly designed as antiaircraft cruisers, a few of these ships were reduced to four turrets after 1940, effectively converting them into heavy destroyers.

The Cabinet knew, of course, that naval rearmament would be an expensive proposition; consequently, an even larger program that called for twenty battleships and 100 cruisers received no consideration. But, whatever size the rearmament program, the main difficulty was actually getting the ships built. David Beatty had feared that the hiatus in capital shipbuilding imposed by the Washington Naval Conference would lead to a precipitous decline in the specialized workforce necessary to build such ships. He was right, ironically so because German naval expansion encountered similar difficulties. Many contracts offered throughout Britain went unfulfilled because the firms did not have the workers and machinery needed for the required tasks. The shipyards themselves had to rebuild their capacities after years of neglect. The British steel industry could not produce all the necessary plating. A contract was let to Czechoslovakian firms.[25] Delays delivering highly technical fire control systems and radio equipment, and difficulties assembling ASDIC instruments (ASDIC, an anagram for Allied Submarine Detection Investigation Committee) caused disruption. What was conspicuously absent from the new naval program were the escort vessels that could have benefited the most from the available ASDIC equipment.

The British Admiralty should have learned from World War I that German U-boats, now allowed under the Anglo-German Naval Agreement in contravention of the Versailles Treaty, posed a potent threat to British commerce. The Admiralty was blinded by their bias favoring capital ships, by the Submarine Protocol requiring U-boats to approach merchantmen on the surface, and by an untested faith in ASDIC.

ASDIC, conceived in 1918 and developed through the 1920s, was operational by 1936. The principle was simple enough. A quartz crystal suspended beneath a ship was charged with electricity, causing it to expand and contract, thus sending a pulse through the water. If the pulsations encountered an object they were reflected, like an echo, back to the originating crystal. A technician then interpreted the echo to determine its source. Consequently, the dreaded submerged submarine could be located, attacked with depth charges, and sunk. The fear subsided that the unrestricted U-boat attacks of World War I would be repeated.[26] This rather smug complacency overlooked the annoying fact that ASDIC instruments were not installed on ships specifically designed to attack submarines—escorts. These vessels were not even on the drawing boards in 1936.

The reason behind the omission, ASDIC notwithstanding, was that escort vessels shepherded convoys, anathema to many naval officers who believed the convoy concept defensive—and defensive thinking invited weakness. For their part, the Admiralty believed "convoy" always referred to fast ship formations carrying military equipment and troops "screened by an outer ring of cruisers, battlecruisers and [with] a close destroyer escort."[27] They did not bother about merchant ship convoys, what would become the life blood of Britain's survival. As Stephen Roskill emphasized, "*not one exercise in the protection of a slow mercantile convoy against submarine or air attack took place between 1919 and 1939.*"[28] The big-ship, big-gun philosophy prevailed.

For seventeen years Britain and the continental nations watched as Germany grew more united and militarily powerful, reaching an apogee under Adolf Hitler. Nonetheless, Western Europe seemed strangely apathetic toward Germany or at least content with that nation's transformation from a defeated nation to a powerful presence. And why not? Treaties, pacts, conferences, and agreements curbed overt aggression. War ceased to be a viable extension of politics. Turning a blind eye to Japanese aggression in Manchuria, the British government believed that negotiations made all things right. Hitler, despite his bellicose nature, was not really a bad man. Had not the great Lloyd George, Britain's wartime prime minister, visited Hitler in

1936? He reported that yes, Germany would resist any invasion, but did not harbor territorial ambitions. And he was quite taken by Hitler at a personal level. A.J.P. Taylor wrote that beginning with the Armistice of 1918 through 1936 there existed an appealing belief that precautions against a German-made war were unnecessary.[29]

What needed attention were German grievances. Unsurprisingly, as it were a series of placations, all the treaties, pacts, and agreements signed in the postwar years usually favored Germany: reparations were renegotiated in Germany's favor; loans, especially from the United States, flowed into German coffers; the British took the bold step of committing themselves to continental peace by guaranteeing, along with Italy under the Locarno agreement, the integrity of Belgian, French, and German borders; and the Germans rearmed without any sanctions imposed, despite continual and flagrant violations of the Versailles Treaty. At nearly every political turn, Germany was left to decide on her own terms whether to agree or not, to sign or not, to obey or not, to comply or not. Again, as Taylor stated, appeasement of Germany did not begin with the tenure of British Prime Minister Neville Chamberlain in 1937; it originated shortly after World War I.[30]

Britain's indecisiveness or indeterminate attitude toward Germany and toward her own rearmament program was twice tested in mid-1936.

Allied troops occupied the Rhineland following the war with the proviso that they would withdraw in 1930, leaving it a demilitarized zone. On 7 March 1936, German Army units marched into the Rhineland despite Hitler's passionate oratory of May 1935, when he promised that Germany would fulfill all the obligations of the Locarno Treaty and respect the demilitarization of the Rhineland. But he had watched the fumbling gestures of Britain and France during the Abyssinian War. He was convinced, despite his generals' hesitancy, the two great powers would be just as fumbling over his reoccupation of the Rhineland. He was right. The French army, ill-equipped and ill-trained, could stop the Germans only by using overwhelming numbers. That involved general mobilization. The French would not take that step for fear Hitler would view such a move as provocation for a larger war. The French looked to the British for help but there was none forthcoming. True, the British had been guarantors of both French and German boundaries but, technically speaking, the Germans were taking back German territory; therefore, the British were not obligated to respond militarily. Besides, Britain lacked sufficient forces to support a French counter-strike, and there was a widespread sentiment in Britain against any possibility of repeating World War I.

Nothing was done about the German incursion for, in reality, neither Britain nor France wanted to do anything. So they blamed each other for

Czech delegation barred from the conference, the pact was signed 29 September 1938. Chamberlain returned to London where, at the airport, holding the document aloft for the assembled crowd, cameramen, and reporters to see, he announced "peace in our time."

Not everyone was certain Chamberlain accomplished a miracle at Munich. Planning committees within the armed services, procurement departments, designers, and politicians such as Churchill—now convinced that war was imminent—pushed rearmament forward with an urgency born of a present danger. The Admiralty at long last admitted the fleet needed escort vessels specifically designed to protect British shipping. In June 1938, they approved the Black Swan Class of sloops. They were literally light destroyers that displaced 1,470 tons, were 300 feet long, and made just over 19 knots. They mounted six 4-inch dual-purpose guns plus ten guns of smaller caliber. They did not carry torpedo tubes. Seven ships were laid down between 1937 and 1942, and proved so successful that an additional eighteen were ordered in the next two years. But the ships that received the greatest recognition were those of another new class called corvettes. Churchill referred to them as "cheap and nasties"—cheap for the British to build and nasty to the Germans. These little ships, the Flower Class, were based on a well-known whaler design. They certainly were cheaper and faster to build than destroyers, and much less expensive to operate. Fifty-six of the class were laid down under a 1939 supplementary navy budget and, remarkably, over 150 more were ordered by war's end. The corvettes carried one 3- or 4-inch gun, a pompom gun aft of the funnel, up to six 20-mm antiaircraft guns, and depth charges. The Flowers made 16 knots, quite sufficient for slow mercantile convoys where the highest speed was determined by the slowest vessel. The first of the class became operational in 1940. Naval reserve officers, the so-called "Wavy Navy" because the rank stripes on their jackets undulated instead of staying straight, typically commanded these little ships with skill and bravery.

Yet the new escort ships did not shake the Admiralty's conviction that submarine warfare was a diminished threat. They firmly believed the real danger to British shipping would be from German surface raiders. The ships best suited to find these raiders were cruisers. Alas, the launching by 1939 of new cruisers could not match the demand for their services. Thus, the available cruiser force was inadequate, a realization first voiced in the 1920s and repeated in the early 1930s but generally ignored. The Shipping Defense Advisory Committee recommended a World War I solution: commandeer fast passenger liners, arm them with leftover World War I 6-inch guns, and send them out as armed merchant cruisers (AMCs). Some would patrol the North Sea and the waters east and south of Iceland and, to the west, the

Denmark Strait, establishing a blockade of Germany. Other AMCs would escort merchant convoys from Canada. Still others would join the South Atlantic cruiser squadron.

One need only look at a pre–World War II map to see the extent of the Royal Navy's problems in 1939. To borrow a British officer's apt description of British arms about to engage in a war eighty years before, "[Our force] is like a steam engine whose boiler is in Halifax, its cylinders in China, and its other machinery distributed in bits and pieces wherever the map of the world is colored red and for which machine neither water . . . nor oil nor repair tools are kept at hand."[37]

The Royal Navy lurched toward what seemed an inevitable war.

They were not alone. In truth, by 1937, the naval agreements of Washington and London had fallen apart. Yes, the Royal Navy was entranced by battleships but so too were Hitler and the German admirals. And so, too, were Italy, France, the United States, and Japan. In 1937, the Italians laid down the first of a three-ship class of 35,000-ton battleships mounting 15-inch guns. France, in 1935 and 1936, started construction on the *Dunkerque* and *Strasbourg*, both 26,000 tons and carrying eight 13-inch guns. The United States in 1938 laid down the first of ten battleships that displaced from 42,000 to 45,000 tons and mounted nine 16-inch guns. The Japanese planned two super battleships (1938–1942), the *Musashi* and *Yamato*, that would displace nearly 70,000 tons fully loaded, and carry nine 18-inch guns. The naval arms race was charging ahead with nothing to stop it. All the lessons of World War I, all the good intentions, pacts, treaties, and agreements finally came to nothing.

CHAPTER 4

WAR: SEPTEMBER 1939 TO NOVEMBER 1940

OPENING PLANS, OPENING MOVES

Whatever else the Versailles Treaty meant to the German people, no provision was more universally despised than the creation of the Polish Corridor. That strip of land gave Poland access to the Baltic Sea by separating East Prussia from the rest of Germany. Danzig was the corridor's major city, not Polish territory but a free city created by the League of Nations and governed by a league-appointed high commissioner.

Hitler, doubtlessly dissembling, but in a negotiating mood nonetheless, wanted Polish concessions to build a six-lane highway and a rail line across the corridor, the land on either side ceded to and governed by Germany. He demanded that Danzig be returned to German rule, for he wanted to reunite all German people, one of his rationales for earlier taking the Czech Sudetenland. The corridor gave him ammunition by which to provoke the Poles and, by one means or another, fulfill his ambition.

In late October 1938, Nazi Foreign Minister Joachim von Ribbentrop transmitted Hitler's demands to the Polish Foreign Ministry. Although Poland was reborn as a democracy after World War I, Joseph Pilsudski led a military coup in 1926 and created a dictatorship. When he died in 1935, a council of colonels continued his authoritarian rule. One of these was Foreign Minister Colonel Joseph Beck. He modified Hitler's wish list insisting that even though the highway could be constructed the adjacent land would remain Polish. Danzig would remain a free city. Hitler, barely hiding his claws, called Beck to Berlin in January 1939. "Danzig is German," he declared, "will always remain German, and will sooner or later become part of Germany."[1]

Beck's responses over the next weeks fended off Hitler. He also ignored the Russians who did not like the idea of Germany expanding eastward. And he played the French, with whom Poland had a mutual support agreement, and the British for all the political clout he could get. He doubted that would be much. Beck's apparent cynicism toward his hoped-for allies was well founded; he realized Hitler had made a fool of Chamberlain at the Munich Conference. Yet Beck's calls for political backing nevertheless gave Chamberlain an opportunity to appear forceful for once. Indeed, he made a fateful decision. Informed of German troop movements near the Polish Corridor, appraised of Hitler's demands to the Poles, and with Beck's approval, Chamberlain rose in Parliament on 31 March 1939 and announced that Polish sovereignty was now protected by Britain and should any action threaten that nation's independence both Britain and France would immediately lend Poland all their support. There was one small omission: He did not give the French advanced warning of this announcement. Technically, it did not matter because of the earlier Franco-Polish agreement. However, as Leonard Molsey wrote, "The last thing [the French] wanted was to be reminded of it."[2]

Hitler met with his general staff on 3 April. He told them he had lost all patience with the Poles and if no new avenues of rapprochement opened he would crush them. He then issued a directive to his armed forces. Two items stand out. First: "The task of the armed forces is to destroy the Polish armed forces. To this end a surprise attack is to be aimed and prepared." Second: "Preparations must be made in such a way that the operation is carried out at any time from September 1, 1939, onward."[3]

Hitler did not stop there. He called his military leaders to a meeting in the Reich Chancellory on 23 May and announced that war was inevitable. Of course, any of the assembled officers who heard him in April realized as much. But now he pointedly condemned the British as the principal force against Germany. Therefore, it was necessary to invade Holland, Belgium, and France, thus creating an Atlantic and English Channel front for air and naval bases from which Britain could be defeated. "The aim [of the war] will always be to force England to her knees."[4] The means of victory were the bombing of Britain, developing a submarine blockade to starve out the island, and defeat of the Royal Navy. Grand Admiral Raeder, knowing the *Kriegsmarine* could not fight Hitler's war, was aghast. All Hitler's promises, timetables, and plans for the new navy apparently meant nothing.

But Poland came first. The Germans attacked 1 September 1939. The invasion was made possible by a last-minute nonaggression pact between Germany and the Soviet Union, signed on 23 August, by which Germany would invade Poland but not go beyond the Vistula River east of Warsaw. The Soviets took a measure of comfort from the deal. They occupied eastern Poland as well as the Baltic States of Estonia, Latvia, and Lithuania. This land grab created a buffer zone between Russia and Germany.

The German Navy, using the old battleships *Schleswig-Holstein* and *Schlesien,* bombarded Polish shore forts and troop concentrations with considerable effect. Their guns may have been antiques but their shells were no less dangerous. The *Wehrmacht* and *Luftwaffe* worked in a coordinated fashion never before seen in warfare. The Polish air force did not exist after the first day. By 27 September, encircled, bombed, and shelled, Warsaw surrendered. On 6 October the campaign was over and the world had a new word for the unstoppable fury of the German advance—*blitzkrieg,* lightning war.

Was Britain actually to be the ultimate target of the next war? Raeder, still unbelieving, had repeatedly warned Hitler that the *Kriegsmarine* was ill prepared to fight an all-out war against the Royal Navy. The British possessed fifteen battleships, the Germans two (reclassifying the *Scharnhorst* and *Gneisenau* from their usual battlecruiser status). The three pocket battleships were potent weapons but, designed as commerce raiders, they were of little value against the new and more heavily gunned King George V class British battleships. The British counted fifteen heavy cruisers and forty-nine light cruisers, the Germans three and five, respectively. The two fleets each had fifty-seven submarines. On 1 September, however, only eighteen German U-boats were on war stations in the Atlantic. The remaining vessels were needed elsewhere or were small coastal submarines restricted to short Baltic and North Sea patrols. Raeder estimated that only eight or nine boats would be regularly in the Atlantic because the others would be going to or from the war zone, be resupplying, or in repair facilities.[5]

What Raeder did not anticipate, given repeated reassurances during recent years, was the "bomb shell" the Führer threw him on 3 September when they met in the chancellory: Britain and France had just declared war on Germany. "[The Führer] was embarrassed over his faulty judgment," Raeder observed. Hitler told him, "I have not been able to avoid war with England."[6] The admiral bitterly commented in his memoirs "The German Navy could do little more than go down fighting . . . [and] show that it knew how to die valiantly."[7] Dönitz was equally thunderstruck by the declarations of war. "Seldom," he wrote, "has any branch of the armed services of a country gone to war so poorly equipped [as the U-boat fleet]."[8]

Raeder and Dönitz may appear sincere, if not naive, in their reactions to

Hitler's announcement, but there is also a beguiling note in their shared dismay. Prior to 1 September, U-boats and pocket battleships already had departed Germany for their Atlantic war stations. Such positioning had little to do with a parochial conflict in Central Europe that lacked appreciable sea frontiers. Who else but the British and French were these ships supposed to fight?

One thing was clear: Plan Z was finished. The hoped-for five or six years for fleet development abruptly ended, sacrificed to Hitler's rampant ambitions and his final misreading of British and French intentions. He fully expected the politicians of the two nations to crumble before his aggression in Poland just as they had limped away from the reoccupation of the Rhineland, the absorption of Austria, and the eradication of Czechoslovakia. Hitler now faced opponents who, for all his hyperbole, he did not really want—at least not in 1939. Yet he clung to the belief that he might somehow find a way out of a full-scale war, especially with the British. A peace treaty with them was as good as a military defeat, and either would secure his western flank. But his policies, plans, lies, declarations, contradictions, threats, and desires now crashed into one another.

British and French impotence during the Polish invasion at first buoyed Hitler's belief that the two allies would negotiate a peace, for their pledges of full support amounted to nothing. Not a soldier moved. Not a shot was fired. The Home Fleet did venture into the North Sea, trying to locate something, anything, that might bring the men to action stations and give the appearance of active support to the Poles, but they found nothing.

The Germans were expected to smash west following the Polish invasion and conquest, but an unexpected scenario unfolded that eased tensions along the western front. True, German troops deployed along the French frontier, and the French did man the infamous Maginot Line. But not much happened. The next eight months became known variously as the Twilight War, the Phoney War, and the *Sitzkrieg*. This almost surreal military situation did not, however, match the realities of war exploding on the Atlantic Ocean.

THE WAR AT SEA: THE FIRST MONTHS

By early August, eighteen U-boats were positioned west of Ireland. On 21 August, the *Graf Spee* slipped past Iceland, bound for the Brazilian coast near Pernambuco (Recife). On 24 August, the *Deutschland* (which would be the cover photo for *Life* magazine on 29 November 1939) sailed for the Denmark Strait. All were in their positions to begin commerce raiding. But on 7 September, Hitler and Raeder agreed that the two pocket battleships should move from their assigned operational areas, the *Graf Spee* sailing east to the mid-Atlantic, and the *Deutschland* held above the Denmark Strait. Submarines could attack British merchant ships but there was to be no offensive action against any French ships. Furthermore, no passenger ships would be attacked, even if sailing in convoys. They also ordered nine U-boats from their Atlantic operational areas back to the North Sea. These shifts were "[i]n view of the political and military restraint shown by France and the still hesitant conduct of British warfare."[9] In short, Hitler believed he could still bring the two to the bargaining table.

Hitler further insisted that U-boat commanders obey the 1936 Submarine Protocol. There was one exception: *"Transports which are determined to be on active service and belong to the armed forces were to be considered warships."*[10] The renewed emphasis on the protocol came about because the U-boat skipper necessarily made the determination of whether or not a transport was on active service. This was fraught with subjectivity and possible error. Approaching a transport on the surface was a dangerous maneuver, a lesson learned during World War I when British Q-boats stalked submarines. The decision was therefore made from a submerged position, making observation of the enemy ship much more difficult. Indeed, on 3 September 1939, shortly after the declarations of war, the *U-30*, captained by Lieutenant Fritz Lemp, sighted the 13,500 ton British liner *Athenia*, outward bound from Liverpool, zigzagging and running without lights. Lemp sent a torpedo into her. She went down with 112 lives, including twenty-eight Americans. The destroyers *Electra* and *Escort*, together with some foreign vessels, rescued 1,300 survivors.

The German leaders first learned about the sinking from British news accounts. Hitler denied a U-boat sank the *Athenia*, the statement stemming from his earlier insistence on obedience to the Submarine Protocol. In fact, he did not know exactly what happened. Lemp maintained an ordered radio silence and did not return to Wilhelmshaven until 27 September. Dönitz met him at the dock. Lemp told his commander that he believed the *Athenia* was an armed merchant cruiser. Dönitz ordered Lemp to erase any mention of the sinking from his war diary (*Krieqstaqebuch*). Then Dönitz declared that the *Athenia* struck a mine.[11] Hitler decided the affair should be kept secret and that Lemp would not be court-martialed for exceeding orders. However, in a radio broadcast, Propaganda Minister Joseph Goebbels stated the real culprit behind the sinking was Winston Churchill, recently made first lord of the Admiralty. According to Goebbels, Churchill connived to place a time bomb aboard the *Athenia*, the better to implicate Germany. Both Raeder and Dönitz were taken aback by this obvious lie, coming as it must have with Hitler's approval, but both kept quiet.[12]

The *Athenia* sinking spurred three immediate actions. First, the British

Admiralty accelerated the escort vessel program, despite some strong reservations, and eighty-six trawlers, already on antisubmarine duty, received ASDIC equipment.[13] Second, the British instituted plans for merchant convoys. And third, on the German side, Hitler again ordered that the Submarine Protocol be strictly obeyed, upsetting Raeder and Dönitz who saw value in a more aggressive U-boat strategy.[14] But Hitler still harbored hopes that Britain and France would sue for peace—at any price. Nor did he want Britain screaming about unrestricted U-boat warfare, reawakening memories of World War I, when the Allies cursed the German butchers of the sea for their inhumanity.

Although new destroyer classes, corvettes, and sloops were being built and armed merchant cruisers (AMCs) were being commissioned, the Royal Navy's need for escorts was immediate. The Admiralty looked to the Royal Canadian Navy (RCN) for assistance. Unfortunately, in 1939, there was not much assistance to give. During the 1930s, the RCN entered into tangled negotiations with the British Admiralty about building destroyers, especially of the Tribal Class, in Canadian yards. But questions about how many would be built and who would have jurisdiction over the ships once launched precluded a coordinated program. The sudden declaration of war on 3 September certainly caught the Canadians off guard and unprepared. To fill the duties thrust upon them, the RCN, by December 1939, commandeered some sixty auxiliary vessels for harbor defense, mine sweeping, and antisubmarine patrols. None of these ships was particularly worthy and all were unreliable.[15] A few of the commandeered ships nonetheless performed quite well within their limitations. Three of these—HMCSs *Prince David*, *Prince Robert*, and *Prince Henry*—were small, fast passenger liners from the Canadian-Pacific Line converted to AMCs. More of them later.

Canadian unpreparedness had many causes but two stand out. First, the senior officers in the RCN believed their first and most important task would be coastal defense against German capital ships sent to bombard them. In that way, they shared the British Admiralty's prewar assumption that big guns on big ships would rule the seas. Second, the Canadians also shared an unbounded faith in ASDIC, concluding that submarines no longer presented a major problem.

Actual sea duty proved that ASDIC had its shortcomings. There were several limitations. The instrument established an echo's bearing and relative range along a narrow beam at a fixed angle and worked best at speeds less than 8 knots. The instrument's range did not exceed 1,500 yards. Best readings were obtained when the sea was relatively calm and the water not too cold. However, even under optimum conditions, errors up to 25 yards were commonplace, a considerable weakness when depth charges needed to explode within 20 feet of a U-boat to sink it, and within 50 feet to do damage. Moreover, once an echo registered it needed interpretation. Submarines did not reflect a consistent configuration; so, was a U-boat really out there, or was it a whale, or a school of fish, or a temperature anomaly?[16]

Another problem loomed in the war at sea. Enlightened officers of both sides of the Atlantic worried about air attacks against naval and merchant shipping, especially along Britain's east coast. They begged for antiaircraft weapons. Machine-guns and four-barreled pompom guns that fired 2-pound projectiles were the only weapons readily available in 1939 and early 1940. More sophisticated 20-mm guns and 40-mm Bofors guns became available only later in 1940 after production problems were solved. To make matters worse, very few 3-inch and 4.1-inch guns were dual-purpose weapons.

Whatever the antiaircraft weapons, they shared the same fundamental problem. The probability of hitting anything was remote. Antiaircraft fire control, even on destroyers, was nonexistent or ineffective. The two fusing mechanisms used by the larger antiaircraft guns presented problems. Contact fuses necessitated a direct hit on the target before exploding. The second type of fuse exploded the projectile after a set time. Both types involved extraordinary luck. A direct hit on a plane flying at a guesstimated height and speed was a rarity. Time fuses offered little more because the second or two between setting the time, loading, and firing often meant a miss up to 2,000 yards. Consequently, gunnery officers filled the sky with as much steel as possible in the hope that one or more aircraft would run into the barrage.

The biggest problem was complacency. Shortly after the war started, a strong Royal Navy patrol headed for Helgoland Bight off Denmark and came under attack from the *Luftwaffe*. A Heinkel 111 bomber aimed for the aircraft carrier *Ark Royal*, its bomb missing her bow by only 20 yards. A bomb that blew a great slab of armor from the hull hit HMS *Hood*. The conclusion in high places was that damage to ships from air attacks was much overrated.[17]

Thus, escort vessels rolled into the northern seas inadequately armed with imprecise weapons, lacking any tactical coordination for combating U-boats, and manned by half-trained crews who learned as they went.

Nevertheless, on 2 September, the first escorted convoy of some eight ships sailed from Sierra Leone. The first escorted convoy in home waters sailed from the Thames Estuary to the Firth of Forth on 6 September. The next day the first westward or outbound convoy sailed from Liverpool to Canada. The first homeward or inbound convoy, code-numbered HX-1, left Halifax, Nova Scotia, on 16 September.

Each westbound convoy was escorted in these early months by a small cluster of ships—perhaps a destroyer or a sloop and some trawlers—to a position about 150 miles west of Ireland. Because U-boats did not initially operate much beyond that point, the convoy then scattered, each ship sailing independently to its destination. Meantime, an eastbound convoy was escorted across the Atlantic by an older battleship, or a single destroyer, sloop, or AMC to a point where they met the escorts of the recently released westbound convoy. Those warships took them into a British port.[18]

The Admiralty was comforted by the results. Forty-one ships were lost in September 1939; twenty-seven ships were sunk in October; twenty-one went down in November; and twenty-five in December. These figures translated into a total loss of 421,156 tons. That compared very favorably to the May 1917 slaughter of over 800,000 tons. The Admiralty believed that ASDIC was working, overlooking the fact that most of the ships lost in those first four months either sailed independently or lagged behind their convoys, usually because of mechanical breakdown.

As much as the British needed ships for convoy duty, they also needed to blockade the North Sea. The supposition existed, based on World War I strategy, that the Germans could be starved into surrender. Few in Britain appreciated the difference between 1914–1918 and September 1939. The Nazis, by taking Austria, Czechoslovakia, and Poland gained food supplies, factories, and raw materials they did not possess during World War I. For example, as reported in the London *Times*, 12 November 1940, an agreement with Romania guaranteed Germany a steady oil supply. Also, the Nazis conquest of Europe enabled them to create a huge slave labor force that freed many able-bodied men for military service. The British faced a contrasting situation. In the summer of 1940, Britain was alone and without allies. Most everything needed to fight the war much less exist as an island people had to be imported along vulnerable sea-lanes. The expense was enormous and Britain was nearly broke.[19] Thus, the race between Germany and Britain to see which won the war at sea meant survival for one, defeat for the other. Raeder and Dönitz gnashed their teeth at the restricted U-boat operations imposed by Hitler. The British needed to strengthen their fleet and that meant more ships. The Admiralty accepted the Shipping Defense Advisory Committee's recommendation to commandeer and commission passenger liners for use as AMCs, thus plugging the cruiser gap. By February 1940, forty-eight liners were outfitted as AMCs. Their assignments were numerous and varied. Ten AMCs joined the Freetown Escort Force, and four—HMSs *Alaunia*, *Laconia*, *Montclare*, and eventually *Jervis Bay*—escorted Halifax convoys. Seven more AMCs were scattered about the Mediterranean, off East Africa, and in the Indian Ocean. In April 1940, for instance, HMSs *Chakdina*, *Chantala*, and *Laomedon* helped evacuate troops and civilians from Berbera, British Somaliland, before the Italians took it.

But the AMCs' principal job was reinforcing the Northern Patrol, securing the sea-lanes between Iceland and the Faroe Island to the southeast, and the Denmark Strait between Iceland and Greenland to the west. Twenty-five AMCs were allocated to the 7th and 12th Cruiser Squadrons. This released older regular cruisers for other duties, fifteen being assigned to North Atlantic convoys and hunter groups and four to South Atlantic stations.[20]

North Atlantic AMCs worked under arduous conditions—tempestuous, unpredictable seas, rain, sleet, ice, and heavy mists that restricted observation. And there was an ever-present sense of isolation, of being alone on a slate gray sea surrounded by steel sharks—U-boats.

These odd warships worked diligently. Between 12 and 16 September 1939, HMSs *Scotstoun* and *Transylvania*, steaming together, stopped six German ships attempting to get home through the British blockade. The AMCs captured three but the crews of the other three scuttled their ships to avoid capture. In March 1940, HMS *Maloga* intercepted the steamer *La Coruna* but her crew scuttled their ship. On 28 March, the *Transylvania*, operating alone, encountered the *Mimi Horn* trying to run the blockade. The freighter was scuttled by her crew. HMS *California* patrolled Iceland's eastern fjords during May 1940 to prevent German trawlers landing saboteurs who might damage the trans-Atlantic telegraph cables that came ashore at Seydisfjord. Between September 1939 and early 1940, the Northern Patrol cruiser squadrons, both regular cruisers and AMCs, intercepted 300 ships, sending 171 to port for cargo inspection. During the first six weeks of the war 338,000 tons of contraband were seized. Many Germany-bound ships were scuttled; however, seventeen were captured.[21] The numbers probably would have been fewer were it not for the AMCs filling the gap. All seemed to being going well.

Then reality hit.

THE FATE OF HMS *RAWALPINDI*

HMS *Rawalpindi*, a 16,697 tons converted passenger liner, was one of the AMCs sent to war. Although she was armed with eight 6-inch guns, the fire control system was rather along the lines of aim-shoot-pray. *Rawalpindi* had no armor, torpedoes, or mines. There was no radar (but few ships at that time had it), and no ASDIC or other antisubmarine weapons. Although she had a speed of 15 knots, *Rawalpindi* lacked the maneuverability of warships. Thus, without the speed to flee from a cruiser or pocket battleship, and lacking firepower for a serious attack, *Rawalpindi*, like her cousins, was labeled a death ship. She joined the Northern Patrol, coursing between Iceland and the Faroe Islands, looking for merchant ships carrying contraband and reporting German surface raiders striking into the Atlantic.

The pocket battleship *Graf Spee* was already in the South Atlantic in a holding pattern off Brazil and the *Deutschland* was waiting near the Denmark Strait. Hans Langsdorff, the *Graf Spee*'s commander, did not receive orders to attack the enemy until 26 September. As we shall see, he had some success.

Skipping ahead for the moment, by November *Graf Spee* had sailed 30,000 miles and her engines showed signs of wear. Captain Langsdorff, believing he could urge some further mileage from his ship, planned a raid around the River Plate before returning to Germany after the New Year. Grand Admiral Raeder devised a plan to take pressure off the *Graf Spee* by distracting the Allied ships sent to hunt her down. On 13 November, he ordered the new battlecruisers *Scharnhorst* (1939) and *Gneisenau* (1938) south of Iceland to raid British shipping, at the same time avoiding encounters with superior enemy naval forces.

On 23 November 1939, late afternoon, as the two German ships bludgeoned their way through heavy seas between Iceland and the Faroes, the *Scharnhorst* suddenly turned north, signaling *Gneisenau* that they spotted a large ship on a parallel course. *Scharnhorst*, commanded by Captain Kurt Hoffman, identified the intruder as an AMC. The two enemies closed on one another. *Scharnhorst* signaled the AMC to stop and identify herself, but the steamer kept coming toward the battlecruiser. *Scharnhorst* fired a warning shot across the ship's bow, but HMS *Rawalpindi*, commanded by Captain Edward Kennedy, stayed its course. Kennedy, at last seeing what he was up against, ordered smoke canisters thrown into the sea. They did not ignite. Kennedy, his ship now in great danger, attempted to escape by changing course, simultaneously opening fire with his 6-inch guns. The range was too great and the shells dropped harmlessly into the sea. The *Scharnhorst* replied with a salvo from her 11-inch guns. The shells crashed into the starboard side of the unarmored merchant cruiser, knocking out the electrical system. The radio operator rigged an emergency generator and sent a message that *Rawalpindi* was being attacked by the pocket battleship *Deutschland*. No sooner was the message transmitted than another 11-inch salvo hit the steamer, destroying the radio, smashing the bridge, and killing Kennedy and his officers. *Scharnhorst* allegedly passed astern of *Rawalpindi* and around to the port side. This was a moment of confusion in the fight, for it is unclear whether the *Gneisenau* joined the bombardment. In any event, 11-inch projectiles battered *Rawalpindi*, destroying what was left of her 6-inch guns, killing their crews, and reducing the merchant cruiser to a helpless burning hulk. Someone aboard Rawalpindi flashed a signal to *Scharnhorst* to send boats. Hoffman quickly responded but picked up only twenty-seven survivors because the cruiser HMS *Newcastle*, having received *Rawalpindi's* distress call, was sighted steaming toward the action. *Scharnhorst* and *Gneisenau* made hasty exits even though they could have blown the *Newcastle* out of the water. But they had orders not to engage British warships. Only eleven more *Rawalpindi* crewmen were plucked from the sea the next day; 270 died with their ship.

When news of the sinking reached the Admiralty, Churchill was in a meeting with First Sea Lord Admiral Sir Dudley Pound and Admiral Sir Tom Phillips. Churchill and Pound stood aghast, each accepting responsibility for the tragedy. Churchill grimly concluded that public reaction to the sinking would require him to answer the question "Why was so weak a ship exposed without effective support?"[22] This was an absurd situation. Armed merchant cruisers were needed for patrol and for escorting convoys. Thus, as a consequence of their inherent weaknesses as warships, it seems that Churchill thought they needed individual reinforcement from the very ships they were supposed to replace. However, as Stephen Roskill pointed out, the Admiralty could not find any other way to increase the cruiser force except by commissioning AMCs. The modern guns, fire control equipment, radar, and well-trained crews needed to give these ships "even a reasonable chance of engaging a German raider successfully simply did not exist in 1939."[23]

From the start of the war, Churchill certainly had reservations about the AMCs. The ships were expensive to outfit and operate. He resisted improving their 6-inch gun mounts because the task would be costly and time consuming at already overworked shipyards. Of course, his primary and justifiable concern was the vulnerability of the merchant cruisers to U-boat attacks. He was aware that they were particularly defenseless when intercepting a suspicious vessel. Both ships would have to stop and a boarding party sent from the AMC. The AMC would be a perfect target for a torpedo attack. And, as bad weather diminished U-boat operations against merchant shipping in the Atlantic, Churchill forewarned they would attack ships of the Northern Patrol with consequent heavy losses among the AMCs.[24]

RETRIBUTION: THE FATE OF THE *GRAF SPEE*

Churchill's *mea culpa* notwithstanding, AMCs continued sailing the Northern Patrol and escorting convoys. Churchill had actually worsened their situation when he initially embraced the conventional wisdom of many Royal Navy officers that convoys reflected a defensive strategy. He pushed "unremittingly" for offensive actions,[25] supporting nine so-called hunter groups positioned down the Atlantic and into the Indian Ocean to Ceylon.[26] Among the groups was Force G, operating from the Falkland Islands and comprising the heavy cruisers *Cumberland* and *Exeter* and the light cruisers *Ajax* and *Achilles*, the last from the New Zealand Navy. The French battleship *Strasbourg*, together with three French AMCs that had served in the Norwegian campaign—*El Kantara*, *El Djazair*, and *El Mansour*—and the cruiser HMS *Neptune* were stationed at Dakar. They formed Force Y. Force X, two French heavy cruisers, the aircraft carrier HMS *Hermes*, and the AMC HMS *Pretoria Castle* operated from St. Helena Island. These assignments sometimes changed as ships were shifted about between groups depending on regional needs. In all, the hunter groups literally commandeered from the Royal Navy's Home Fleet and from the Mediterranean Command three battleships, five aircraft carriers, two battlecruisers, and eleven cruisers. The French added one battleship and three cruisers. Three additional British battleships and two cruisers were made available to the Halifax convoys.

And what exactly excited this reorganizational activity? News reached the Admiralty on 1 October that the 5,000-ton steamer *Clement* had been sunk the previous day by the *Graf Spee* off Bahia, Brazil. Hitler, nettled by his failure to bring Britain and France to peace terms, unleashed his pocket battleships *Graf Spee* and *Deutschland*. Certainly Churchill and the admirals thought the hunter groups the best solution to the surface raiders. The firepower of any single group could sink either raider.

But were both the *Graf Spee* and *Deutschland* at sea? What were Hitler's intentions regarding the *Scharnhorst* and *Gneisenau*? Did he also send out surface raiders disguised as merchant ships? The Admiralty lacked reliable intelligence, long-range air patrols, and radar. The hunter groups consequently groped about rather than systematically hunted for the German ships. Admiral Raeder knew all along that the threat of his capital ships loose in the Atlantic would disperse the Royal Navy's strength and worry and confuse its leaders.[27] His strategy was working.

But sinking the *Clement* proved an inauspicious if not embarrassing beginning for the *Graf Spee*. Her commander Hans Langsdorff had signaled the *Clement* to stop. The *Spee*'s seaplane, without orders from Langsdorff, strafed the *Clement*'s bridge as if encouraging compliance. The *Clement*'s skipper Captain Harris heaved-to and ordered his crew to abandon ship. He and his chief engineer were brought aboard the *Graf Spee* but the *Clement*'s crew remained in their lifeboats. The Germans gave them provisions and a compass bearing for the nearest Brazilian port, then set about sinking the *Clement*. Two of *Graf Spee*'s torpedoes ripped through the calm waters toward the steamer—and missed. Then the raider's 5.9-inch guns opened fire. Twenty-five rounds failed to sink the ship. Finally, five 11-inch projectiles sent *Clement* to the bottom of the sea. Langsdorff was not pleased by the ineffective gunnery.[28]

Langsdorff now headed for West Africa, knowing full well the British would scour the waters off Brazil for his ship. On 5 October, he intercepted the British freighter *Newton Beach*, which was retained to transport prisoners. On 7 October, *Graf Spee* sank a freighter and two days later rendezvoused with the supply ship *Altmark*. What captives *Graf Spee* held were transferred to the *Altmark*, and *Newton Beach* was sunk.

That same week, *Deutschland* sank a freighter near Bermuda but not before her radio operator sent a R-R-R message, indicating they were under attack by a surface raider. This confirmed that two pocket battleships were in the Atlantic. To confuse the British Admiralty, Raeder sent *Gneisenau*, the cruiser *Köln*, and some destroyers on a sortie to Norway, then turned them back to Wilhelmshaven. By mid-November, the *Deutschland* was ordered back to Gotenhafen (Gdynia). Hitler awaited her return much like a parent wondering about an absent child, and promptly changed the ship's name to *Lützow*. There was no sense in tempting fate by putting in harm's way a ship named *Deutschland*. But the British Admiralty, oblivious of her return home, kept searching for her well into December. Churchill remarked that *Deutschland* "imposed . . . a serious strain on our escorts and hunting groups in the North Atlantic. We should have in fact preferred her activity to the vague menace she embodied."[29]

Graf Spee, meantime, entered the Indian Ocean but sank only two ships. Langsdorff turned back to the Atlantic. Although *Graf Spee's* engines needed overhauling, he intended further operations around the River Plate before returning home. At that point, Raeder sent the *Scharnhorst* and *Gneisenau* into the Northern Patrol zone to distract the British and take some pressure off Langsdorff.

On 27 November, *Graf Spee* again linked with the *Altmark*, taking on fuel and needed supplies. Two days later, the two ships parted, *Graf Spee* sailing northeast toward Africa. Four days later the British refrigerator ship *Doric Star* was sighted. Langsdorff ordered a warning shot fired toward the merchant ship. *Doric Star* either did not notice the shot or chose to ignore it and kept on course. Drawing closer, *Graf Spee* fired again, barely missing the vessel. *Doric Star* heaved-to and awaited the Nazi raider but, given the few miles distance still between the ships, the British radio operator sent the R-R-R raider attacking signal over and over. Langsdorff ordered the steamer to shut down its wireless immediately or he would open fire. No contest—*Doric Star* stopped transmitting.

The Freetown British naval base had received the signals and relayed them to the Admiralty in London. Hunter groups put to sea, searching the trade routes from Capetown to the North African coast. Commodore Henry Harwood, commanding Force G at the Falklands, received a message from Freetown that the *Admiral Scheer* was off West Africa. The hunt was on. The misidentification exemplified British confusion caused by poor and unverified information. But Harwood did not believe the pocket battleship would remain around West Africa. He came to a risky, lucky, and unaccountably accurate conclusion: The raider was headed for the River Plate and its rich shipping lanes. Using the light cruiser *Ajax* and his flagship, Harwood ordered the heavy cruiser *Exeter* from the Falklands and the *Achilles* from Montevideo, all to meet 12 December about 150 miles east of the River Plate. However, Langsdorff had not yet moved, beset by delays to a point when time became precious. First, the boarding party sent to inspect the *Doric Star* barely glanced at the cargo. Instead, their attention was focused on a cache of silver bars, which they desperately wanted, and transferred to *Graf Spee*. They took their time. Then the *Spee's* scout plane went missing, the victim of an empty petrol tank, and was not recovered until sundown. Only then, just as Harwood predicted, *Graf Spee* headed for Montevideo. On the way, she intercepted and sank the steamer *Tairoa*. Three days later, she again met the *Altmark*, taking on further stores and transferring prisoners to the supply ship. On 7 December, the freighter *Streonshalh* was sunk.

Harwood's Force G rendezvoused as planned. Early in the morning of 13 December, smoke was seen on the horizon. *Exeter* steamed off to investigate. Her signal came back to Harwood: "Pocket battleship."

Graf Spee's crew was at battle stations before *Exeter* sighted their ship. The height of the pocket battleship's masts and the acuity of her rangefinder allowed her lookouts to see further than the enemy. The ratio of one pocket battleship to three cruisers did not especially faze Langsdorff. His ship outgunned the British cruisers and her armor was thick enough to withstand hits even from the *Exeter's* 8-inch guns. Thus, he did nothing to avoid the British force. But neither was Harwood alarmed by the pocket battleship. His cruisers possessed superior speed and maneuverability and his 3-to-1 odds gave him, he believed, a tactical advantage.

Langsdorff expected the cruisers to follow from a safe distance but Harwood attacked. *Exeter* steamed northwest at a range of some 19,400 yards. *Ajax* and *Achilles* moved northeast at about 19,200 yards. This maneuver, already practiced by Harwood's ships, forced Langsdorff to divide his firepower by aiming one turret at the *Exeter* and the other at the light cruisers. *Ajax* and *Achilles* scored repeated hits on the *Graf Spee* but nothing critical was damaged. *Exeter*, in contrast, was blanketed by 11-inch gunfire, which shattered her starboard torpedo tubes and scout planes. With the range closing, the gun turret in front of the bridge took a direct hit, killing all within and turning the bridge and forward superstructure into a tangled, bloody mess.

Two more 11-inch shells put the other forward turret out of action. *Exeter* was in trouble.

Yet the heavy cruiser still had fight left in her. Captain Frederick Bell, commanding his ship from emergency steering gear and sending runners through the ship in place of the destroyed communications apparatus, kept his stern turret firing. An 8-inch shell pierced the *Graf Spee*'s deck armor, and another tore through the superstructure. Another hit put a big hole in the bow. Bell ordered his starboard torpedo tubes to fire one salvo. He turned his ship and fired a second salvo from his port tubes. No hits. Then another 8-inch shell hit the *Graf Spee*. Langsdorff fired back, striking *Exeter* yet again. Bell desperately wanted to continue the fight, even if it meant ramming the German ship. But the *Exeter* was settling and the electrical system was out of commission. Bell reluctantly turned his ship away from the action, setting course for the Falklands. *Ajax* and *Achilles* continued the fight, firing at 17,000 yards, then again at 11,000 yards. Their guns peppered the *Graf Spee*'s decks and superstructure. Some 6-inch shells hit the water, shredding the armor belt but not piercing the hull itself. The pocket battleship fired a salvo at the *Ajax*, destroying her two aft turrets. *Ajax* retaliated by launching four torpedoes, forcing Langsdorff to temporarily change course to avoid being hit.

Langsdorff had had enough of the cruisers! He launched four torpedoes at *Ajax*—they missed—then steamed west toward the River Plate and Montevideo. The battle had lasted an hour and a half.

The two British cruisers fired occasional 6-inch shells at *Graf Spee* as if to hurry her along. *Graf Spee* returned fire with salvoes from her 11-inch stern turret. But Langsdorff was running out of ammunition for his main guns and his ship was wounded. The cruisers had scored twenty hits on her; yet, none had caused critical damage except for the hole in the bow. Langsdorff needed time to repair the bow hole and to bury his dead. Only the Uruguayan government could grant the time because, under international law, a belligerent ship could stay in a neutral port only twenty-four hours and make only those repairs necessary to make her seaworthy. Langsdorff radioed the German ambassador that he needed more time. After anchoring, a Uruguayan naval inspection team declared *Graf Spee* could stay for seventy-two hours.

In the meantime, Harwood signaled the Admiralty for assistance. The heavy cruiser HMS *Cumberland* arrived from the Falklands on 14 December to replace the *Exeter*. The cruisers *Dorsetshire*, *Shropshire*, and *Neptune*, the battlecruiser *Renown*, and the aircraft carrier *Ark Royal* all headed for the River Plate—but long journeys lay ahead of them.[30]

Admiral Raeder, with Hitler's consent, left the decision of what to do in Langsdorff's hands, with the exception that *Graf Spee* was not to be interned.

In the event she was scuttled, Raeder ordered that the sinking must be done "with effective destruction."[31] Hitler grumbled that *Graf Spee* should fight her way through the British patrols and sink a few ships along the way. The problem was that no one in Berlin, much less in Montevideo, knew which British ships were waiting.

At 6:00 P.M., 17 December, all diplomatic negotiations to extend her time in port exhausted, *Graf Spee* weighed anchor and left Montevideo harbor. Unbeknownst to anyone but the crew, only Langsdorff, his senior officers, and eight petty officers manned the pocket battleship. She steamed down the estuary and into international waters where three British cruisers were waiting for her. Suddenly Langsdorff turned his ship away from the British force and anchored. He and his skeleton crew climbed into a motor launch and made for Buenos Aires. At 8:00 P.M., explosions rocked the *Graf Spee*, tearing her apart.

Langsdorf, exhausted, dispirited, and alone, shot himself.

THE HAPPY TIME—FOR THE GERMANS

Hitler avoided a tantrum over losing the *Graf Spee* but a silent humiliation persisted over losing her to mere cruisers. That mood deepened when, on 16 February 1940, the *Altmark*, headed for Germany with 300 British seamen taken off the *Graf Spee*, was intercepted by the destroyer HMS *Cossack* in Jossing Fjord, Norway. The prisoners were forcibly rescued despite the presence of Norwegian torpedo boats.

Such a provocative maneuver was evidence to Hitler and Raeder that Britain had no intention of respecting Norwegian neutrality and that their next step would be the establishment of Royal Navy and Royal Air Force bases in Norway. Such thinking may have been either a classic rationalization or a burst of political reality for what was about to occur because Raeder long-wanted northern bases. Here was a reason to get them. Hitler ordered an interservice planning committee get the jump on the British by taking Norway first. The *Kriegsmarine* representative was Captain Theodor Krancke, soon to command the *Admiral Scheer*. Thus, on 9 April, the Nazis invaded Denmark and Norway.[32] By 7 June, all resistance ended. But the *Kriegsmarine* suffered losses. The new cruiser *Blücher* went down in Oslo Fjord from coast artillery and torpedo fire, and ten destroyers were sunk by the Royal Navy at Narvik. Nonetheless, the Germans gained valuable military assets: air bases to protect their northern flank; relatively unfettered access to the North Sea; and Raeder's coveted naval bases for U-boats and capital ships.

On 10 May, Prime Minister Chamberlain stepped aside. He was replaced by Winston Churchill, who was charged with forming a national or coalition government. That Churchill, vehemently anti-Nazi, was now Britain's leader did not bother Hitler. He believed Churchill's support, thin at best, would soon diminish and level heads would "recognize the futility of warring against [Germany]" and seek peace.[33]

Ironically, the long-awaited "hot war" on the western front opened that same day. The Germans overran Holland, Belgium, and France in a sledgehammer offensive lasting only six weeks. Now the Nazis could literally look across the English Channel to Britain. The *Luftwaffe*, from bases along the channel coast, bombed and strafed British east coast shipping, RAF bases, and factories in southern England. Then the bombing shifted to British cities. This was total war. U-boats operated from French ports from L'Orient south along the Bay of Biscay, their travel time to the Atlantic trade routes and their chances of discovery much reduced. The Nazi army, poised in France, was getting ready to invade Britain in Operation Sea Lion.[34]

The British Admiralty faced a dilemma of enormous proportions. To guard against invasion meant withdrawing from convoy duty and the Northern Patrol essential cruisers and destroyers. The situation was made more critical by the loss of nine destroyers during the Dunkirk evacuation early in June. The invasion threat loomed large because of the possible starvation of Britain caused by decimated convoys.

The Germans also had problems. Hitler needed a successful *Luftwaffe* air campaign to soften Britain for invasion but, as the summer wore on, the results were inconclusive. The RAF fought back tenaciously, inflicting heavy losses on German bombers and escort fighters. Also German assembly ports for the invasion, from Le Havre to Antwerp, were hit hard by long-range British coast artillery, motor gunboat raids, and RAF raids. The German naval staff, on 17 September, declared the ports to be too vulnerable. Hitler indefinitely postponed Operation Sea Lion. Admiral Raeder was not displeased, knowing his fleet could not realistically fulfill the demands of a cross-channel invasion. Indeed, earlier on 19 July 1940, Raeder stated that Sea Lion "is out of proportion to the Navy's strength and bears no relation to the tasks that are set to the Army and Air Force."[35]

Now it was up to the *Kriegsmarine* to throttle Britain's supply lines. Unfortunately for the Germans, Dönitz's U-boats lacked the numbers to do the job properly. His fleet began the war with fifty-seven boats. A year later he still commanded the same number because newly built boats did not exceed the number sunk, and several were always retained for training. For instance, in September 1940, of thirty-nine operational U-boats, there were about twelve at sea at one time. Of those, according to Dönitz, about only six were actually on war patrol. The number rose to eight by October.[36] The problem magnified. An unacceptable number of the torpedoes fired by these U-boats failed to explode. This "torpedo crisis" was eventually solved by the development of a new firing mechanism or "pistol," but the U-boat crews were the ones who, in the interim, risked their lives with the ever-present possibility of no results. That was a sour draught to swallow.

Dönitz made two tactical changes that frustrated the British and gave his submariners needed advantages. First, he found a way to beat ASDIC by having his U-boats attack at night and on the surface—so often, in fact, that one might consider the submarines to be surface raiders, which had the capacity to submerge, for ASDIC did not respond to surface contacts. Convoy escorts were not equipped with radar, and the combination of a submarine's low silhouette and the darkness made the attackers nearly impossible to detect. The impact intensified when the U-boats attacked in groups, Dönitz's second tactical change, called wolf packs. He stationed his boats in line across probable convoy routes, enhancing interception. When a submarine sighted a convoy, that U-boat commander signaled the other boats in the group to gather on him. On the night of 18 October, for example, five U-boats attacked convoy SC-7, steaming for Nova Scotia. Seventeen merchant ships went down. The next night the pack intercepted convoy HX-79, which was escorted by two sloops, two corvettes, and four armed trawlers. The U-boats sank fourteen of forty-nine ships, then attacked convoy HX-79A and sank another seven ships. Not a single U-boat was lost.[37] No wonder that the U-boat crews sailed from their bases brimming invincibility and singing "We're sailing to England."

Despite the small number of U-boats, the British felt the decline in available food. For their part, they sang the music hall ditty "Oh, when can I have a banana again?"

AMCs appeared as vulnerable to U-boats as Churchill feared. Not only did they present bulky targets but their patrol assignments placed them in dangerous situations without the means to fight back.[38] By November 1940, eight AMCs had been torpedoed and sunk—*Carinthia*, 6 June by U-46; *Andania*, 16 June by UA; *Transylvania*, 10 August by U-56; *Dunvegan Castle*, 8 August by U-46; *Cheshire* mid-October by U-137. On 3 November, HMSs *Laurentic* and *Patroclus* fell victim to Otto Kretschmer's U-99.[39]

On 3 November 1940, 10:02 p.m., Kretschmer, cruising on the surface, intercepted three large ships heading east. The first ship to be sunk was the merchantman *Casanare*. The second ship, a liner, turned and sped away. Then another liner with two funnels and a foremast came into range. Her forward scuttles were not blacked out—perhaps in preparation for swinging out hidden 6-inch guns, Kretschmer concluded she was an AMC. At 10:50, U-99 sent a torpedo into the ship, hitting below the forward funnel. Then U-99 picked up a message sent in the clear from the ship, "Torpedoed engine-room, all [boiler] fires out." Suddenly, the liner was ablaze with lights. She was the AMC HMS *Laurentic* (18,7245 tons). U-99 fired a second torpedo that missed. A third seemed to have no effect. The *Laurentic*, recovering from the surprise attack, fired star shells to locate the U-boat and opened fire with her 6-inch guns. The other liner reappeared on the scene, heaved-to, and was picking up those of the *Laurentic*'s crew that took to her lifeboats. Kretschmer fired a torpedo at the rescue ship, the AMC HMS *Patroclus* (11,314 tons). Empty barrels gushed from a hole in the stern. Another torpedo hit—more barrels. A third torpedo hit—still more barrels. These had been placed in the ship's holds to increase her buoyancy, a common practice among AMCs. Kretschmer sent his deck gun crew to finish off *Patroclus*, but the AMC's guns were returning fire. Kretschmer submerged to reload his torpedo tubes.

At 4:53 A.M., Kretschmer returned to the *Laurentic*. A torpedo fired into her stern finished the ship. Then, at 5:16 A.M., he sent a fifth torpedo into *Patroclus*, breaking the ship in two. According to the London *Times* (5 November 1940), rescue ships picked up fifty-two officers and 318 men from the *Laurentic*, and thirty-three officers and 128 men from the *Patroclus*.

Dönitz noted that the number of torpedoes used to sink the two AMCs was disproportionately high but disturbingly typical of such attacks. Thus, U-boats often lacked sufficient torpedoes to attack other targets and so returned to their bases earlier than expected.[40]

On 1 December Kretschmer posted a record third sinking of an AMC when he torpedoed HMS *Forfar*, which was escorting convoy HX-90. He put one torpedo into her that evening, but *Forfar* kept steaming west. Later, he fired four more torpedoes into the AMC, sending her to the bottom. Kretschmer's attacks were Churchill's worst nightmare about the merchant cruisers; yet, the AMCs kept sailing.

The British faced another maritime threat. Beginning in March 1940 and continuing throughout the year, Admiral Raeder sent out seven auxiliary cruisers to raid the shipping lanes. These were *Atlantis*, *Orion*, *Widder*, *Thor*, *Pinguin*, *Komet*, and *Kormoran*.[41] The *Komet* sailed to the Pacific Ocean via the Arctic Circle. All the others broke through the British North Sea blockade to raid the Atlantic and Indian oceans. The auxiliary cruisers, known as *Handels-Stor-Kreuzer*, commerce raiding cruisers, were not liners but common freighters. Their disguised armaments usually included six to eight 5.9-inch guns and various smaller antiaircraft guns. Some carried 21-inch torpedo tubes, some carried mines, and a couple were equipped with scout planes. They chased down or drew to them single merchant ships, as it were Q-boats in reverse, dropped their disguises, then sank their quarry and took the crews captive.

The *Thor*, commanded by Otto Kähler, is of particular interest. Before the war she was the banana boat *Santa Cruz* of 3,144 tons with a maximum speed of 17 knots. In two cruises over 1940 and 1941 lasting 653 days, *Thor* sank eighteen ships for an aggregate loss of 152,134 tons. She was the only auxiliary cruiser to eventually battle three AMCs, all during her first cruise.

In mid-July, Rear Admiral Henry Harwood (promoted for his action against *Graf Spee*), and still commanding British warships in the South Atlantic, received a report that a German raider disguised as a freighter was operating off Anguilla in the West Indies. Harwood ordered the AMC *Alcantara* to search for and destroy the raider, thought to be the *Widder*, which he believed would sail on toward the coast of South America. The *Alcantara* was a 22,209-ton liner armed with eight 6-inch guns, two 3-inch guns, and various lighter weapons. She could make 19 knots.[42]

Early on 28 July, *Alcantara*'s lookouts spotted an unidentified ship off the Argentine coast. The range was 28,000 yards. The ship changed course, after sighting the AMC, and sped away. *Alcantara* gave chase. After some hours, the AMC had gained 8,000 yards. At 12:57 P.M., at a range of 15,000 yards, the stranger slowed and began turning. *Alcantara* signalled for identification. The Nazi ensign snapped up the mast. This ship was the *Thor*, not the *Widder*. She fired a broadside at *Alcantara*. The British AMC turned and delivered her own broadside, but the sun was in the gunner's eyes and the shells missed. The scene must have looked much like a battle between frigates of old. The Germans delivered two more broadsides, damaging *Alcantara*'s engine room, one of its 6-inch guns, and the fire control system. Yet, the British gunners fired back, one shell going into one side of *Thor*'s hull and exiting the other, and a second damaging an ammunition hoist. Then another 6-inch shell hit the boat deck, putting *Thor*'s torpedo tube fire control system out of commission.

Alcantara was temporarily dead in the water. Captain Kähler of the *Thor* decided enough was enough. He was under orders not to engage enemy warships of any kind, and there was the likelihood that other British naval vessels were coming to the scene. *Thor* steamed away, disappearing over the horizon and eventually slowing to make necessary repairs.

Kähler rendezvoused with the supply ship *Rekum* on 25 August, then continued raiding with minimal results. On 8 October, they encountered the refrigerator ship *Natia* just north of the Equator. A chase ensued but *Thor* overtook *Natia* in the early afternoon and opened fire at 9,000 yards. The Germans shot 175 rounds at the cargo vessel but scored only nine hits. The *Natia* sank, *Thor* rescuing eighty-four of her crew. A month later *Thor* rendezvoused with the supply ship *Rio Grande*, taking on supplies and transferring prisoners.[43]

The Royal Navy actively searched for the raider, committing a battleship, ten cruisers, and several AMCs. One of these was the *Carnarvon Castle*. She carried eight 6-inch guns, a couple of 3-inch guns, and machine guns. At 20,122 tons she was big but could make 19 knots. On 5 December, at 5:30 A.M., while steaming through a thick mist, an unidentified freighter was spotted. The British ordered the ship to stop and be identified. She paid no heed. A warning shot was fired but fell short. With that, Captain Kähler on the *Thor*, orders to the contrary, decided there was nothing else for it but to fight. The *Thor*'s disguises dropped and the battle ensign was hoisted.

The two ships circled each other, firing sporadically. Kähler launched two torpedoes. Neither hit. Then *Thor*'s gunners found the range: one, two, three—then four, then five shells hit *Carnarvon Castle*! Flames leaped skyward fore and aft of the bridge. Worse, the fire control system was destroyed. The British gunners were on their own and, try as they might, they could not find their target. Still, the two ships kept pounding away at each other. After an hour, *Carnarvon Castle* had been hit eight times. Her bridge and funnel were damaged, some waterline plates were buckled or punctured, and she was beginning to list. Six of her crew were dead and thirty-two lay wounded. Her skipper, Captain Hardy, pulled out of the fight and made for Montevideo.

Kähler let his enemy go. Nothing could be accomplished by pursuing the merchant cruiser. *Thor*'s guns had overheated and jammed, and the gunners had used two-thirds of their ammunition. And there was the high probability that regular Royal Navy cruisers were rushing to the rescue. The *Thor* slipped away.

Meantime, during November 1940, Dönitz agonized over his U-boat shortage. In fact, the ocean was free of submarines for two or three weeks. Not only did appalling weather conditions make operations impossible but most boats needed some repairs, resupply, and rest for the crews. Dönitz did not want just six or eight boats in the Atlantic; he wanted a hundred U-boats at sea. He wrote with some frustration that "out there in the Atlantic a handful of U-boats was being called upon to fight a battle . . . that the continentally-minded German government and High Command . . . were both, unfortunately, quite incapable of grasping."[44]

In October, to bolster the war against Britain's supply lines, the pocket battleship *Admiral Scheer* cast off from the naval base at Brunsbüttel, its ultimate destination the Atlantic.

CHAPTER 5

THE BATTLE BETWEEN HMS *JERVIS BAY* AND THE *ADMIRAL SCHEER*

PRELIMINARIES: THE *ADMIRAL SCHEER*

The *Admiral Scheer* did not burst upon the war scene, as did her sister ship *Graf Spee*. Rather, in September 1939, the *Scheer* rode peacefully at anchor in the Schillig Roads off the Wilhelmshaven naval base. The heavy cruiser *Admiral Hipper* was moored nearby. All seemed well. But that quiet scene was about to change. RAF Bomber Command, fearing the *Scheer* might make a run into the Atlantic, mounted an air raid against the pocket battleship on 4 September, as if it were a sitting duck in its German pond. Two bomber flights, each of five twin-engined Bristol Blenheims, cut across the North Sea. Their top speed was 287 mph with a full load of two 500-pound bombs. The machines carried little armor and their only defense was a dorsal-mounted turret carrying two .303-caliber machine guns.

The young airmen probably did not dwell on their vulnerability; after all, the planned high-altitude bomb run and the element of surprise seemed protection enough. But deteriorating weather conditions reduced visibility and forced a lower approach to their target. The first flight from 110 Squadron went in at allegedly masthead height (about 25 or 30 feet) but more likely between 50 and 100 feet. The astonished Germans on the *Scheer* managed to shoot down one plane. The remaining four Blenheims dropped their bombs. Two exploded in the water near the *Scheer*, one hit the deck and bounced off, and the remaining bombs failed to explode. The second flight from 107 Squadron met heavy fire from the now-alert Germans. Four Blenheims went down. The *Scheer* was undamaged.[1] The raid was a tactical flop but it at least let the Germans at Wilhelmshaven know they were not entirely safe.

That same day, nine Vickers-Armstrong Wellington medium bombers mounted a raid against the *Scharnhorst* and *Gneisenau*, both moored at Brunsbüttel base near the mouth of the Elbe River. Again, the raid failed to damage either ship and two bombers were shot down. On 29 September, Handley Page Hampden medium bombers attacked two German destroyers off Helgoland. The bombers could each carry a 4,000-pound bomb load but, like the Blenheims, they had inadequate defenses. The first flight's attack missed their target but escaped without loss. Not so the second flight. The five attacking Hampdens were all shot down, the victims of Messerschmitt ME-109 fighter interception.

As the historian Edwyn Gray concluded, British Bomber Command awakened to the high cost of daylight raids against heavy defenses. The Germans, for their part, abruptly discovered from these small raids that, "unlike the High Seas Fleet in the First World War," their capital ships could not avoid attack by staying in their bases.[2] Certainly the RAF was not through with the German Navy and, as the war churned on, their raids influenced German command decisions.

Nonetheless, the *Scheer* remained at Wilhelmshaven. In November 1939, Captain Theodor Krancke, age forty-nine, came aboard as her new commander. By that time, half the old crew had been transferred ashore to train the large number of men entering the rapidly expanding navy. Those who remained with the *Scheer* knew little of their captain except that he came from command of the *Kriegsmarine* naval academy. Many concluded he was more of a naval theorist or scientist than a deep-water sailor.[3]

In February 1940, the *Scheer* was dry-docked for refitting. The crew did not get to know their commander any better during this downtime. Although he retained command, he was ordered to Berlin where he served as naval representative to the High Command, helping plan the invasion of Norway.[4] Following the campaign, he went to Norway as navy chief of staff.

Krancke returned to the *Admiral Scheer* in June, finding his ship much altered. The rather archaic-looking straight bow line, reminiscent of designs from the 1910s and 1920s, was replaced by a raked bow that gave her the look of a speedy clipper, more in keeping with those of the *Scharnhorst* and *Gneisenau*. The heavily armored trapezoidal forward control mast was gone, replaced by a lighter model similar again to the two new battlecruisers. This new mast contained more accurate radar and fire control equipment. More light antiaircraft guns had been added, doubtless a response to the earlier bomber raids. On 27 July 1940, the *Scheer* was pronounced ready for sea trials.

Captain Krancke knew there was much work ahead for his ship and crew before they went to battle. Although open-sea trials would inevitably reveal needed mechanical adjustments, it was integration of his crew that was essential, a task for which he was well suited. Krancke entered the navy in 1912 as a cadet. Promoted to lieutenant in 1915, he served in destroyers during much of World War I, a young officer upon whom his superiors looked with favor. Thus, despite the navy's decimation following the war, Krancke was retained, working his way up the promotional ladder: lieutenant in 1922; the equal of lieutenant commander in 1930; commander in 1935; and captain-commandant of the Navy Academy in 1937—an appointment that gave him insight into the kind of new junior officers with whom he would soon go to sea.

Any reservations the crew harbored about their captain were dispelled as the *Scheer* entered the Baltic for sea trials and training.[5] Krancke worked his ship and his men night and day. They practiced reporting to their various duty stations—some twenty different posts for each man. They learned how to operate new machinery, they practiced gunnery again and again, they did torpedo runs and responded to simulated air attacks. The crew quickly learned the basic three rules of any good warship: do your job the way you were trained to do it; focus on that job and let the other men do theirs; expect the unexpected.

Krancke was relentless. A normal peacetime crew was 1,100 men. He commanded a diverse lot of 1,300: a cadre of experienced men; reservists; some merchant sailors; and—the overwhelming number—green recruits who had never seen a body of water larger than a rain puddle. They needed to be welded into a unified crew within which each man could depend on his shipmates. Teamwork was essential for, once in the Atlantic, they were on their own except for an occasional rendezvous with a supply ship. The *Graf Spee's* fate demonstrated that there were no friendly harbors. And once the *Scheer* was in the Atlantic and her presence known, the largest navy in the world would be hunting them. No reinforcements would come to their rescue. Everything depended on the crew's seamanship, their fighting ability, and their confidence in their captain and each other.

Fully supplied at Gotenhafen (Gdynia), the *Admiral Scheer* sailed west on 24 October, ostensibly to move secretly into the North Sea via the Great Belt and Kattegat Strait along Denmark's east coast. But the *Luftwaffe* reported increased British aerial and submarine activity around the Skagerrak, putting an end to the breakout plan. Krancke and his superiors at Naval Group Command North agreed that the *Scheer* should reverse course, pass through the Kiel Canal, and anchor overnight at Brunsbüttel.[6]

The *Admiral Scheer* left Brunsbüttel at about 11:00 A.M. on 27 October escorted by an armed merchant ship (this one classified a *Sperrbrecher*—literally a barrier or blockade breaker but in reality not so well-muscled) and a torpedo boat flotilla (rather like light or small destroyers). The secrecy of this departure was utmost in the minds of the High Command.

The British were, in fact, completely unaware of the *Scheer's* departure. Despite the *Luftwaffe's* reports of British patrol activity, no RAF reconnaissance planes overflew the German naval bases, and North Sea patrols watched more for invasion activity than a single ship.[7] Thus, Krancke sailed his ship into the growing darkness, forging unseen across the North Sea and reaching a fjord near Stavanger, Norway, by late morning of the 28 October. That evening at 7:30, leaving her escorts in the fjord, the *Scheer* continued north. By 10:00 A.M. on 29 October she was off Trondheim. By midday on 30 October, *Scheer* had reached the apex of her generally northern course and was now northeast of Iceland. Krancke turned his ship southwest and headed for the Denmark Strait (Map 2).

PREPARATIONS: HMS *JERVIS BAY*

Who before the war could have foretold the fate of *Jervis Bay*? Launched in 1922, one of five Bay class ships, she displaced 14,164 tons, was a 550-foot-long passenger ship with a 68-foot beam sailing under the pennant of the Aberdeen and Commonwealth Line on a route between Britain and Australia. Structurally, she had a long fo'c'sle. The forward cargo well was equipped with a mast and cargo booms. Aft of the cargo well, a step up defined the cabin deck framed forward by a three-tiered bridge structure. Behind the lowest tier and above the cabins was the boat deck with the chart house and radio room. The boat deck was surmounted by a single funnel. Another cargo well, mast, and cargo booms were in the stern quarter. A covered viewing deck wrapped around the stern. Sleek enough, *Jervis Bay* could steam at 15 knots. By any estimation, she was a sound ship, sturdy and comfortable.

Anticipating war, the Royal Navy commandeered *Jervis Bay* on 24 August 1939, and commissioned her some six days later with orders to prepare for sea as quickly as possible. She was dressed for war at the Royal Albert Dock as an armed merchant cruiser. The forward and aft masts remained but the cargo booms were removed, as was the aft viewing deck. Seven antique 6-inch guns, two dating from the 1890s, were mounted—two atop the fo'c'sle, one on each side of the forward cargo well deck, two on the aft well deck, and one on the aft housing. Two 3-inch antiaircraft guns, taken from the cruiser HMS *Raleigh* (wrecked in 1921), were placed at the aft end of the boat deck.[8] A request for additional 3-inch guns was made but denied.[9]

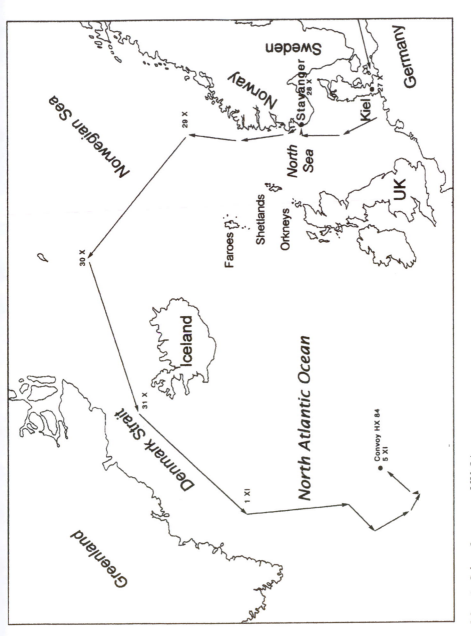

Map 2. *Scheer* Intercepts HX-84

Workers installed fire control equipment near the radio room area behind the funnel. They also made internal alterations because one does not just strap some guns to the decks and go to war. They stripped much woodwork and tore out the aft passenger cabins to create common messes for the seaman. Forward of those were the messes for the stewards and engine room crew. Ammunition magazines and hoists to the guns above had to be built in the cargo holds. The decks beneath the guns were hastily reinforced to take their recoil. Remaining cargo hold spaces were loaded with timber and empty 40-gallon drums to increase the ship's buoyancy in the event she was hit by enemy gunfire or torpedoes. An alarm system was strung stem to stern for sounding action stations. After painting the ship gray, HMS *Jervis Bay* was war-ready, in a manner of speaking. She had no radar or ASDIC equipment, no torpedo tubes or depth charges. She was helpless against submarines and a target of convenience against large surface raiders carrying big guns. One is left with the uneasy conclusion that, as convoy escorts, AMCs were so many psychological balms to the merchant ship crews; as it were scant measures of assurance.

The first voyage, under Captain H. G. Harris—called out of retirement—was north to Scapa Flow where her anchor caught a cable and, in the effort to get free, the windlass for retrieving the anchor was damaged.[10] Other mishaps followed. *Jervis Bay* was ordered south for repairs. She put into Rosyth on the Scottish coast and clipped a destroyer, her anchor penetrating the side plates. The destroyer went down until only her upper works were above water. Moving on to Tyne near Newcastle, *Jervis Bay* broke her moorings, drifted toward a mud flat, and had to be hauled back into place by a tug. *Jervis Bay* went into dry dock for further refitting and war-readiness.

Around the New Year, 1940, *Jervis Bay* sailed south to Freetown, Sierra Leone, a gathering point for convoys headed for India, Egypt, and those returning to Britain. She escorted ships north to the English Channel then returned to Freetown to escort the next group of merchant ships. Boring.

Captain Harris fell ill in February 1940 and Commander J.A.P. Blackburn, *Jervis Bay*'s first officer, was made temporary skipper. He had earned the crew's respect with his seamanship and dedication to gunnery practice. Shortly thereafter the freighter *Hartesmere* went adrift mid-ocean with a broken propeller shaft. *Jervis Bay* departed Freetown, found the freighter with great navigating efficiency, and towed her back—a 10-day trip at a 6-knot speed to keep the towline from breaking. *Jervis Bay*'s entry into the war began with uncertainty but ended on a high note: the crew's confidence increased from a job well done. They had eight months to enjoy the feeling.

In March 1940, 49-year-old Captain Edward Stephen Fogarty Fegen took command of *Jervis Bay*.[11] Born in Chatham in 1891, he was the younger son of Vice Admiral F. F. Fegen of Tipperary, Ireland. Fegen entered the Royal Navy in 1904 as a midshipman. In 1912, he was made a sub-lieutenant and the next year was promoted to full lieutenant. With Britain's entry into World War I, Fegen specialized in gunnery, qualifying as a full-fledged gunnery officer in 1916. In 1921, considered an officer of promise, he was promoted to lieutenant commander and in 1927 was made a commander and appointed executive officer of the Royal Naval College. Beginning in 1929, he commanded the cruiser *Suffolk* and, in 1931, he was awarded the Life Saving Medal of the Dutch government for rescuing crewmen of the storm-battered freighter *Hedwig*.

Fegen found that *Jervis Bay*'s crew of 255 was a diverse lot. Exact figures are lacking but best estimates put their age range from eighteen to sixty-one, most in their late twenties and thirties. Over thirty men were Canadians and Newfoundlanders, most of them Royal Canadian Navy Reservists. About fifty men were Royal Navy regulars but another seventy or so were Royal Navy Reservists, including eighteen men from Caithness in northeast Scotland.[12] Over eighty men listed Chatham as their home.

Another group of about ninety-five men were civilian merchant seamen classified as Naval Auxiliary Personnel (T.124s). Obtaining a full crew for an AMC was not an easy task. Crews were urgently needed for the expanding number of escort vessels and regular warships. Thus, when the navy fell short, volunteers for the AMCs were called from the civilian merchant seamen pool. Terry Hughes and John Costello, in their book *The Battle of the Atlantic*, tell the tale of sixteen-year-old John Harrison who was looking for a ship's berth at the Liverpool seamen's hiring hall. One opening was for a scullion on an AMC. Harris told the attending Royal Navy petty officer that he would take the position, but he was turned down because he was not yet seventeen. An older seaman told young Harris not to ship out on an AMC because they were considered death traps. The petty officer finally shouted out, "Isn't there one man amongst you who will take the job?" Someone shouted back, "Stick it, mate!" The now-impatient petty officer asked Harris if he was still interested. He signed on for two years at £2.10 a week,[13] becoming one of 11,000 merchant seamen serving as Naval Auxiliary Personnel.

Among the Merchant Navy serving on *Jervis Bay* were six officers, three radio officers, three electricians, a painter, a plumber, a half-dozen watch keepers, a couple of writers, and seven carpenters. Thirteen more formed the kitchen staff from cooks to the scullions. Twenty-one men were aboard as stewards and storekeepers. And another twenty-one worked various engine room positions, most as firemen and greasers (see Appendixes C and D). The tale of young Harris notwithstanding, the *Jervis Bay* crew comprised a solid core of experienced seamen, whether men of the regular navy, reservists, or merchant seamen. Experienced or not, very few had ever been in battle.

George Pollock wrote of Captain Fegen that he "exerted remarkable control over his men."[14] Fegen was athletic in appearance, quiet, and always in control of himself, exuding a kind of innner strength which, coupled with his vast experience, appealed to the crew. The day after assuming command, Fegen gathered his men together on the promenade deck. He extended the usual greetings then came to the crux of the meeting. "So far, we haven't seen any real action, but I promise you this much. . . . [I]f the gods are good to us and we meet the enemy, I shall take you in as close as I possibly can."[15] That promise was soon enough fulfilled.

Jervis Bay sailed to Bermuda, and went north to escort HX convoys, originating out of Halifax, or SC convoys, originating out of Sydney, Cape Breton Island. Nothing much occurred.

On 10 June 1940, *Jervis Bay* was ordered to Halifax, there to await instructions. She subsequently was sent to St. John, New Brunswick, in the Bay of Fundy west of Nova Scotia, docking at the St. John Iron Works to undergo degaussing.[16]

This strange word, not much seen today, refers to the demagnetizing of ships. Any steel-hulled vessel produces a magnetic field. The Germans took advantage of this by developing magnetic mines, their firing mechanisms activated by ships passing near them. The mines were both effective and inexpensive. In November 1939, five ships were torpedoed by U-boats but magnetic mines sank thirteen, and the next month, while U-boats sank six ships, mines accounted for twelve.[17] Experiments at the Portsmouth naval base demonstrated that a ship's magnetic field could be substantially reduced by placing coils or cables around the hull and passing an electric charge through them that was produced by the ship's own generator. To hasten the process, cables were at first strung horizontally around the exterior of the hulls. When time and materials allowed, they were fitted to the ship's interior. As Winston Churchill noted, even though the process was simple enough, degaussing absorbed 1,500 miles of cable a week. Nevertheless, from January to early March 1940, 219 warships and 312 merchant ships underwent degaussing.[18]

When *Jervis Bay* left St. John for Halifax in September 1940, the degaussing equipment installed at a cost of $7,000 (Canadian) did not work properly. Rain at the end of August had saturated the unpainted canvas cable covers and penetrated their porous insulation material. That caused shrinkage, which pulled at the cable-holding clips, grounding them and rendering them ineffective. A flurry of memoranda passed between the commandants at St. John and Halifax, and between the Iron Works and naval headquarters in Ottawa. How was the job approved in the first place? Obviously, a competent degaussing officer was needed to oversee installations. Who was going to pay for reinstallation?

All the memos notwithstanding, things were finally made right (but the matter of who would make payment was still being argued in February 1941). *Jervis Bay* returned to escort duty in September 1940, becoming part of the 3rd Battle Squadron. She shepherded Convoy HX-72, forty-one cargo vessels, to a mid-Atlantic point where, on 20 September, they were transferred to an escort force of a destroyer, three corvettes, and a sloop.[19] *Jervis Bay* turned around and headed for Halifax. On 21 September, U-100 attacked the convoy and sank one ship.

In about mid-October, Commander Blackburn was promoted to captain and given command of his own AMC, HMS *Voltaire*, a ship we will learn about later.

On 28 October, at about 2:00 P.M., convoy HX-84, accompanied by HMS *Jervis Bay*, departed Halifax harbor. There were thirty-seven ships in the convoy (see Appendix B), an average number for this stage of the war. Anything larger was considered unmanageable in Atlantic storms. Once clear of the harbor, they formed nine columns, each a thousand yards apart and each ship 600 yards from the ship ahead. Thus, the convoy was a horizontal box about 5 miles wide. The only long-range escort was HMS *Jervis Bay*. Captain Fegen was therefore senior officer escort. The convoy commodore, responsible for maintaining the merchant ships' formation, was Rear Admiral H. B. Maltby under whom Fegen had briefly served in World War I. The convoy commodores were typically retired Royal Navy captains and rear admirals who volunteered for convoy duty. Maltby sailed aboard the steamer *Cornish City*. In the event of an attack Maltby, was obliged to take orders from Fegen. Communications between convoy vessels was very restricted. No wireless transmissions were allowed because they were easily intercepted by the Germans. And, since radiophones were not yet available, signals were sent by code lamps, signal flags, and rockets. The signalmen were often young reservists or conscripts who nonetheless did their work with considerable skill.[20] Off went HX-84 into the Atlantic where most anything could happen.

Two Canadian destroyers accompanied the convoy for the first couple of days, some 400 miles, and then returned to Halifax. A strict watch discipline was followed aboard *Jervis Bay*. Lookouts were atop the mainmast, on either side of the boat deck, on either side of the bridge, and bow and stern. The guns stood ready twenty-four hours a day and, at dawn and dusk—the hours when a raider was most likely to strike—everyone was at action stations.[21] Below in the engine room Commander (E) James Chappell, RNR, worked his men with precision as speeds were often altered to coincide with changes in course and the various alarms that might be raised.

THE BATTLE

On 30 October, the *Admiral Scheer* entered the Denmark Strait, the slot between Greenland and Iceland. Four hundred to 200 miles wide in good weather, sometimes narrowing to fifty miles when ice sheets develop, the strait is like a funnel that squeezes water, wind, sleet, and snow its length, whipping them into ferocious storms. Thus, what had been a fairly pleasant trip from Norway turned grim as the *Scheer* pitched and rolled in deepening troughs. The wind intensified and rain pelted down. But Captain Krancke kept his ship moving ahead at a steady 20 knots.[22] The *Scheer*'s bow plunged into the deepening swells, waves crashing over her decks. The few men moving about wore life ropes lest they be swept overboard. At that, two men were lost and another was slammed into a bulkhead so hard that he suffered two broken legs.

Visibility worsened. Now the seas looked like a series of great walls, one after another. The wind, reaching hurricane velocity and cutting like a thousand knives, howled along the decks. Havoc reigned below. Ventilators, wrenched off by the storm's impact, poured seawater into passageways and compartments, drenching men and equipment. Lockers tore open under the force, sinks and toilets wrenched loose, furniture turned to kindling, and drawers spilled open, their contents whipped about. The experienced sailors, some worried about the sharp listing to and fro of their ship, nonetheless survived the battering in good shape. The young sailors turned green, their seasickness adding a vile mixture to the tumult. Some wished for nothing more than a quick death.

By the morning of 1 November, with visibility only 300 yards, the *Scheer* was abreast of Greenland's southern tip. The hurricane subsided during the early hours to gale-force winds and, although the sea was still high and waves continued crashing onto the deck, the ship seemed steadier. Krancke ordered a damage inspection and repairs. Later that day, the *Scheer* slipped into Atlantic waters, her presence completely undetected. The storm, as bad as it was, cloaked her arrival.

On Sunday, 3 November at noon, the *Scheer* "was somewhere around 50° North latitude when Captain Krancke turned her bow northward again,"[23] searching for a convoy. Even though Nazi intelligence knew from which ports convoys departed, nothing was known of their exact routes. Given the sea's expanse, it was no easier to find a convoy of forty ships than to intercept one vessel. There was no specific information about the type and number of escort ships provided convoys, and the Germans did not know the exact position at which HX and SC convoy escorts transferred their duties to those warships that had sailed from Britain. Given the sophisticated detection equipment available in our time, the *Scheer's* operation must seem crude. But that was war in 1940. Krancke did receive information based on wireless intercepts that two HX convoys would be passing through his patrol area between 52° and 54° north and 32° and 35° west.[24] Even with that information, their discovery would not be easy.

Late in the afternoon of 3 November, a tanker was spotted sailing west. Krancke let her pass on because she was sailing in ballast—that is, without a cargo—and was, therefore, of little value. Moreover, an attack would doubtless prompt a R-R-R distress call, the signal that a raider was attacking, thus revealing the *Scheer's* presence and prompting any nearby convoy to scatter. Krancke wanted an entire convoy. By Tuesday morning, 5 November, the *Scheer* was within the designated search zone on a course to intercept either of the Halifax convoys. To facilitate the search Krancke ordered his Arado Ar 196-A scout plane aloft flown by Lieutenant Pietsch. The little float plane, with a range of a thousand miles, immediately extended the *Scheer's* range of vision. But Pietsch found nothing during his first sweep. Refueled, the Arado again catapulted into the sky. Sooner than expected, the plane returned, dipping its wings and Pietsch signaling, "Eight eighty sea miles."[25] Once back on board the *Scheer*, he rushed to the bridge, reporting that a large convoy was eighty-eight miles ahead and moving at about 9 knots. That meant the *Scheer* could overtake the convoy in about three hours, or around 4:00 P.M. Dusk already would be upon them and night would quickly follow. Waiting till morning, however, probably would put the convoy close to the estimated zone where the transfer of escorts took place. What kind of ships might be in that mix was unknown to Krancke but a cruiser or older battleship was not out of the question. He decided to attack as soon as possible.[26]

At 3:27 P.M., lookouts saw a single ship. She was the 5,389-ton banana boat SS *Mopan*. Krancke drew close to the merchantman, ordering her to stop and not use her wireless. The crew took to their lifeboats and slowly rowed toward the *Scheer*. Krancke ordered his 5.9-inch guns to sink the vessel. Shells punctured her hull but she would not go down. Not until her hatch covers were blown away, releasing the air pressure built-up in the cargo holds, did the *Mopan* roll over and slip into the depths. The attack, although forestalling a R-R-R signal that might have resulted in the convoys scattering, consumed ninety minutes. There was some trepidation aboard the *Scheer* that a convoy might have been missed.

Fate was with the pocket battleship, for a convoy came hauling over the southwestern horizon. The *Mopan* incident unexpectedly delivered HX-84 into Krancke's hands.

The time was 4:55 P.M. Visibility was good, the sea was calm, and the wind was but 4 mph. The position was about a thousand miles east of Halifax at latitude 52° 45' north, longitude 32° 13' west.

Lookouts on several convoy vessels, the tanker *Erodona* among them, sighted a large ship steaming eastward at 336° on a converging course. Understandably, she was difficult to identify at a distance of fifteen miles. Suddenly the unknown ship turned and headed bow-on toward the convoy. Captain Fegen brought his ship to full speed and, sounding action stations, steered away from the convoy and north northwest toward the oncoming ship (Map 3). At the same time, Rear Admiral Maltby, the convoy commodore, ordered an emergency turn 40° starboard and an increase in speed (Map 4).

The officers on the *Scheer's* bridge at first thought the convoy did not have an escort, which indeed, would have been strange. But Lieutenant Peterson spotted a ship with unusual lines for a freighter. Krancke, looking at her through his binoculars, thought she might be an AMC (*Hilfskreuzer*). This was confirmed when the ship pulled away from the convoy and signalled the letter "A" over and over, using a code lamp larger and more powerful than a cargo vessel typically carried. Then the AMC signalled "M-G-A." Krancke states in his memoir *Pocket Battleship* that he attempted a ruse by signalling back the same letters immediately as if requesting the British AMC for recognition. But the *Scheer's* war diary (*Kriegstagebuch*) states, "I refrained from answering" ("*Ich lasse nicht antworten*").[27] More than fifteen years had passed between the event and the memoir. Either Krancke forgot what exactly happened or he and his coauthor decided to add some intrigue.

In any event, Captain Fegen took no chances and fired red rockets, signalling the convoy to disperse (Map 5). At the same time he had smoke floats tossed overboard to screen his own movements. No easy job this: about the size of dustbins, weighing fifty pounds, and weighted at the bottom, they had to be manhandled over the ship's railing. The merchant ships launched their own smoke floats as they scattered, and sent message after message announcing a German surface raider, perhaps a pocket battleship, was attacking the convoy.[28] Meanwhile, the crew of *Jervis Bay* was trying to identify the oncoming ship. Was she the battleship *Ramilles*? Perhaps the *Rodney*? Or maybe the battle cruiser *Resolution* or the *Revenge*? The battleship *Barham*? Finally, Lieutenant Commander Arthur Driscoll dashed these optimistic guesses, concluding she was a German pocket battleship.[29]

The *Scheer*, now just under eight miles from the *Jervis Bay*, turned to port and aimed her 11-inch guns at the approaching AMC. *Jervis Bay* turned 40°

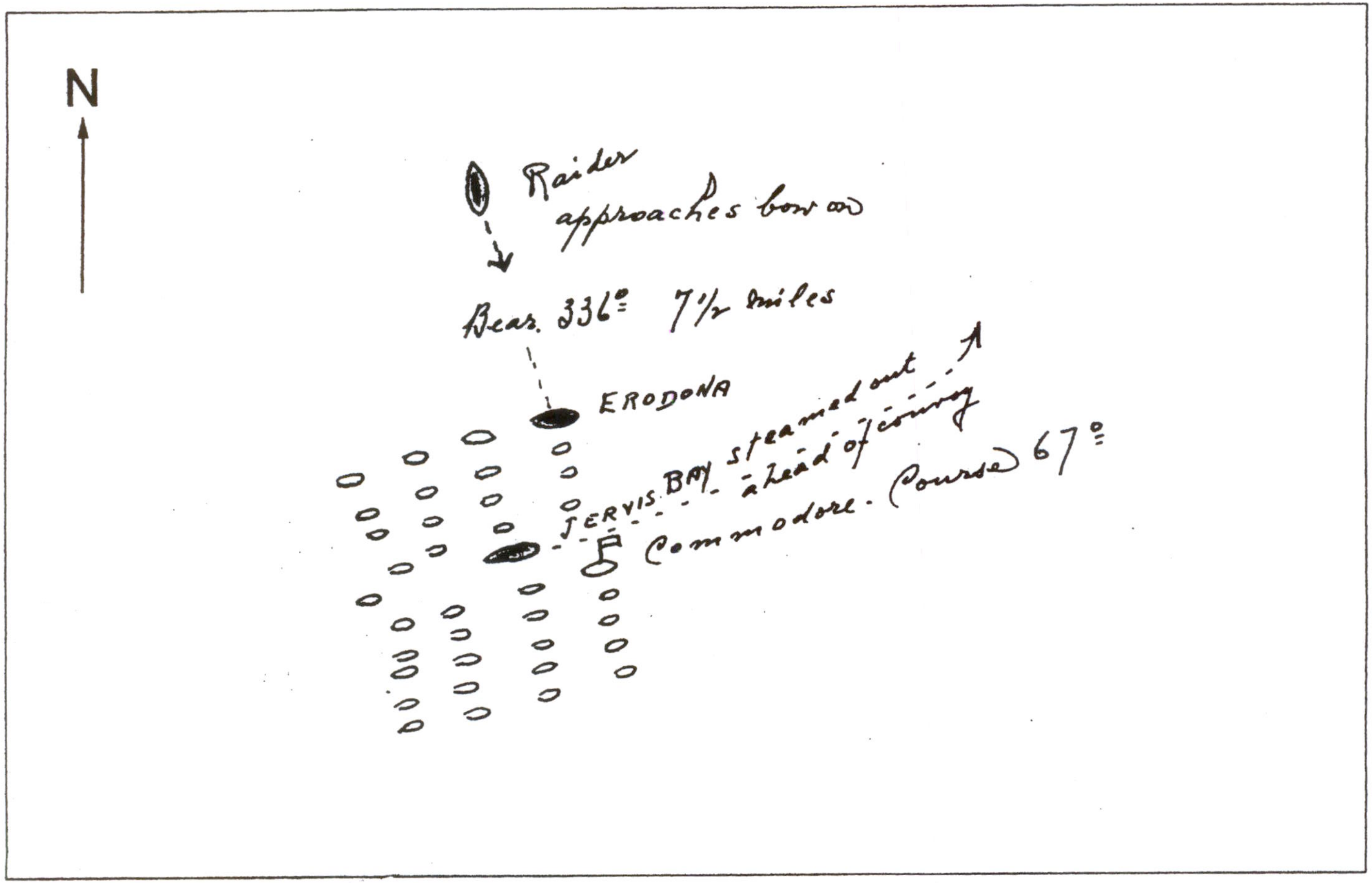

Map 3. The Attack: Phase 1 (Courtesy U.S. National Archives.)

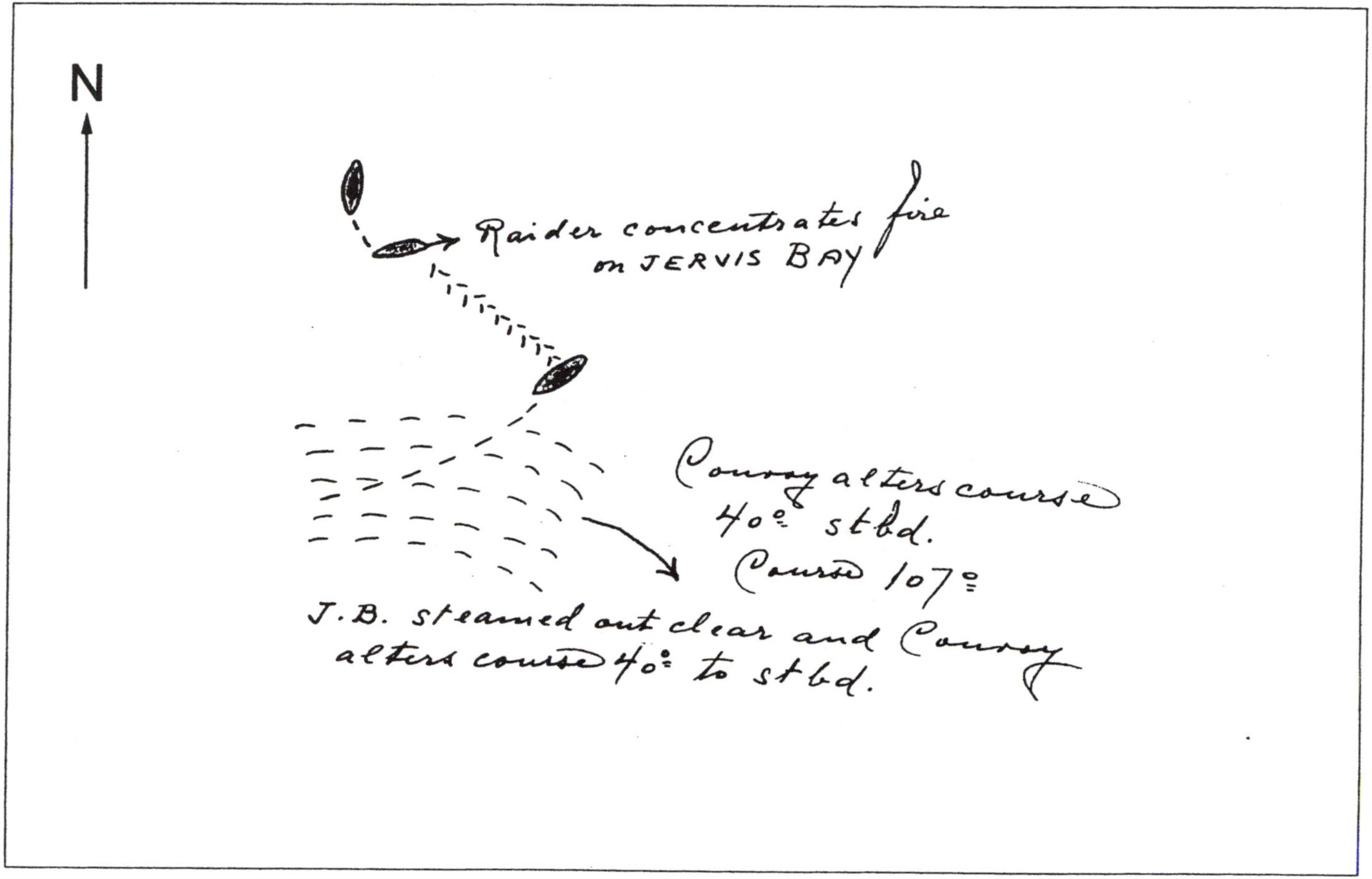

Map 4. The Attack: Phase 2 (Courtesy U.S. National Archives.)

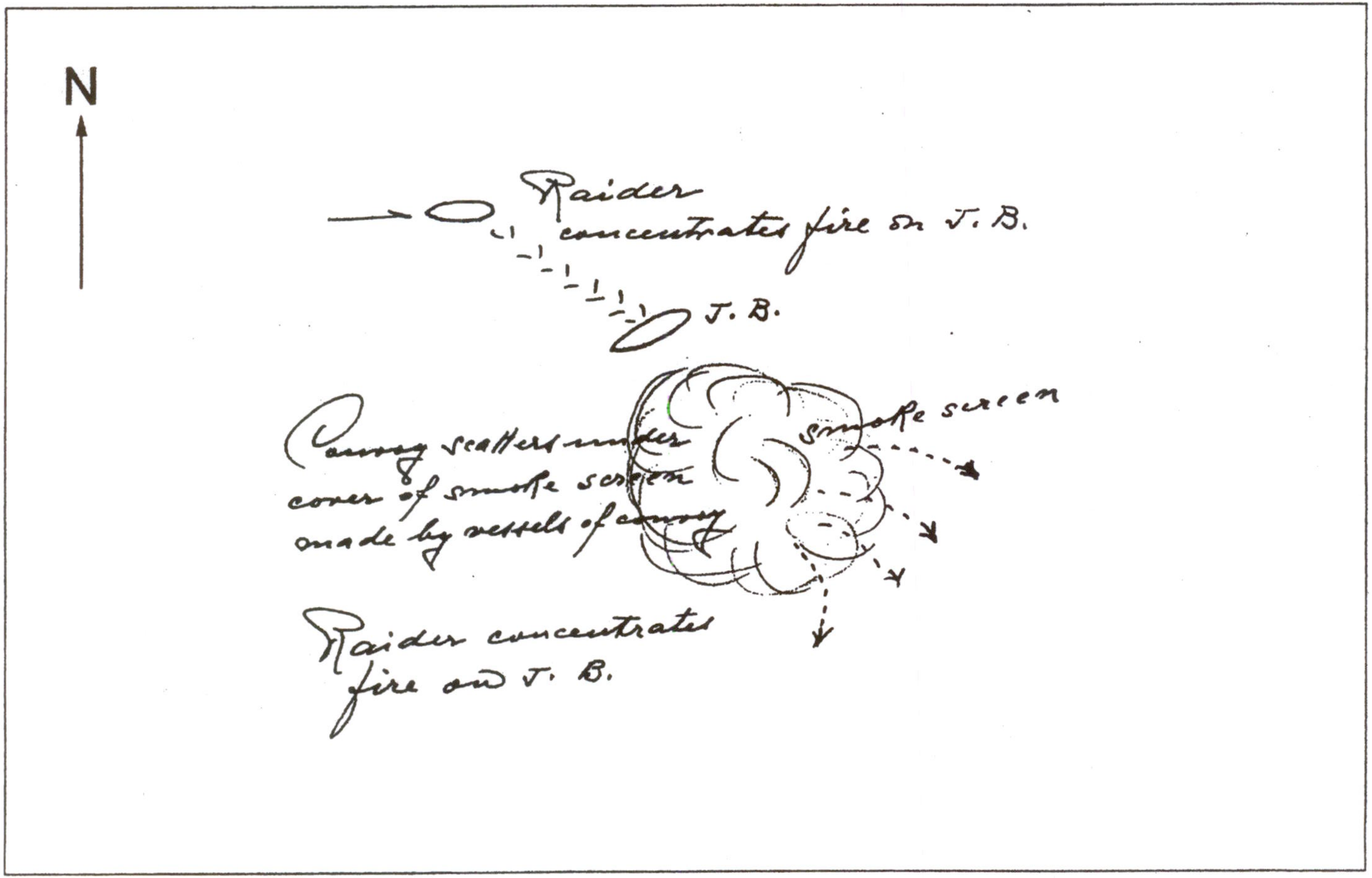

Map 5. The Attack: Phase 3 (Courtesy U.S. National Archives.)

to port for maximum use of four of her 6-inch guns. Captain Fegen and his entire crew realized how impossible were the odds in the duel. As one unidentified officer later said, "I think everybody aboard was proud as our ship turned toward the enemy. Our captain knew just what we were going to get, but it did not matter."[30] The convoy needed time to escape. *Jervis Bay*'s job was to give them that gift of time.

Jervis Bay was now positioned between the convoy and the *Admiral Scheer*. Although his old guns could not reach the pocket battleship at their extensive range, Fegen ordered them to open fire, various merchant ship captains testifying later that these were the first shots of the battle; in contrast, those aboard *Jervis Bay* believed the *Scheer* fired first.[31] The British crew grimly worked their action stations, knowing that Fegen was intentionally attracting the fire of the German ship. Unlike a land battle, where some soldiers might shirk from the maelstrom or even run away, a warship does not provide such options. The ship's crew must fight the fight to which their commander brings them. The men of *Jervis Bay* unflinchingly did their duty.

An AMC was a fearful place to be in battle. The guns had only wraparound shields, rather than turrets, which left the gunners exposed to all the blast, fire, tearing, and splintering surrounding them. There was no armor, so anyone could be swept away in a moment by an exploding shell. Fires could range down passageways because there was inadequate compartmentalization. Another hell emerged below deck. The 6-inch guns set up a horrendous beat that thumped, thumped, thumped throughout the ship. Sometimes gangways shook loose, pipes burst, rivets popped. An exploding shell, penetrating the hull, killed everyone around, tore into the ship's inner fabric, and, between the smoke and steam, created toxic clouds in which the crew tried to work or from which they tried to escape. Or they suffocated and died.

The German sailors, some surprised, some awed by the British ship's attack, realized she was firing as best she could and, given the rapid response to the *Scheer*'s maneuvering, that the guns "were served by trained naval men."[32] In fact, *Jervis Bay*'s gunners were a mixed lot and their efficiency was the result of the determined training given them aboard ship by Commander Blackburn and then Captain Fegen. Captain Krancke knew full well that his was the superior ship but he could not let the AMC maneuver and fire freely. She just might be carrying torpedo tubes or a lucky shot might hit some vital gear. There was nothing else for it: He had to first concentrate his fire on the AMC in order to mount the most efficient attack against the convoy (Map 5).

Open fire! A salvo from three 11-inch guns roared, flames belching from their barrels, smoke seemingly covering everything as shock waves reverberated across the *Scheer*'s deck. Three great projectiles, each weighing over 600 pounds, hurtled toward *Jervis Bay*. They missed; hitting 200 yards short and sending up huge water geysers. The *Scheer*'s gunnery officer adjusted the range and another salvo roared forth—a little long and to one side. As Krancke and Brennecke point out in *Pocket Battleship*, hitting *Jervis Bay* was no easy matter. Both ships were moving forward and pitching and rolling in the sea. Also, a target such as *Jervis Bay* could take evasive actions, speeding up or slowing down or making course changes, to avoid being hit. Furthermore, at first sighting, *Jervis Bay* "looked like a thin pencil floating in the water."[33]

A third salvo did not miss. One shell smashed into the forward well deck, bringing down the foremast. Another shell hit behind the wheelhouse of the bridge, shattering the radio room, killing Richard Williamson, the 1st Radio Officer. The shell also destroyed the fire control equipment and generators, killing or wounding all the operators, and cutting the wires for the communications system to the guns. The fire control room had been the action station for Paymaster Sub-Lieutenant John Gordon Sergeant. Fortunately, he was called away just before the fatal shell hit. Looking forward, he saw another shell carry away one of the forward guns and all its crew. Stoker 1st Class George Crowson was taking a bath when action stations sounded. Barely dressed, he reported for duty to the forward magazine. After sending up some fourteen powder bags to the 6-inch guns above, the gun crews stopped responding. He clambered up a ladder to find two guns completely demolished and body parts scattered all over the deck. He helped move some of the wounded to the sick bay. Moments after he left, a shell crashed into the sick bay. Then another hit, slamming the door shut and literally welding it in place. There was no escape forward from the surgery.[34]

The ship's wheel was not working, probably because the link to the steering motor that operated the rudder was cut. Amid a continuing rain of shells descending on his ship. Captain Fegen ordered that the aft emergency steering station be manned.[35] At that moment, a shell hit the bridge, a piece of shrapnel shattering Captain Fegen's left arm. Accompanied by Dennis Moore, chief yeoman of signals, Fegen made it to the aft control station where he tried to command his dying ship.

Engine room mechanics managed to connect the aft steering wheel to the aft control room from which directions could be given for the ship's proper course. That accomplished, Fegen and Moore started forward but never made it. They were cut down on the deck. But no directions came from the aft control room for, no sooner were new connections made, than a shell landed in the compartment, killing everyone there. Lieutenant Commander George Roe was now the senior officer remaining. Only one of *Jervis Bay*'s guns kept firing.

Kranke ordered all his light guns, the 5.9-inch and 3-inch batteries, to fire on *Jervis Bay*. Their intense bombardment "[split] open her thin plates as though she were made of glass and [let] the sea rush into her holds."[36]

Ordinary Seaman George Squires, in the navy only eight months, and Able Seaman Henry Lane, a former London taxi driver, testified to the horror descending upon them. The shells exploded in vivid yellow flashes, which resembled incendiary projectiles. Shell splinters and bits and pieces of the ship slashed through the air and fires were everywhere. Squires had the impression that the shells did not so much blow things up as they tore things apart, and everything that was supposed to be inflammable was on fire,[37] engulfing the ship from bow to stern.

The men below tending the boilers and engines had little idea of what was going on above them. When Captain Fegen ordered action stations and full speed ahead, all the engineering officers went below. It was up to them to give him all they could coax from the engines.[38] But they were soon working in light provided by hand-held torches. The same shell that cut the communications wiring had also cut the lights to the engine boiler rooms. The first major damage they sustained was when the funnel on the boat deck was hit. This altered the draught necessary to keep the boilers working properly. Their air choked off, the furnaces blew back, spewing flame and filling the room with acrid smoke and soot. Then the condenser in the engine room was hit, releasing a torrent of water across the floor at the same time seawater poured through the shell hole in the hull. The engines were soon submerged in twenty feet of water. The engine room gang made it topside. Not so those in the boiler room. *Jervis Bay* was now dead in the sea.

But the Germans kept firing at the AMC; even though it was obvious she was no threat at all. As Leading Seaman Thomas Hanlon asked of nearby Lieutenant Commander Keith Morrison who was soon to die, "What's the sense of them banging away at us like this, sir? They know we're finished."[39]

Lieutenant Commander George Roe, navigator and now senior officer by elimination, and Chief Petty Officer Walter Wallis looked at the remains of their ship and agreed there was nothing more anyone could do. Perhaps getting away from the ship could save some lives. Roe ordered, "abandon ship."

What happened next was confusion. Some lifeboats were smashed or set afire by the *Scheer's* gunnery. Those interviewed at least fifteen years later by George Pollock for his book *The Jervis Bay* indicated that only one lifeboat was launched. Some survivors, debriefed upon their return to Halifax, testified that two boats were launched. The lifeboat with George Crowson aboard filled with water and only its air tanks kept it afloat. His boat pulled away with twenty-one men aboard, some badly burned, others with shell fragment wounds. Able Seaman Henry Lane stated that he swam to another lifeboat drifting ahead of the ship. Others soon joined him and they searched for survivors.[40]

Men still aboard *Jervis Bay* launched two, perhaps three or more rafts—one of them damaged—or pitched timbers and anything else that would float into the sea, then jumped from the ship into the cold water. Cries for help sounded as crewmen struggled to stay alive.

Still the *Admiral Scheer* kept firing at *Jervis Bay*, now using her lighter dual-purpose antiaircraft guns, even though she was obviously sinking and the crew was abandoning ship.[41] Captain Daniel of the SS *Trewellard*, one of the convoy ships, later reported that the Germans kept firing for five to ten minutes after *Jervis Bay*'s guns were silenced. Captain Waite of the tanker *San Demetrio* also reported that the *Scheer* kept firing—while *Jervis Bay* was sinking.[42]

The officer in charge at Halifax, after interviewing the survivors, summarized their experiences when he wrote that the sinking of *Jervis Bay* was "peculiarly brutal" and "murderous," as if the *Scheer* were deliberately trying to create as many casualties as possible.[43] Paymaster Sergeant stated in an interview published in *Life* (25 November 1940) that, although *Jervis Bay* was completely disabled within fifteen minutes of the first shot, the German ship kept pumping shells into her. He probably expressed the collective bitterness of his fellow crewmen when he concluded "It was just firing practice for them." Captain Sven Olander of the Swedish steamer *Stureholm*, which was part of HX-84, reported another view to Arthur Bryant of the *Illustrated London News* (23 November 1940), when he stated, "[The battle] was glorious. Never shall I forget the gallantry of the British captain, sailing forward to meet the enemy."

The battle between the *Scheer* and *Jervis Bay* lasted only twenty-two minutes, but the AMC, reduced to a blazing hulk, did not capsize and sink until 8:00 P.M., taking Captain Fegen and most of his crew to the bottom. The tactical value of this *beau geste* was about to be tested as the *Admiral Scheer* turned toward the scattered ships of the convoy. Had *Jervis Bay*'s hard-earned, even desperately earned, twenty-two minutes been a sufficient gift of time?

PURSUING THE CONVOY

Captain Krancke, finally satisfied *Jervis Bay* no longer posed a threat of any kind, turned his gunners loose on the convoy, "preying like a hawk in a chicken yard," as stated in the apt but *ex post facto* London *Times* report (8 November 1940). A few shots by the *Scheer*'s 5.9-inch guns had already been fired at a couple of ships but now the full weight of the pocket battleship's guns searched for the scattering convoy vessels that sped away as fast as their engines could manage (Map 6). Even though smoke floats cast overboard by

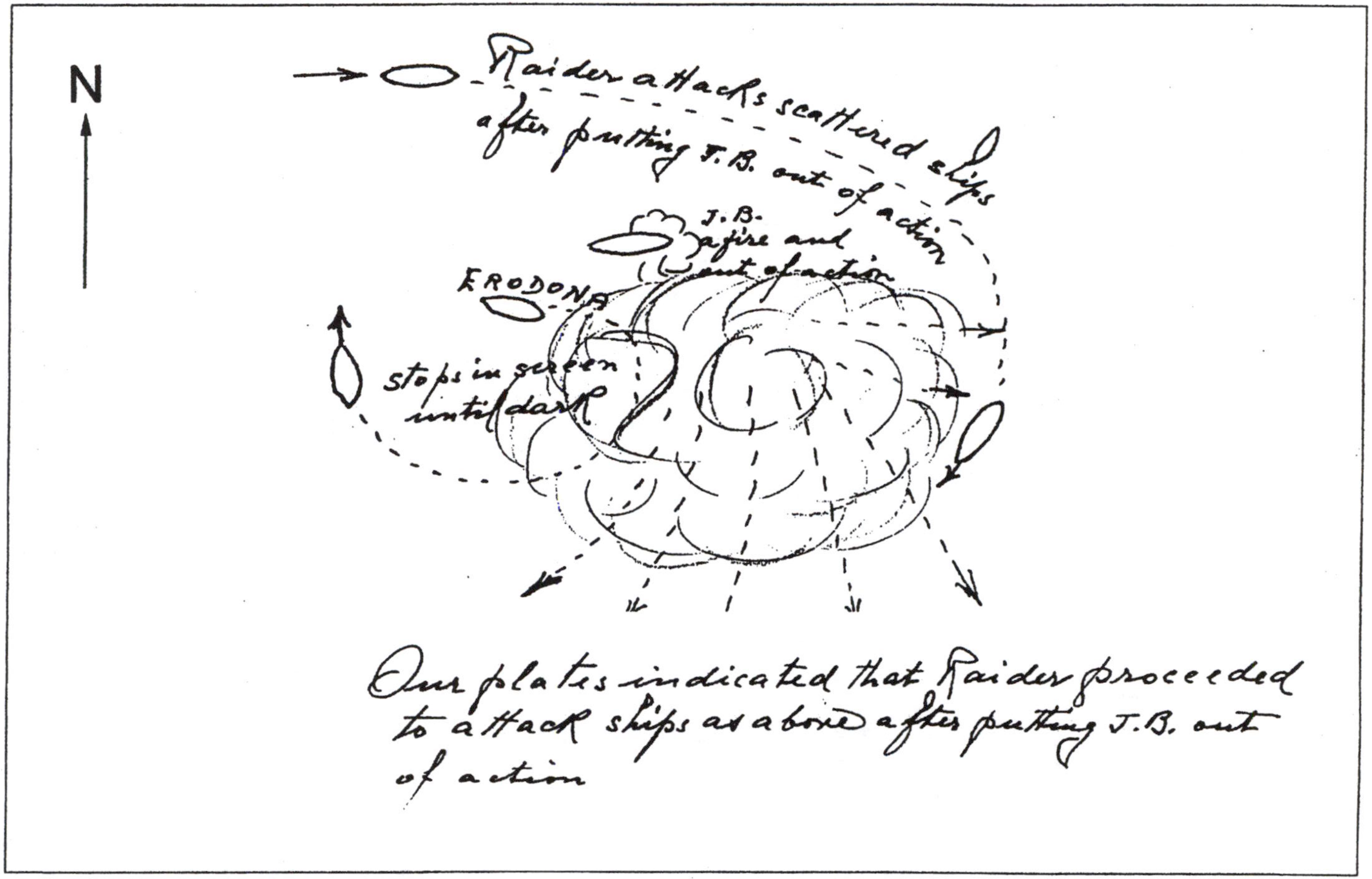

Map 6. The Attack: Phase 4 (Courtesy U.S. National Archives.)

Table 1

List of Ships Sunk or Damaged by the *Admiral Scheer* during the Raid on Convoy HX-84

Target	Name	Type	Sunk	Damaged
1	HMS *Jervis Bay*	AMC	14,164	—
2	*Rangitiki*	Transport	—	16,700
3	*Trewellard*	Freighter	5,201	—
4	*Kenbane Head*	Freighter	5,225	
5	*Erodona* (?)	Tanker	—	—
6	*San Demetrio*	Tanker	—	8,073
7	*Maidan*	Freighter	7,908	—
8	*San Demetrio*	Shelled a second time		
9	*Beaverford*	Freighter	10,000	—
10	*Fresno City*	Freighter	4,995	—

Sources: Translated and edited from *Kriegstagebuch* "Admiral Scheer" RM/92/5228; also Krancke and Brennecke, *Pocket Battleship*, pp. 59–60, and Hague, *The Allied Convoy System*, p. 131. The *Mopam*, listed in both sources, is omitted here. The war diary otherwise lists eleven targets, one of which was the reshelling of the *San Demetrio* but was left unidentified. *Pocket Battleship* lists thirteen targets. One was probably the *Erodona*. Another was not identified. A third was the freighter *Andalusian* listed as damaged. These last two ships lack confirmation and were omitted from the table. Target sequence has been altered to conform to British reports cited in the text.

the fleeing ships created a dense screen for their escape, visibility remained good in the late afternoon hours and the sea remained calm.

The *Rangitiki*, a 16,700 ton transport or what used to be called an auxiliary freighter that carried both cargo and passengers—here seventy-five of them—was the *Scheer*'s first target (see Table 1 for an edited summary of targets and sinkings).[44] Shells hit all around the ship, sending fragments spewing as high as the funnel and the forward superstructure.[45] She sped away at full speed through the smokescreen on a south southwest course, thus avoiding further damage. No matter. Another target was immediately available, the 5,201 ton freighter SS *Trewellard*.[46] Captain Daniel, skipper of the vessel, ordered his first mate in charge of the aft 4-inch gun to open fire on the *Scheer*. They managed to shoot eight rounds at the great gray ship but the range was far too long and their projectiles went harmlessly into the sea. The *Scheer* responded, the first shot hitting the aft hold filled with pig iron. The cargo went up like a giant shrapnel shell, scything across the deck, cutting down some of the gunners. Those left alive quickly abandoned their gun—it was useless anyway. A salvo from the *Scheer's* 11-inch guns hit behind the funnel and penetrated the bowels of the *Trewellard*. Her engines shuddered to a halt as steam poured up through gaping holes and wreckage.

Captain Daniel gave orders to abandon ship. All confidential papers and code books were put in a weighted bag and thrown overboard. The crew launched three lifeboats. One made it away with twelve men aboard, another with nine. A third boat capsized when launched but righted itself. Four men clambered in but Daniel had them standby as he checked for any survivors. Fortunately, the *Scheer* had ceased fire for the moment. He found one man badly dazed and another severely burned on his face and arms. Both were put in the standby boat. With Daniel on board, they shoved off but had to use floorboards for paddles because the oars and sail were lost when the boat tipped over during launching. No sooner had they loosed the painter than the *Scheer* opened fire again. The bridge was smashed, erupting in a sheet of flame. When Daniel's boat was about 150 yards away, the *Trewellard* tilted upward and sank stern first. He later estimated that his ship had been hit thirty times.[47]

Thomas Milner, master of the SS *Kenbane Head*, a 5,225-ton freighter, watched helplessly as the *Scheer* kept firing at *Jervis Bay*, even though she was all afire. He thought he saw a shell hit the *Rangitiki* and he saw the *Trewellard* go down. He knew that if those big guns were turned on his ship there was no chance of surviving the onslaught. He put his ship on a course 255° at full speed to escape that fate. But, at 6:15 P.M., as dusk drew across the gray Atlantic, three shells struck *Kenbane Head* near the stern.[48] The poop hatch and magazine burst into flames, the main and emergency wireless aerials were carried away, and the steering gear was destroyed. Another salvo destroyed the engine rooms. Within a few minutes fires raged the length of the ship and she started to settle.

Milner ordered his crew to abandon ship. Assembling at their lifeboat station, the men assigned to Number 1 boat found it shot to pieces, so they moved to Number 2 boat that had been partially lowered. But another salvo from the *Scheer* struck beside the *Kenbane Head*, a shell fragment holing the lifeboat. When launched, it filled with water. The men climbed back aboard their ship and helped launch boats 3 and 4 and a raft. By 7:00 P.M., *Kenbane Head*, still fiercely burning, listed heavily to starboard and sank rapidly.

When later debriefed, the various ships masters made no mention of the tanker *Erodona* being hit by a salvo. Only in the U.S. Navy's Intelligence Report by Commander Ben Wyatt, USN, is this attack mentioned,[49] and it is listed here in Table 1 as Target 5. In fact, there are a several discrepancies regarding the exact order of targeting. This is quite understandable. The firing by the *Scheer* of its secondary guns may have been overlooked or not seen at all by witnesses aboard various convoy ships. Certainly it is doubtful that those later interviewed saw the same events at the same time. Furthermore, their distance from any given action differed and so did their angle of vision. At any rate, the *Erodona* disappeared into the smokescreen and evaded harm. Two more of *Scheer's* salvoes missed an unidentified target, but another may have damaged the freighter *Andalusia*; however, that lacks confirmation.

Then began the saga—no overstatement here—of the *San Demetrio*, an 8,073-ton tanker.[50] She had sailed to Halifax loaded with petrol from Aruba in what was then the Dutch West Indies. On 1 November at 6:00 P.M., the worst nightmare a merchant seaman could imagine was realized. The ship's engine cracked a piston head and the *San Demetrio* glided to a stop as the rest of the convoy sailed on. Alone, her deck gun useless against a submerged U-boat, helpless against a surface raider, they wallowed in the sea as the engineers worked furiously. At 7:55 P.M. the next day, repairs completed, the tanker surged ahead to catch the convoy. By 8:30 A.M. on 5 November, they were back in column. Luck had been with them.

Then their luck ran out. At 4:55 P.M., all hell broke loose. The *Admiral Scheer* was sighted. John Lewis Jones, an apprentice seaman aboard the *San Demetrio*, had a photograph of the *Deutschland*. He observed that the forward main turret on the approaching ship had the same configuration as that on the pocket battleship. Captain George Waite certainly thought it was a German capital ship. Thus, when the convoy commodore signalled a change in course and *Jervis Bay* sent up "scatter" rockets, the *San Demetrio* readily increased speed to 12 knots and dropped smoke floats. Waite ordered battle stations. The ship's 4-inch and 12-pounder guns were manned and the lifeboats swung out.

The crew watched as the *Jervis Bay* fell victim to the *Scheer's* concentrated gunfire, appalled that the pocket battleship kept firing even after the AMC was awash in flames. They saw the *Rangitiki* straddled and race away into the smokescreen. Then the *Trewellard* went down and soon after the *Kenbane Head* was ablaze and sinking. Out of anger more than the certainty of doing any damage, Waite ordered his 12-pounder to open fire on the *Scheer*. Suddenly, he ordered them to cease fire. "For God's sake," he shouted, suddenly realizing the consequences of his previous order, "stop firing. It'll only get her back up."

Too late. The *Scheer* turned her guns on the tanker. The first salvo straddled the ship. Waite ordered the crew to abandon ship. It would have been suicide to stay: The Germans had the range and the next salvo would doubtless set the whole ship afire. The crew took to their lifeboats but, just in case a return to the ship was possible, Jacob's ladders were lowered from the deck. Two lifeboats got away with nineteen men aboard each. Waite's boat, the last to leave, contained a three-man crew. As they lowered away, a salvo hit the San Demetrio, setting her ablaze and destroying the bridge, but they made it safely to the water. Without sufficient crew to row, their boat drifted. At dawn the next morning, Waite and his few men met boat Number 4. One of the ship's officers was among the survivors and he reported seeing the San Demetrio one massive sheet of flames. Waite concluded his ship was a total loss. He had but one question: Where was the other lifeboat?

Meantime, the Scheer fired on two other ships but missed them both in the diminishing visibility. Radar located another ship directly ahead on the same course as the Scheer—the 7,908-ton freighter Maidan. Krancke brought all his guns to bear.[51] Shells ripped into the ship, turning her into a helpless, blazing wreck. As with the sinking of Jervis Bay, there was no let-up as projectiles from the 3-pounders and then the lighter guns, their tracer rounds etching paths across the water, cut into the Maidan. The freighter rolled back on her stern and plummeted beneath the waves. There were no survivors.

The Scheer moved on at 23 knots, looking for more of the convoy. Once again they passed the San Demetrio, still afloat, still afire, and abandoned. More shells from the Scheer smashed into her. Krancke sailed on, writing her off as a sunken ship.[52]

The Scheer's radar found another ship to the southwest. Closing at full speed, they came upon the 10,000 Beaverford, originally a freighter for the Canadian Pacific Railways. Her decks were heavily laden with cargo. The Scheer's 3-pounders and 37-mm and 20-mm guns opened fire first, their rounds bursting and lighting "up the ship and surrounding sea in an uncanny orange light."[53] Then the Scheer's larger guns scored nineteen hits on the freighter—three 11-inch rounds and sixteen 5.9-inch rounds. Hugh Pettigrew, her captain, had his guns fire back—with no effect—but their action kept the Scheer focused on them, allowing others in the convoy to put distance between their ships and the raider. Soon enough, the sea was lapping the deck of the Beaverford, but she did not sink because the deck cargo kept her afloat. Krancke ordered a torpedo fired into her that hit in the fore quarter, ripping a great hole in the hull. The Beaverford heeled over, spilling the deck cargo into the sea. She was gone in another minute, taking the crew with her.

The Scheer's radar picked out yet another victim, the 4,955-ton freighter Fresno City.[54] Krancke opened fire at less than 3,000 yards, the 11-inch guns hitting freighter four times, exploding the hatches and the forepeak, and puncturing the hull. Flames belched through the hole, up the side, and along the deck. The ship's engines suddenly stopped. Abandon ship! Two boats were lowered, the port boat with the chief officer and the starboard boat with the captain. All hands were accounted for. The two lifeboats lay a short distance apart but, by 3:00 A.M., the chief officer lost contact with the captain's boat. The captain and his men were never seen again.

The attack on Convoy HX-84 was over. In some six hours, the German raider destroyed over 52,000 tons of British shipping.

SURVIVING

Abandon ship! Not easily done. Escaping an engine room filled with steam, smoke, and rising water involved crawling up through the wreckage of twisted steel, jagged holes, and smoke and fire. Above deck was a purgatory of its own. The hail of steel shell fragments and the concussive impact of explosions cut men down. Fires raged through passageways. And for all, a heaving ship, a dying ship, could pitch a seaman into the water or down a dark hole never to be seen again. To the lifeboat! What lifeboat? It might be on fire or shattered. Try another boat! The davits might be jammed and refuse to swing the boat clear of the ship. Or the boat starts down the falls, but one runs smoothly and the other catches in the tackle, tipping the boat forward and spilling the crew into the sea. Those without boats jump for it— twenty-five feet, fifty feet into the water that is filled with wreckage, bodies, and oil—which might be aflame. For those who leave the ship there is a cardinal rule—get away from it. Swim, pull the oars. She may roll over onto the drifting rafts and lifeboats, crushing them with her weight. The suction caused by her sinking can capsize lifeboats, and anyone in the water will be sucked under as she goes down.

The men in the water, if they are lucky, swim to a lifeboat or a raft and are pulled on board. If the craft is crowded, then they must cling to the side until someone on board dies and room is made for another. Most in the water will die from drowning or, within a short time, from hypothermia. The lifeboats and rafts try to stay together. The men are cold, and some are bleeding from unattended wounds or sick from swallowing seawater made worse if it was covered with oil. Some are in unbelievable pain from burns. Others have broken bones and torn muscles suffered while abandoning ship. One and all, they share a common circumstance: they have no place to go. They are a thousand miles from port, the convoy is scattering, and the enemy is lurking not far away. Only a damned fool of a ship's captain would stop to pick up survivors. Unless a miracle happens, there is little hope of survival.

But sometimes miracles do happen and captains can be damned fools.

The sea turned nasty by dusk on 5 November. The wind picked up, increasing from Force 5 (around 20 mph) to Force 8 (between 39 and 46 mph), a gale that created heavy seas and brought rainsqualls. Lifeboats were swept apart as the painters, which tied them together, snapped. Sea anchors were dropped from the sterns and the men rowed mightily to keep their lifeboats headed into the wind. Others bailed to keep their small craft afloat. How the men on rafts kept from being swept away is unimaginable.

By mid-morning, 6 November, the gale diminished. San Demetrio's lifeboat Number 1, the one whose whereabouts troubled Captain Waite, had survived the awful night intact. The boat held Chief Engineer Charles Pollard, suffering a smashed hand, Second Mate A. Hawkins, John Jones, and another apprentice, the ship's two radio officers. Third Engineer Willey, the boatswain, four able seamen, two ordinary seamen, the leading cook, and three stewards.[55] At noon, they sighted a ship. Stepping the boat's sail, they steered toward her. The ship was afire and abandoned. It was the San Demetrio, very much a wreck but still afloat. To a man, those in the lifeboat agreed to board her. Jacob's ladders dangled down from the deck but the steel lifeboat had to approach cautiously to keep from banging against the hull and cause a spark that might ignite more fires. The men wrapped the boat's gunwales in blankets for safety. The crewmen made it back aboard, tying the lifeboat alongside just in case. But the painter broke and the little boat drifted away.

The men set to work, realizing they had to save the tanker or die in the attempt. They restored electricity by using the generator used for the degaussing cables. Cables in the engine room were repaired and the starboard auxiliary boiler was lit. Using steam hoses fed by the boiler together with remaining fire extinguishers the crew first controlled and then put out the ship's fires. Auxiliary steering gear located aft was badly damaged but not a total loss. Repairs were made and a steering wheel with only four spokes left was mounted. At 2:00 P.M. on 8 November, the engines were started. The San Demetrio steamed east.

The battered tanker chugged into Blacksod Bay, County Mayo, Ireland, on 13 November. Three days later, the destroyer HMS Arrow arrived and, taking the tanker in tow, brought her to Rothesay Bay on the Firth of Clyde, Scotland. Unbelievably, the San Demetrio lived to sail again in Atlantic convoys.

What was the fate of those who did not make it back aboard? Number 3 lifeboat, containing Captain Waite, made it through the gale-swept night of 5 November and through the next day. On the morning of 7 November, they stepped their sail and headed east. At 9:30 A.M., they sighted a ship, the freighter Gloucester City captained by S. G. Smith. She had been in a westbound convoy from the United Kingdom but, with a top speed of only 9 knots, fell behind and lost contact with the other ships. Her radio operator picked up a message from the *Rangitiki* that HX-84 was being attacked. Captain Smith, rather than avoiding the battle zone, sailed his ship to the *Rangitiki*'s reported position and, cruising in fifteen-mile circles, searched for survivors. They first came upon *San Demetrio*'s Number 4 boat, containing Chief Officer Wilson and eighteen men,[56] and then Number 3. Boat Number 1, however, was still missing and, reluctantly, the *San Demetrio*'s survivors concluded it was lost at sea.

The *Trewellard*'s Number 1 boat with Captain Daniel aboard rigged a sea anchor during the gale and erected a protective canvas forward.[57] A deckhand named Turley who ran the ship's auxiliary motors and pumps (called a donkeyman on merchant ships) was badly scalded. Daniel gave him two morphia tablets and another later to reduce the excruciating pain. He was put under the canopy and slept all night. The 2nd Engineer, Mr. Gow, was badly wounded on the back of his head and suffered burned legs, but his only complaint was being cold. He awakened around midnight with leg cramps but went back to sleep. In the morning he was dead. Turley died about 10:00 A.M. Both were slipped over the side of the boat.

Turley died just as two sightings were made, one a ship to the north and then a sail to the west. The second was *Trewellard*'s Number 2 boat with nine men aboard. They steered alongside Daniel's boat, passing over some drinking water and two oars. Daniel told them to sail north, find the ship they had sighted, and report his position. About 1:00 P.M., *Gloucester City* rescued Daniel and his men. Once aboard, he discovered that Captain Smith had also rescued survivors from *Trewellard*'s Number 3 boat.

When the gale hit the night of 5 November, the men in the port lifeboat of the *Fresno City* rigged their sea anchor. The crew weathered the storm and at 7:00 A.M., they stepped the boat's sail and headed east northeast in still-heavy seas. At 2:40 P.M., they sighted *Gloucester City* and were picked up an hour later.

Captain Smith and the *Gloucester City*'s crew, at great risk to themselves and their ship, spent fifteen hours rescuing ninety-two men from the sea—twenty-five from the *Trewellard*, twenty-three from the *San Demetrio*, twenty-four from the *Fresno City*, and twenty from the *Kenbane Head*. Captain Smith, probably with a mixture of reluctance and satisfaction, turned his ship west and docked at St. John on 12 November at 5:00 P.M.[58]

When the *Scheer* attacked HX-84, Sven Olander and the crew of the Swedish freighter *Stureholm* must have wondered what they were doing in the company of vessels that invited attack. Not every captain liked sailing in convoys, many thinking they would be better off sailing independently. Fortunately, Olander was a clever and experienced seaman. When the scatter order came, he carefully maneuvered his ship to starboard and, by small alterations in course and speed, kept the smoke floats between his ship and the *Scheer*.[59]

That evening, with darkness shrouding his ship's movements, Olander called his crew on deck to ask if they should stay in the area and look for survivors. As reported in the London *Times* (14 November), the crew unanimously voted to stay and search. At 11:00 P.M., they picked up twenty *Jervis Bay* survivors from a lifeboat. They told Olander that more survivors were about on rafts. Surviving on the rafts was cruel. The gale pitched them about, tilting them at acute angles that made it impossible for some men to hold on. The waves swept around them and crashed onto them. The wind tore at them. Wet, cold, and exhausted, more men disappeared into the depths.

Seamen from the *Stureholm* climbed into the *Jervis Bay*'s lifeboat and searched for the rafts. They picked up about fifteen survivors from a reported two rafts. But other rafts were missing, and the lifeboat manned by the *Stureholm*'s crew had developed some serious leaks. They returned to their ship. Further searching from the ship yielded men from two more rafts. At about 4:00 A.M., an SOS from a hand-held light was spotted. The signal was being sent by Able Seaman Tom Davison.

Davison had just finished washing his clothes and was about to bathe when action stations sounded. He grabbed what clothing he could, went to the port gun aft of the superstructure, and donned headphones that linked him with the fire control room. But given the angle of *Jervis Bay* to the *Scheer*, his gun had no opportunity to fire. No matter. The fire control connection had been cut. He and the rest of his gun crew spent their time ducking shrapnel and debris. When the order came to abandon ship he went over the side, torch in one hand, a lifebelt in the other (he could not swim), and looked for a raft. The first he found was too full so he paddled away. He soon sighted a second raft crowded so tightly that the men had to stand up. Their collective weight submerged the craft about a foot beneath the surface. But Davison hung on. For ten horrific hours they withstood the gale's onslaught until it seemed all were ready to die. In that last moment, with Davison signalling SOS, the *Stureholm* heaved into view and rescued those who were left.[60]

Stureholm rescued a total of sixty-eight men from *Jervis Bay*. But three died and were buried at sea late in the afternoon of Wednesday, 6 November.[61] The remaining sixty-five were the only survivors (see Appendix D). *Jervis Bay* lost 190 men that day (see Appendix C). Two hundred and six other merchant seaman also died.[62]

With the return to Halifax of the convoy's survivors, both men and ships, the navy began the arduous task of sorting out exactly what happened. Survivors aboard *Gloucester City* and *Stureholm* were transferred ashore and subsequently interviewed by Naval Intelligence officers. Crew members from the merchant ships sunk as well as the officers from two surviving convoy ships, the *Cordelia* and *Pacific Enterprise*, were also interviewed.

The commodore of the Chatham Barracks sent telegrams on 13 November to survivor families, including Davison's wife. "GLAD TO INFORM YOU THAT YOUR HUSBAND IS A SURVIVOR FROM HMS JERVIS BAY." Davison, in early December, was allowed to cable his wife and daughter in Dover "Quite safe. Don't worry."[63]

The Admiralty in London initially did not want any of *Jervis Bay*'s crew to speak to the press but quickly relented, probably because their story was judged worth more to civilian morale than it would reveal potentially valuable information they might possess—which was very little if any. Several of the crew were interviewed by newspapers and three were interviewed by the Canadian Broadcasting Corporation for radio news.[64] That recording was awkward and brief, probably the result of careful scripting by the navy.

The story of *Jervis Bay*'s heroism was soon known on both sides of the Atlantic. One of the Royal Navy's great legends was born.

A tragic addendum followed. The *Stureholm* was rescheduled to sail in Convoy HX-91. Several of the Swedish crew, including Captain Olander, refused to sail in her and were paid off in Halifax. But that left the freighter short-handed. Their places were partially taken by some survivors of the *San Demetrio* and HMS *Jervis Bay*. HX-91 left Halifax in early December. On 11 December she was torpedoed by U-96. With steel and machinery in her holds, she went down like a rock.

Admiral Karl Dönitz. He objected strenuously to Erich Raeder's strategy of using surface raiders at the expense of building a large U-boat fleet. Reproduced by courtesy of the U.S. National Archives, Washington, DC.

Admiral Sir John Tovey (*left*), leader of the *Bismarck* hunt, inspects U.S. troops in Iceland. Reproduced by courtesy of the U.S. National Archives, Washington, DC.

German battleship *Scharnhorst* after a refit in September 1939. This dangerous raider was destroyed by the Royal Navy off North Cape, 26 December 1943, in the last capital ship engagement of the Atlantic war. Reproduced by courtesy of the U.S. Naval Historical Center, Washington, DC.

The refrigerator ship *Santa Cruz*, a "banana boat" that was converted to the disguised raider *Thor*. She battled three British AMCs, damaging two and sinking one. Reproduced by permission of the Hauptstaatsarchiv Stuttgart/Württembergische Landesbibliothek.

The British AMC *Alcantara*, which battled the German raider *Thor*. The placement of the 6-inch guns is clear. Reproduced by permission of the Trustees of the Imperial War Museum, London.

HMCS *Prince David*, a former passenger ship of the Canadian-Pacific Line, searched in vain for the AMC *Voltaire*, sunk by the raider *Thor*. Reproduced by courtesy of the Canadian Department of Defense.

HMCS *Prince David*, after conversion to an infantry landing ship. Most of her 4-inch guns were replaced with light antiaircraft weapons, and five landing craft were placed the length of the boat deck. Reproduced by courtesy of the Canadian Department of Defense.

The end of the *Admiral Scheer*. Hit by RAF bombers, the ship capsized in the Kiel dockyard 10 April 1945. She was subsequently covered in rubble as part of a postwar landfill project. Reproduced by permission of the Trustees of the Imperial War Museum, London.

· CHAPTER 6 ·

THE CONTINUED VOYAGE OF THE *ADMIRAL SCHEER*

Captain Fegen's wireless transmissions warning that a pocket battleship was attacking Convoy HX-84 hit the British Admiralty like a shock wave. Their first response was to recall two HX convoys and a Bermuda-Halifax convoy, and to delay departure of those still assembling. The harbors at Sydney and Halifax filled with ships as the United Kingdom anxiously awaited much-needed supplies. The regular convoy schedule did not resume until 17 November.[1] Captain Krancke would have rejoiced had he known all this. News that a raider the size and power of a pocket battleship was loose in the Atlantic created precisely the confusion the German naval command wished. Indeed, the British befuddlement was almost as satisfying as ship sinkings.

The Admiralty deployed ships to find the raider—exactly which one was still unknown—and sink it. Not an easy task. The *Admiral Scheer* already had eluded British aerial and sea patrols during its passage into the Atlantic, a feat that revealed British shortcomings, their worries about a Nazi invasion of Britain notwithstanding. But Sir Charles Forbes, commander in chief, Home Fleet, concluded that the pocket battleship's breakout and attack served one of two German plans. Either she was on a short raiding foray and, having hit HX-84, would head back to Germany or sail to a French port, or the raid on HX-84 was just the beginning of a longer cruise and she would head for the South Atlantic.[2]

In case the first scenario was correct, Forbes sent the battlecruisers *Hood* and *Repulse*, the cruisers *Dido*, *Naiad*, and *Phoebe*, and six destroyers to cover Brest and L'Orient. Simultaneously, the battleships *Rodney* and *Nelson* scouted the waters between Iceland and the Faroe Islands. But Forbes's deployment was inexplicably altered by the Admiralty, the *Rodney* and her escorts sent to the position where HX-84 was attacked. What they were expected to find remains a mystery. As for the second scenario, any attempt to intercept the *Scheer* if she sailed south collapsed when Force H, earlier transferred to Gibraltar from Capetown, was needed for Mediterranean operations.[3] Force H probably had the best chance of finding the *Scheer* because the aircraft carrier *Illustrious* was part of that hunter group and its planes could have significantly extended the search area.

Captain Krancke, well aware that the Royal Navy would be after him, turned the *Scheer* south on the night of 5 November. The great ship raced toward a position 45° west and 25° north, the prearranged rendezvous point with the supply ship *Nordmark*.[4]

The guns of Convoy HX-84 did not damage the *Admiral Scheer* but this did not mean the ship was unscathed. The blast of her own guns damaged the Arado scout plane and the ship's radar apparatus. The *Scheer* needed a good cleaning because anything not secured was sent flying with each salvo. The *Scheer* also needed resupplying. Her fuel tanks and food lockers needed topping off and her ammunition magazines needed to be replenished. Her gunners had used half their 5.9-inch shells and almost as many 11-inch shells.[5]

On 12 November, the *Scheer* reached the designated rendezvous point only to find the *Nordmark* was nowhere to be seen. Instead, a rusty old tanker, the *Eurofeld*, hauled into view. This ship had been docked at Tenerife, the Canary Islands, in September 1939 with her engines needing repair and with little hope of getting back to Germany. As luck would have it, the unfolding of the Atlantic war placed the *Eurofeld* in a good position to function as a supply ship for German surface raiders, particularly the commerce raider *Thor*.[6] However, the *Eurofeld* was ordered by naval operations to weigh anchor and meet the *Admiral Scheer* so that the warship's skilled engineering department could make the necessary repairs to the tanker's engines.

The *Nordmark* joined the other ships on 14 November. She was a 22,850-ton tanker converted to a general supply ship that carried both general and refrigerated food supplies, ammunition, and fuel. The ship also could hold, if needed, nearly 300 prisoners. An American flag snapped smartly from the *Nordmark's* mast and her bows sported the initials USA painted in large letters, an allowable subterfuge under international law because the United States was still a neutral nation.

Despite deep swells rolling across the sea, a towing hawser was passed between the *Nordmark* and the *Scheer* and then oil lines were hauled aboard the warship. At the same time, all available small boats from both ships were lowered to bring supplies to the *Scheer*. Included were foods of all kinds, clothing, spare parts, and some luxury items, such as sweets and tobacco. Other boats transferred ammunition. The 11-inch shells were lowered by hoist and sling to an awaiting boat. Then the boat, heaving through the swells, made its way to *Scheer* where another hook was lowered, the sling attached, and the shell hoisted aboard.

Resupply took two full days and nights of exhausting labor. But a few crewmen could look back to World War I and remember when coal, the fuel of most warships, was heaved and hauled in hundred-weight sacks from one ship to another, the men choking and their skin turning black as the dust mixed with their sweat. The two wars were much the same so far, but thank God for the differences.

On 20 November, Captain Krancke bade a temporary goodbye to the *Nordmark* and headed for the West Indies. On Sunday, 24 November, one of *Scheer*'s lookouts spotted the British 7,448-ton freighter, *Port Hobart*. The British ship, in turn, saw the *Scheer* bearing down and immediately sent the R-R-R signal—indication that a surface raider was attacking them. Even though the *Scheer* sent a message to heave-to, the freighter kept moving away. Krancke ordered a shot put across her bow. The freighter sent another message, "Opened fire on me." An American warship received the signal and relayed it to the Royal Navy base in Bermuda. The *Port Hobart*, duty done, came to a stop. A prize crew from the *Scheer* boarded her and transferred sixty-eight crewmen and passengers, including seven women, to the *Scheer*. Finding nothing of value in her cargo, the prize crew set explosive charges and left. The freighter shuddered as the charges exploded but she would not sink. A 5.9-inch shell administered the coup de grace.

Krancke did not mind, in this instance, that *Port Hobart* sent wireless messages reporting the attack and giving their position. Let the British search for him in the West Indies; he turned his ship east and sped away toward the Cape Verde Islands (see Map 7 for this and subsequent locations of the voyage).

The Admiralty was in a high state of alarm. Was the *Port Hobart* attacked by a pocket battleship, the same one that fell upon Convoy HX-84, or was the enemy a disguised commerce raider? The R-R-R signal sent by the freighter gave no specific identification of type. The Admiralty organized three hunter groups or, better said, added a few ships to those already committed to finding the *Scheer*.[7] The carrier *Formidable* and the heavy cruisers *Norfolk* and *Berwick*, now designated Force K, sailed to the Freetown area of the South Atlantic but did not arrive until January. The St. Helena zone was patrolled by the carrier *Hermes*, a light cruiser, and an armed merchant cruiser. The heavy cruiser *Cumberland* and the light cruiser *Newcastle* rein-

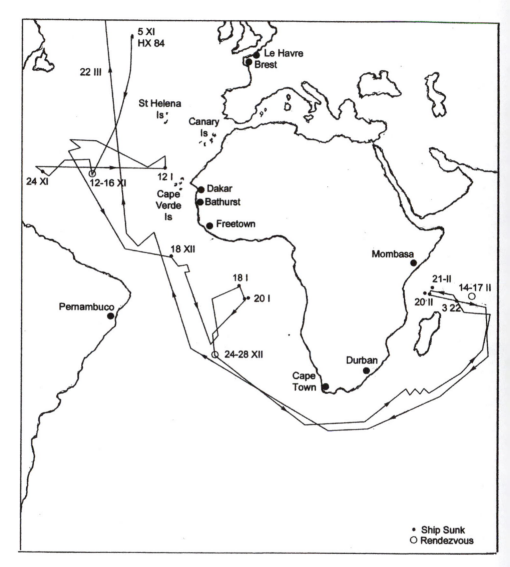

5 XI
HX 84

22 III

Le Havre
Brest

St Helena
Is

Canary
Is

24 XI

12-16 XI

12 I

Dakar

Bathurst

Cape
Verde
Is

Freetown

18 XII

Mombasa

18 I

20 I

21-II

14-17 II

20 II

3 22

Pernambuco

24-28 XII

Durban

Cape
Town

• Ship Sunk
O Rendezvous

Map 7. *Scheer's* Continuing Raid

forced the area further south toward the Falkland Islands. As a safety measure, South Atlantic convoys were rerouted east to the channel between the Cape Verde Islands and Dakar, where the narrower waters increased the possibility of seeing an oncoming raider.

Despite the fairly well established convoy system, some ships still sailed independently. On 1 December, the *Scheer* sank the freighter *Tribesman* several hundred miles west of Bathurst, Gambia. She mounted a gun on the stern. As the *Scheer* drew near, the *Tribesman* opened fire. Surprised by the merchant ship's feeble attempt at self-defense, the *Scheer* fired back, setting *Tribesman*'s stern afire. Finally, after considerable shelling, the *Tribesman* started to go down. Some of the crew made it to a lifeboat and others jumped into the sea. Krancke took the time to pick up the survivors, seventy-eight in all.

To keep his pursuers guessing, Krancke turned west again to intercept any ships on the routes between South America and Freetown. On 18 December, he intercepted the refrigerator ship *Duquesa*, which was carrying food, including 900 tons of eggs. The freighter sent the R-R-R code message—to signal that it was being attacked by a surface raider—over and over, the wireless crew aboard the *Scheer* vainly attempting to jam their transmission. Krancke ordered a warning shot sent over her bow but the *Duquesa* continued to move away from the raider and send the attack signal. The British station at Freetown responded, so Krancke sent another shot toward the *Duquesa*, this one landing very close. The freighter heaved to.[8] Krancke decided not to sink her but keep her as a supply ship to restock the *Scheer*, the *Thor* and, if necessary, even the *Nordmark*.

Royal Navy hunter groups searched for the *Scheer*, one sailing west from Freetown, another patrolling northeast from St. Helena, the third moving southwest of the Azores. But the *Scheer* moved ever south to a rendezvous point scheduled for 24 and 25 December. The *Scheer* needed some further cleaning, some new paint, and a thorough check of the electrical system. The ship's engines, which had run continuously for two months, needed an overhaul. When the *Nordmark* arrived, the *Scheer*'s fuel tanks were once again topped.

Krancke never allowed his fuel supply to reach a critical point. Running a 13,000-ton ship at full speed consumed a tremendous amount of fuel. Krancke and his engineers never knew precisely when and for how long they would have to sail at full speed. Nor did Krancke know, given the chance occurrences of a raiding foray, how many miles the *Scheer* would have to cruise in any given direction. A fuel shortage at a critical juncture could spell the death of the great ship—as another raider commander would soon learn.

Naval operational command instructed Captain Krancke and the *Thor*'s skipper, Captain Otto Kähler, to join forces through January of 1941. Neither captain liked the idea. The *Scheer's* presence would compromise the *Thor's* disguise. The *Thor*, in turn, was slower than the *Scheer*, carried much lighter gunnery, and was unarmored. Although one might invent some interesting joint tactical situations, the disadvantages far outweighed any imagined scenarios. When both captains met at the rendezvous, they agreed to reject headquarters' instructions and continue working independently.

The *Scheer* and *Thor* made separate journeys to yet another rendezvous point, arriving 27 December. And what a rendezvous it was! The *Duquesa* was already there. Then the old *Eurofeld* and the *Nordmark* joined them. It seemed the ships could meet with impunity just about anywhere they wanted. The *Scheer* again took on fuel, and the electrical and engine overhauls were completed. Krancke sent a message to naval operations on 6 January that he was taking the *Scheer* alone to the Gulf of Guinea where he could intercept ships on their way to Egypt via the Cape of Good Hope.

Yet, it was not until 10:15 A.M., 18 January, that the *Scheer* spotted the 8,038-ton tanker *Sandefjord*. Krancke followed at a distance so that his lookouts in the *Scheer's* foremast could see the tanker but, heavily laden and riding low in the water, lookouts on the tanker could not see the raider. Krancke decided on a night attack. The tanker crew would be less certain of the raider's identity and the element of surprise would reduce the possibility of an R-R-R message, something he did not need with hunter groups about, for neither Freetown nor St. Helena were that far away. Also, Krancke received a message from German intelligence that the carrier *Hermes* was at St. Helena.

When the night was darkest, Krancke brought the *Scheer* a few hundred yards abreast of the tanker's starboard side. He then ordered his ship's searchlights to sweep the *Sandefjord*; at the same time a 5.9-inch gun put a shell across her bow. The men on the tanker were taken completely off guard and the ship stopped. The prize crew put aboard the tanker found her to be a Norwegian vessel operating for the British under the authority of the Norwegian exile government in London. The tanker's crew were locked away below deck and the prize crew set course for another rendezvous point.

The *Scheer* sailed on, sinking two ships on 20 January. The first was the 5,597-ton Dutch freighter *Barneveld*, which was carrying war materiel in her cargo—five American-built Northrop light bombers, eighty-six military vehicles, and a thousand tons of ammunition. The crew, together with three Royal Navy officers and forty-eight Royal Marines, were taken aboard the *Scheer* and the freighter was scuttled. Shortly after, the *Scheer* intercepted the 5,103-ton British freighter *Stanpark*, carrying potatoes and cotton from Egypt to Freetown. The ship's crew were imprisoned aboard the raider. This time Krancke torpedoed his captive ship. Alas, the first torpedo missed. A second went awry as it ejected from the tube, smashed the stern of a launch coming under the stern of the *Scheer*, dropped into the water, and ran for a few hundred yards before it turned around a came back toward the *Scheer*. Fortunately for the Germans, it sank before making contact. The third torpedo struck home and the *Stanpark* went to the bottom. The torpedo officer doubtless noted that his men needed more drill.

For four days, beginning 24 January, the *Scheer* again rendezvoused with the *Nordmark* and the *Duquesa*. The *Thor* and *Eurofeld* soon joined them. Last to arrive was the tanker *Sandefjord*. Krancke transferred to the tanker 250 prisoners being held on the *Scheer*, including the seven ladies from the *Port Hobart*, and sent the vessel with its valuable 11,000 tons of crude oil to Bordeaux. The *Scheer* left the rendezvous on 28 January after Krancke received permission to operate in the Indian Ocean. On 6 February, he was off the southern tip of Madagascar.

The *Scheer* searched for five days and found nothing. Naval operations arranged a rendezvous with the disguised commerce raider *Atlantis*, believing that intelligence gathered by the commerce raider's commander Bernhard Rogge might be valuable to Krancke. *Atlantis* had sailed the Indian Ocean from Africa to the East Indies for nearly a year and Rogge knew all the sea-lanes. *Atlantis* arrived leading a small flotilla: the captured freighter *Speybank*, the German supply ship *Tannenfels*, and the captured tanker *Ketty Brovig*. The tanker, built in 1918, had seen better days but her high-quality oil was greatly valued by the ever-thirsty raiders.[9] Rogge suggested that Krancke operate north and west of Madagascar where the shipping lanes from Zanzibar and Mombasa, serving the Tanganyikan territory, would provide good hunting.

On 20 February, Lieutenant Pietsch, scouting in the Arado, sighted the 6,994-ton tanker *British Advocate*. The *Scheer*, pretending she was a British warship, exchanged messages with the tanker, all the while closing in on her. Then Krancke signalled, "Heave to! Don't use your wireless or I'll blow you out of the water." The tanker's gun crew ran to their battle stations, ready to fight the Goliath that was broadside to them. Krancke sent a cautionary message—"No hope here"—and the tanker stopped. A prize crew went aboard with orders to rendezvous the tanker with the *Atlantis*.

That afternoon, Pietsch sighted another ship from his Arado, the 2,546-ton Greek freighter *Gregorios*, allegedly a neutral ship. But inspection of the ship's manifest and cargo showed they did not match. Supposedly carrying Red Cross supplies, she actually was loaded with machine-gun parts, airplane tires, and armor plate. This was contraband materiel. The *Gregorios* was unceremoniously sunk.

Lieutenant Pietsch, his luck running high, spotted another ship at about 6:30 P.M. Signals flew back and forth between the *Scheer* and the freighter. The *Scheer* tried to convince them that she was really a British warship. The freighter tried to convince Krancke that she was a neutral American vessel and even flew the American flag to "prove" it. Both captains had reasons to be skeptical. The freighter was not an American vessel but the SS *Canadian Cruiser* out of Halifax. Suspicious of the approaching warship, her captain sent the R-R-R signal, adding, "Being chased by battle cruiser"; however, having used the British naval attack code, the captain unwittingly shed his disguise. Krancke opened fire with his 37-mm guns, hoping to encourage the ship to shut down its wireless. Bits and pieces of the bridge flew in all directions. Too late, for the R-R-R message was received by stations in Aden, Mombasa, Zanzibar, and Mauritius. After bringing the freighter's crew aboard the *Scheer*, the *Canadian Cruiser* joined the *Gregorios* beneath the waves. The next day, the *Scheer* repeated the drill by sinking the Dutch freighter *Rantau Pandtang*, carrying 3,000 tons of coal from Durban to Singapore.

Royal Navy ships were in short supply. The Indian Ocean's 28 million square miles was a vast arena and the limited number of ships could not be everywhere at once. Consequently, those available were poorly positioned. Even though three heavy cruisers and two light cruisers and the newly arrived carrier *Hermes* went after the pocket battleship, only the light cruiser *Glasgow* was anywhere near the raider—and that was 140 miles away. But on 22 February, the *Glasgow* launched its scout plane, a biwinged, push-engine Supermarine Walrus that chugged along at 125 mph. The little machine spotted the *Scheer* off the north coast of Madagascar around noon and signalled the position. A half hour later, the Walrus unfortunately lost contact as the *Scheer* first sped east then switched back west. Now beyond the ability of British warships to catch her, Krancke steered a southwesterly course for passage around the Cape of Good Hope. On 26 February he received orders to return to Germany. That same day Krancke received a message that he had been awarded the Knight's Cross, one of Germany's highest decorations.

On 3 March, the *Scheer* steamed into the South Atlantic.

Krancke was determined to prevent the Royal Navy from finding his ship as it steamed homeward. The *Scheer* had thus far proved to be a lucky ship—locating vessels to sink, avoiding British hunter groups, and not losing a man to enemy action. However, the only ships to oppose the *Scheer* were armed merchant ships, including HMS *Jervis Bay*, none of which mounted anything larger than a 6-inch gun. Now was not the time to call down upon his warship the might of the Royal Navy with bigger ships and bigger guns. Krancke therefore decided not to sink any more merchant ships and risk giving away his position. Luck ran just so far.

The *Scheer* needed some work to make the run up the Atlantic. The hull needed to be scraped of barnacles and other marine growth to gain a little more speed. Using a technique harkening back to sailing ships, the empty tanks on one side of the ship were flooded, exposing the hull on the opposite side below the water line. That cleaned, the process was repeated for the other side. The radar, essential for navigating the Denmark Strait, needed a new quartz crystal. Krancke sent a message, requesting the new part. This was sent on the U-124 that was just departing Germany. Fuel and provisions were also needed. The *Scheer* rendezvoused with the *Nordmark* on 10 March, topped off her tanks, and transferred the recent batch of prisoners to the supply ship. He next rendezvoused with the stores ship *Alsterufer* that filled the *Scheer*'s food lockers and delivered the first mail the pocket battleship's crew received since leaving home. Krancke then reversed his course, causing momentary consternation among his men, to meet the U-124. The quartz crystal transferred, Krancke was ready to take his men home.

British wireless messages filled the air as the *Scheer* moved into the North Atlantic around 18 March. But one had nothing to do with the other. The Royal Navy was searching for the surface raiders *Admiral Hipper*, *Scharnhorst*, and *Gneisenau* that had raided British shipping (see Chapter 7). British intelligence did not have the foggiest notion where the *Scheer* might be found. Nonetheless, Krancke would have freely admitted that his ship was always in danger but more from chance encounters than a planned attack. At this, the war's early stage, the Royal Navy thrashed about without much to show for their efforts, the triumph over the *Graf Spee* a stroke of luck.

The situation was no different as the Admiralty deployed ships in a predictably futile effort to track down the *Scharnhorst* and *Gneisenau*. Not only did the big ships make it safely to France but the diversion they created allowed the *Hipper*, whose attack on Convoy SLS-64 in early February sank seven merchantmen and damaged two others, to sail unnoticed through the Denmark Strait on 23 March. She docked at Kiel on 28 March.

With the *Hipper* clear, Krancke received permission from naval operations to enter the Denmark Strait on 24 March. But he tarried, hoping the weather would turn foul. The *Scheer* entered the strait on 26 March, but the weather actually cleared. There was nothing else for it but to sail on. Krancke steered as close to pack ice as he dared, where the temperature dropped and mist and winds diminished visibility. Then he stopped his ship. Only when the mist thickened and snow blew across the decks did Krancke move his ship forward at 23 knots, making for the strait's narrows in the north. Radar located two probable British cruisers but the *Scheer* avoided them. Then a heavy cruiser was spotted in the early evening. Krancke could have maneuvered his ship into an attack position without being seen but, once more, he chose to avoid contact lest his position be revealed. By noon the next day, the *Scheer* cut across the Norwegian Sea, both the air and water thick with cold. At 7:00 A.M., 30 March, the pocket battleship dropped anchor at Bergen.

That evening at 7:30 P.M. the *Scheer*, with a destroyer escort, plunged south, the big ship steaming at nearly 28 knots and leaving the escort behind. On 1 April, with 46,000 miles on her engines, the *Scheer* entered Kiel. The crew was assembled aft and inspected by Grand Admiral Raeder. The great adventure was over. The lives of some of those aboard that day, and the ship itself, were destined for change.

· CHAPTER 7 ·

GÖTTERDÄMMERUNG: TWILIGHT OF THE GERMAN SURFACE RAIDERS

THE ROYAL NAVY: INADEQUATE OR UNLUCKY?

The British Admiralty was chagrined if not exasperated by the safe return of the *Admiral Scheer* and the *Admiral Hipper* to their home bases. The unimpeded voyages through the Denmark Strait and across the Norwegian Sea doubtless left more than one admiral wondering if German capital raiders were ghost ships, great gray apparitions embraced by fog and mist that might be seen fleetingly, only to slip away—but to where? The truth was hard to face: The German Navy's surface raiders outmaneuvered the Royal Navy at every turn. Worse, this was not a matter of two ships getting back safely. It was a consistent pattern that plagued the Admiralty from 1939 to April 1941.

Moreover, six disguised commerce raiders—*Atlantis, Komet, Kormoran, Thor, Widder*, and *Pinguin*—freighters turned into auxiliary warships or *Handels-Stor-Kreuzer*, and their valuable supply ships, coursed the Atlantic with seeming impunity. And even more powerful capital surface raiders were waiting their turn to break into the Atlantic. The *Scharnhorst* and *Gneisenau*, the inseparable twins of the German Navy, left Kiel on 23 January 1941 under the overall command of Vice Admiral Gunther Lütjens. The ships passed between the Shetland Islands and Norway, turned west, and entered the Atlantic south of Iceland. Admiral Sir John Tovey, who replaced Sir Charles Forbes as commander in chief, Home Fleet, received intelligence reports that the two battlecruisers were under way. Tovey dispatched the battleships HMS *Rodney* and *Nelson*, the battlecruiser *Repulse*, eight cruisers, and eleven destroyers to intercept the German ships off Iceland.

The cruiser HMS *Naiad* reported seeing the two raiders early on 28 January. The *Rodney* and *Nelson* moved to support the *Naiad* and a cruiser screen was deployed to pinpoint the Germans' location. Unfortunately for the British, the excellent radar equipment on the *Scharnhorst* and *Gneisenau* located two British cruisers closing range. Lütjens immediately ordered a turnaround and sped north to arctic waters. He carried orders not to engage enemy warships.

After refueling at sea, the *Scharnhorst* and *Gneisenau* again entered the Atlantic. On 8 February, the Germans sighted Convoy HX-106 escorted by the battleship HMS *Ramillies*. Although commissioned in 1916, and with a speed of only 21 knots, she carried eight 15-inch guns. The German ships mounted 11-inch batteries. With caution his standing order, Lütjens once again turned from the enemy. What he did not know was that Winston Churchill had written off the *Ramillies* and the other R-Class battleships as "floating coffins."[1] Finally, on 22 February, much like foxes among panicked chickens, the battlecruisers caught the remnants of a dispersed convoy sailing west toward Halifax. The Germans sank five merchantmen.

Lütjens steered south to raid the Freetown convoys. Indeed, they found a convoy but the battleship HMS *Malaya*, another holdover from World War I, mounting eight 15-inch guns, escorted the convoy. Lütjens turned away, heading north to once again prowl the Halifax convoy routes. He found exactly the targets he wanted. On 15 and 16 March, the two battlecruisers sank or captured sixteen ships from dispersed convoys.[2] Both now needed refueling and the *Scharnhorst*'s engines showed signs of wear. Lütjens sought a port in Germany or in occupied France for the needed overhaul.

HMS *Rodney* spotted Lütjens's force the evening of 16 March, but soon lost contact. Admiral Tovey ordered HMS *King George* V from Halifax to patrol the area where the battlecruisers were first sighted. He also reinforced the cruiser line south of Iceland in the firm belief that the enemy would return to Germany through either the Denmark Strait or the passage between Iceland and the Faroe Islands.

In fact, Lütjens headed his ships northeast toward France. On 20 March, in the late afternoon, a reconnaissance plane from the carrier HMS *Ark Royal* spotted the battlecruisers. Fate intervened at that point. The plane's wireless failed. The pilot turned back to his carrier and on the way overflew the *Renown* with Admiral Sir John Somerville aboard. The pilot sent a visual signal, indicating that he had seen the two German ships but, for some unfathomable reason, he did not give their course. That was not reported until the plane landed aboard the *Ark Royal*.

What the British did not know was that Lütjens, having sighted the scout plane early enough, changed his course to due north, feeding Tovey's conclusion that the ships were going to Germany. Tovey adjusted his forces accordingly. Meanwhile, operating from German Naval Operations guidelines, Lütjens returned to his northeastern course as soon as the scout plane disappeared over the horizon. The next afternoon, the British realized their error and tried to make further adjustments to Lütjens's course change. It was now obvious that he was making for the Bay of Biscay and a French port. Tovey hoped the *Ark Royal* could launch a torpedo plane attack, but time, distance from the enemy, and deteriorating weather conditions conspired against the Royal Navy. Lütjens brought his unscathed ships triumphantly into Brest on 22 March. His distraction of Tovey's ships allowed the *Scheer* and *Hipper* to use the Denmark Strait for their passages home.[3]

Lütjens's splendid maneuvering brought praise from Admiral Raeder. But Raeder also knew the British to be a relentless foe, a point he had tried several times to impress upon Hitler. The German grand admiral knew the great and deadly Atlantic chess game was far from over.

The Royal Navy established patrol squadrons, each with a battleship or battlecruiser, to make certain the German ships stayed right where they were. The Bay of Biscay was heavily mined, and the Royal Air Force flew persistent and heavy raids against Brest. On the night of 30 March, 109 aircraft hit the port and town—but not the battlecruisers. On 4 April, a bomb hit a hotel, killing 200 sailors from the battlecruisers who were dining there. On 6 April, a Bristol Beaufort, a versatile machine just coming on line from 22 Squadron, put a torpedo into the *Gneisenau*, severely damaging its stern. The plane was shot down. On the night of April 11, *Gneisenau* was hit again, this time by four bombs.[4]

Docking the battlecruisers at Brest not only put them in convenient range of the RAF; it also had an unanticipated consequence for the U-boat fleet stationed around the Bay of Biscay. About 800 dockyard workers who maintained and repaired the submarines were sent to Brest to repair the *Scharnhorst* and *Gneisenau*.[5] Karl Dönitz, as commander of the U-boat fleet, protested the transfers. Admittedly, surface raiders sank enemy ships and disrupted the deployment of Royal Navy vessels. But Dönitz passionately believed that his U-boats were the most economical and effective means of sinking enemy shipping. Reducing the services needed to keep the U-boats operational diminished the impact of their "meager numbers."[6] He wrote a terse memorandum to Hitler, stating that workers should be used to build and repair ships "*indispensable to the prosecution of the war*," and battleships and cruisers were emphatically not in that category.[7]

EXERCISE *RHEINÜBUNG*: THE *BISMARCK* LET LOOSE

On 28 January 1940, Churchill asked, "What do we do if the *Bismarck* breaks out in June? What have we got to face her?"[8] He dropped this pregnant question on three of his admirals—Sir Dudley Pound, first sea lord, Sir T.S.V. Phillips, and Sir Bruce Fraser. The *Bismarck* was an enormous ship. She was 823½ feet long and displaced 42,000 tons (52,000 fully loaded). She mounted eight 15-inch guns, twelve 6-inch guns, and bristled with antiaircraft weapons that included sixteen dual-purpose 4-inch guns and sixteen 37-mm guns. An armored belt from 8 to 12 inches thick protected the hull. She could make 28 knots, 30 if necessary, and carried a crew of over 2,000 men. She was a dominating, even intimidating, war machine.

Churchill and his admirals estimated they could throw together a hunter group that included two carriers armed with Fairey Swordfish torpedo planes. This bi-winged machine bucketed along at a top speed of 138 mph but delivered only an 18-inch torpedo from a height of 50 feet at an attack speed of 85 mph. They were humorously, even lovingly, called "Stringbags," because tears in their fabric covering had to be hand stitched. The hunter group also would include HMSs *Rodney* and *Nelson*, which, at 23 knots full speed, could not catch the *Bismarck*. But they did mount powerful 16-inch guns. Some cruisers and a destroyer squadron would be added to the mix. Newer and faster ships—(such as the battleship *Prince of Wales*) rated at 28 knots and mounted newly designed 14-inch guns that delivered more punch than older 15-inch guns—were experiencing construction delays. Churchill and the admirals considered the hunter group the best protection they could provide at the time.

What the British did not know was that the *Bismarck* would not be commissioned until late August 1940. Subsequent sea trials revealed problems necessitating changes and further trials. One problem was not fixed. If, somehow, the rudders jammed, the ship could not be steered by her engines. Further sea trials and crew training pushed forward the *Bismarck*'s readiness for Atlantic operations to April 1941, an unanticipated break for the British, whose new battleships would be almost ready.

On 2 April, Admiral Raeder readied an operational plan codenamed *Rheinübung* (Exercise Rhine), a strategic sweep of the Atlantic by German capital ships. *Bismarck*, the heavy cruiser *Prinz Eugen*, and the *Scharnhorst* and *Gneisenau*, with their own supply ships and tankers, were to slice into the Atlantic to savage British convoys and confuse the Royal Navy's deployments. Coordinated attacks by the U-boat fleet and long-range *Luftwaffe* aircraft would add to the destruction of British merchant shipping.[9] Lütjens, given sea command of the campaign, was initially lukewarm about the plan but Raeder convinced him that it could be done. Captain Ernst Lindemann commanded the *Bismarck*, Lütjens's flagship. Both were good officers but they did not work well together once at sea.

No sooner did Raeder reveal the plan to Hitler than it started to come apart. RAF bomb damage to the *Gneisenau* had removed her from the plan and the *Scharnhorst* still needed engine repairs. Raeder, anxious that his surface fleet make a strategic impact on the Atlantic war, insisted the operation go forward with just the *Bismarck* and *Prinz Eugen*. And so the ships sailed from Gotenhafen on 18 May. Four days later, Raeder told Hitler of their departure.[10] The Führer "expressed considerable doubt and anxiety," but allowed the operation to continue.[11]

On 20 May, *Bismarck*, *Prinz Eugen*, and a destroyer escort sailed north past Denmark's eastern islands and entered the Kattegat, the strait between northern Denmark and Sweden. The Swedish cruiser *Gotland* saw the ships and radioed Swedish intelligence. The message found its way to the British naval attaché in Stockholm who signalled London. The next day, as the German ships approached Kristiansand on Norway's south coast, they were spotted again, this time by members of the Norwegian underground who promptly contacted London.

On 21 May, the *Bismarck* and *Prinz Eugen*, departing their escort ships, dropped anchor in Grimstadfjord, south of Bergen, Norway. *Prinz Eugen* refueled but the *Bismarck* did not. This perplexed Burkard Baron von Müllenheim-Rechberg, the *Bismarck*'s fourth gunnery officer. The battleship's tanks were not completely full when it left Gotenhafen because a hose had ruptured and further refueling was cancelled. Now Lütjens was taking his ship, short of fuel, into the Atlantic for an indeterminate time and over an unknown distance.[12] This was a stark contrast to Captain Theodor Krancke, who topped off the *Scheer*'s tanks at every opportunity. Lütjens blundered.

While at Grimstadfjord, a British reconnaissance Spitfire from Coastal Command flew over the anchorage and took pictures of the ships below, confirming the previous sighting reports. Lütjens, aware that his ships had been reported in Grimstadfjord, nonetheless sailed across the Norwegian Sea and through the Denmark Strait, convinced this latter part of his breakout went unnoticed by the British. This belief was rooted in a report from a *Luftwaffe* aerial reconnaissance flight over the Scapa Flow naval base. No change in Royal Navy ship deployments was observed.[13] They were wrong, very wrong.

As early as 18 May, Admiral Tovey, alerted by increased German aerial reconnaissance over northern waters, signalled Rear Admiral W. F. Wake-Walker, commanding 1st Cruiser Squadron—HMSs *Norfolk* and *Suffolk*—to carefully patrol the northern entrance to the Denmark Strait where the winter pack ice narrowed the passage to about 50 miles. When the German ships were spotted at Grimstadfjord three days later, Tovey sent from Scapa Flow HMSs *Hood* and *Prince of Wales*—so new that civilian workers were still aboard—and six destroyers under the overall command of Vice Admiral Lancelot Holland. They sailed to Hvalfjord, just north of Reykjavik, Iceland's capital. At the same time, the cruisers *Birmingham* and *Manchester*, later joined by the *Arethusa*, patrolled the eastern passage between Iceland and the Faroe Islands. HMS *King George V*, completed but untested, with a cruiser and destroyer force, remained on-call at Scapa Flow. The Admiralty redirected from convoy duty to Tovey's forces the new aircraft carrier *Victorious* and the old battlecruiser *Repulse*.[14] To strip a convoy of its main protection was an extraordinary measure, one that reflects the alarm sent through the Admiralty at the *Bismarck's* sailing.

But Tovey remained calm even when, on 22 May, Coastal Command aerial reconnaissance reported the German ships had left Grimstadfjord. He, in fact, anticipated the move, ordering Holland's ships to cover the Denmark Strait. Tovey, in *King George V*, accompanied by *Victorious*, four cruisers, and six destroyers left Scapa Flow and steamed west. The *Repulse* soon joined them.

The cruiser *Suffolk* discovered the *Bismarck* and *Prinz Eugen* entering the Denmark Strait on the evening of 23 May. The *Suffolk* mounted new radar equipment that ranged some 23,000 yards. Soon after that sighting, the cruiser *Norfolk* spotted the Germans at a range of only six miles. *Bismarck* snapped a few salvoes at the dangerously close ship, but failed to make a hit. Now both British cruisers fell in behind the German ships, doggedly trailing them at high speed through dangerous waters.

Eleven convoys were scattered about the North Atlantic on 23 May. The most important contained five troop transports headed for the North African campaign.[15] They were supposed to be escorted out of Gibraltar by Sir James Somerville's Force H. But he read the *Norfolk's* sighting report and, anticipating his force—including the carrier *Ark Royal*—would be sent to hunt for the *Bismarck*, readied his ships for departure. When the Admiralty ordered Somerville to join the hunt on 24 May, Force H was at sea in two hours.

On 24 May, at 2:00 A.M., the *Hood* and *Prince of Wales* intercepted the *Bismarck* and *Prinz Eugen*. Holland's ships followed the Germans south from the Denmark Strait for a few hours. The *Norfolk* and *Suffolk*, initially unaware of Holland, pursued the Germans at a distance of fifteen miles. Holland's hastily developed battle plan called for the cruisers to close up and attack the *Prinz Eugen* so that the guns of his two big ships, essentially fighting as one, could be concentrated on the *Bismarck*. This was a mistake because it did not allow Captain J.C. Leach commanding the *Prince of Wales* to maneuver independently and distract and/or confuse the German gunners. Furthermore, the two British ships entered the fight with disadvantages. The *Hood*, however much the pride of the Royal Navy, was obsolete. She was a little slower than her opponent and her deck armor was too thin to prevent a plunging shot from penetrating the ship's interior. *Prince of Wales*, barely out of the shipyard, the civilian workers aboard wondering what the gods had against them, was fast enough but her new four-gunned turrets were untested. Both ships suffered inadequate fire control because rough seas blinded their range finders with spray. Furthermore, unbeknownst to Holland, Lütjens had placed *Prinz Eugen* ahead of the *Bismarck*, a switch that foiled Holland's plan.

At 5:53 A.M., Holland brought his two ships to battle at an angle that did not allow the stern guns of either to fix on their targets. Thus, their concentrated fire on the lead ship, the *Prinz Eugen*, was inaccurate and not as powerful as it might have been had Holland executed a more parallel course to the enemy. Both German ships had better angles on the British and fired their guns with great accuracy. The second or third salvo from the *Bismarck* started a fire in the *Hood*'s midship. Then a shell from her fifth salvo penetrated the *Hood*'s aft deck armor, exploding in the after magazine. A huge fireball engulfed the battlecruiser, cracking her open. She was gone in less than four minutes, taking down all but three of her crew.

Prince of Wales, meantime, experienced difficulties. Just six of her ten guns initially opened fire, and those suffered poor range estimates. Then one of her four-gunned turrets jammed on its rotation ring or barbette. Of the eight salvoes she fired, *Prince of Wales* scored only two hits. Both, however, were important. One crippled the *Bismarck*'s Number 2 forward boiler room and tore into fuel tanks, causing a persistent leak into the sea. The second hit passed through both sides of the hull forward of an armored bulkhead "above the waterline but below the bow wave."[16] Two thousand tons of seawater cascaded into the fo'c'sle, bringing the bow down 3° and rendering useless a thousand tons of fuel oil trapped in the forward tanks. Pressure on the bulkhead and the looming probability of a fuel shortage led Lütjens to restrict speed to no more than 28 knots.

The *Bismarck* struck *Prince of Wales* with three 6-inch shells and four 15-inch shells, one of which destroyed her bridge. Captain Leach, one of three survivors from that hit, turned his ship away from further action under cover of a smokescreen. She now became part of Wake-Walker's cruiser command, who decided that his best option was to continue trailing the Germans with *Norfolk* and *Suffolk*, using *Prince of Wales* as support if *Bismarck* turned on his cruisers.

That decision pleased neither Admiral Pound nor Winston Churchill, both of whom were in the Admiralty war room trying to micromanage a situation neither fully understood. They wanted the cruisers to do battle. They wanted heads to roll for inaction against a visible enemy. Divisiveness aside, one goal was clearly understood by all in London and at sea: Sink the *Bismarck*! Fortunately, Admiral Tovey could plot his moves from the bridge of the *King George V* without the mercurial judgments of his two masters distracting him. For their part, the Admiralty diverted HMS *Rodney* from a convoy and the old "floating coffin" *Ramillies* from another. The latter's sister ship, *Revenge*, was called to sea from Halifax. In total, "four battleships, two battlecruisers, twelve cruisers, two aircraft carriers, and a swarm of destroyers were . . . on the move."[17]

Lütjens determined his next move almost as soon as the battle ended. At 8:01 A.M. he notified naval operations: "Battle cruiser, probably Hood, sunk. . . . Intention: to proceed to St. Nazaire."[18] He did not intend to abort his operation; simply to effect some repairs and refuel. *Bismarck* headed south, the trio of British ships following. During midafternoon, in the thick of deteriorating visibility, Lütjens ordered *Prinz Eugen* to sail on independently and begin raiding. The British ships lost contact temporarily at that time, regaining it again after three anxious hours. During this deadly game of hide and seek, salvoes from one or another of the ships rattled across the sky but no damage was done to either side.

Tovey knew the distance was too great between his force and the *Bismarck*. The German had to be slowed down. One action might possibly work. He ordered Captain H. C. Bovell on *Victorious* to mount a torpedo plane attack. This was done at 10:00 P.M. on 24 May, when the carrier was 120 miles from the *Bismarck*. Bovell sent up nine Swordfish and half-dozen Fairey Fulmar fighters to cover them—again an obsolete machine that the Royal Navy used until a better plane was designed. Few planes were available because *Victorious* was packed with Hawker Hurricanes, fighters destined for North Africa. The Swordfish attacked just after midnight. Every antiaircraft gun on the *Bismarck* opened fire on the little machines. Only one torpedo hit the ship and did no damage. Remarkably, not a single Swordfish was shot down. One reason might have been the zigzag course the *Bismarck* was on, throwing off her gunners.[19] Another explanation might be that the fire control for the antiaircraft guns was configured for planes much faster than the Swordfish. To borrow from field artillery jargon, the Stringbags flew "under the guns."

On 25 May, at 3:00 A.M., Lütjens increased *Bismarck*'s speed and changed to a westerly course. At 3:40 A.M., he turned north, and twenty minutes later made a long turn east, then southeast, completing an almost perfect circle.[20]

Unknowingly, he succeeded in breaking contact with his British hounds. The *Suffolk*, whose radar guided Wake-Walker's decisions, was on a southern zigzag course as a precaution against U-boat attacks. As the ship zigged east from the *Bismarck*, Lütjens began his looping maneuver. When Suffolk zagged back, the *Bismarck* was gone. Thinking she must have sailed west, Wake-Walker turned his ships in that direction, increasing the distance between his force and the southeast course *Bismarck* was now steaming. The irony is that Lütjens believed the British knew where he was and saw no reason to observe radio silence. At 7:00 A.M., he sent the message, "A battleship, two heavy cruisers continue to maintain contact."[21] At 9:00 A.M., he sent another message: "Attempts to break contact unsuccessful despite favorable weather conditions" [meaning poor visibility].[22]

Tovey also made an error. Because of confusion about the exact position where Lütjens radio messages had originated, Tovey aimed *King George V* and his force north. Then the Admiralty staff, doubtless prodded by the pragmatic Admiral Phillips, recalculated the locations of Lütjens's messages, concluding that the *Bismarck* was headed for a French port on the Bay of Biscay. Tovey, at the same time, gave in to a growing apprehension that he was going in the wrong direction. Around 6:00 P.M., he reversed his course and sailed southeast. Fuel reserves were becoming a problem, so he sent all his destroyers, *Prince of Wales*, and *Repulse* to various ports to refuel. He kept *King George V*, *Victorious*, and *Suffolk* in the chase but reduced speed to 20 knots to conserve fuel.

Despite the temporary confusion of Tovey and the Admiralty, Admiral Somerville's Force H plowed north through heavy seas that slowed his progress to 21 knots. On 26 May, he was in position to launch an aerial reconnaissance over the Bay of Biscay. The *Ark Royal's* Swordfish carried auxiliary petrol tanks to extend their patrol time. The dawn search on 26 May found nothing. However, that same morning, a Coastal Command Catalina, piloted by Flying Officer Dennis Briggs with a U.S. Navy ensign as neutral trainer/copilot, left Iceland to scan an area further south than the Admiralty calculated was necessary. At 10:30 A.M., they spotted the *Bismarck*, tailing an oil leak, making 20 knots about 700 miles from St. Nazaire. Briggs immediately radioed the ship's position while maintaining visual contact. Around noon, lookouts on the *Bismarck*, by then used to seeing the Catalina, saw something disturbing approaching—a bi-winged fixed-wheeled aircraft. That meant only one thing. An aircraft carrier was near. It was the *Ark Royal* establishing relays of Swordfish to keep the *Bismarck* in view.

Tovey was doing his best to bring his ships to battle but the fuel problem plagued him. Once again, he called upon the Swordfish torpedo planes to slow the *Bismarck*. When he sent the order to the *Ark Royal*, Somerville in

Renown signalled back that a torpedo attack had been launched but registered no hits—and a good thing because the pilots confused the cruiser *Sheffield* for the *Bismarck*. Tovey was soon buoyed by a second signal that another attack had been launched at 8:47 P.M.

Fifteen Swordfish descended on the *Bismarck* through miserable weather. Low clouds, wind, heaving seas, and poor visibility forced the planes so low that the *Bismarck's* crew felt they could touch them.[23] Thirteen torpedoes dropped into the sea. One (possibly two) hit amidship on the port side. A third hit astern, blowing a large hole in the hull and flooding the steering rooms where motors powered the ship's rudders. Captain Lindemann tried steering with the engines but he knew from earlier Baltic Sea trials that the method was really useless.[24]

The *Bismarck's* fate was sealed. The ship could not be steered; yet, to keep her from pitching wildly, they had to maintain headway. Thus, the great ship was reduced to 8 knots as strong winds literally pushed the crippled battleship toward Tovey's oncoming force.

At 8:20 A.M., 27 May, the *King George V* and *Rodney* found the *Bismarck*. Rodney fired two salvoes beginning at 8:47 A.M., and *King George V* fired her first salvo a minute later. *Bismarck* answered at 8:50 A.M., sending salvo after salvo toward the *Rodney* but not a shell hit. Then the *Rodney* fired a third salvo, one shell hitting *Bismarck's* fo'c'sle, another crashing into the superstructure. At 9:02 A.M., the *Rodney* hit the *Bismarck's* foredeck, her 16-inch shells destroying the two forward turrets.

Both British battleships gradually closed their range as firing from the *Bismarck*, already inaccurate, became increasingly sporadic. The British battleships were joined by the guns of the cruisers *Norfolk* and *Dorsetshire*. Ranges closed to a mere 2,900 yards. In all, the British ships fired 2,878 rounds.[25] As Baron Burkard von Müllenheim-Rechberg observed, the British fired from all directions and "were having what amounted to undisturbed target practice."[26]

But for all the shells directed at the *Bismarck*, the British could not sink her by gunfire alone. Tovey ordered the *Dorsetshire* to torpedo her. Two hits were scored at 10:20 A.M. on the starboard side. At 10:36, the cruiser passed the battleship's bow and launched a third torpedo into the port side. Four minutes later the *Bismarck*, listing to port, vanished into the sea. Many years later, interviews of survivors for the television movie production *Sink the Bismarck* put forward anecdotal evidence that the crew scuttled her. If they did, they but hastened her inevitable end. Only 119 survived from the crew of 2,065. British ships might have picked up more, but a submarine warning was issued and they withdrew, leaving many men in the water. Some of these were later rescued by U-boats. Most drowned.

The battle could have been different or never even have occurred if Lüt-jens had topped off the *Bismarck*'s fuel tanks at Grimstadfjord. As Müllen-heim-Rechberg later wrote, full tanks in Norway would have rendered mute the problem of the inaccessible fuel in the fo'c'sle. Thus, the *Bismarck* could have maintained a speed of 28 knots, putting her 160 miles closer to St. Nazaire and under *Luftwaffe* cover.[27]

CONSEQUENCES

"The sinking of the *Bismarck*," Admiral Raeder mused, "was to have last-ing effect upon the whole naval warfare."[28] Hitler, upon receiving the dis-mal battle report, fell into despondency "and his anger was in proportion."[29] He lashed out at every proposal Raeder made, substituting his own unin-formed views as the only acceptable ones. Previously, he had given Raeder relative freedom to deploy the fleet as he saw fit. No longer! Hitler adamantly refused any further Atlantic adventures by capital ships.

Dönitz at first shared Raeder's conviction that sending capital ships into the Atlantic as convoy raiders was "a thoroughly sound strategic hypothe-sis." They would disrupt the Royal Navy's convoy protection deployments, even to using battleships, thus leaving defensive gaps through which the U-boats could slip.[30] The *Bismarck* sinking told a different story. Where once a raider such as the *Admiral Scheer* broke out into the Atlantic, raided at will, and took on supplies at a rendezvous that lasted days, the British pursuit and sinking of the *Bismarck* demonstrated Britain's new determination, an im-provement in their air and sea patrols, and a coordination between forces hitherto unseen by the Germans. The only surface raiders left in the At-lantic were the *Handels-Stor-Kreuzer* together with their supply ships.

The Achilles' heel of Raeder's Atlantic strategy was that the German Navy lacked overseas bases. Those disappeared with the Treaty of Versailles. When the *Bismarck* went down and the *Prinz Eugen* limped back to port with engine trouble, the Royal Navy searched for the vessels they knew the Ger-mans sent out to service and supply the big ships. Moreover, ULTRA inter-ceptions of German ENIGMA messages gradually revealed the pattern of German supply ships rendezvousing for the entire Atlantic. This enabled the Royal Navy to seriously impact further incursions by capital ship raiders (the Admiralty was, of course, unaware of Hitler's order prohibiting such forays) and rein in the disguised raiders as well.

British code decipherment advanced on 9 May 1941. The U-110, skip-pered by Fritz Lemp, who sank the liner *Athenia* in 1939, was forced to the surface. The corvette *Aubretia*, the destroyer *Bulldog*, and the sloop *Broadway* opened fire, the *Broadway* closing in to fire depth charges directly at the U-boat. Many of the submarine's crew, already panicked by their near-underwater death, jumped overboard. *Bulldog* sped toward the stricken U-boat in what Lemp thought was an attempt to ram his submarine. He leaped from the conning tower, the last to leave. He did not survive. But the *Bulldog* veered away and sent over a boarding party. They captured the ENIGMA machine and codebooks, one of which was used for following convoys and calling in wolf packs. *Bulldog* took U-110 in tow but she sank the next morning.

The Royal Navy's hunt was on![31] On 3 June, The cruisers *Kenya* and *Aurora* sank the tanker *Belchen*, which was to supply the *Bismarck* and *Prinz Eugen*. Three more supply ships were lost the next day: the freighter *Gonzenheim* sank beneath an aerial attack; the tanker *Gedania* was captured by HMS *Marsdale*; and the *Esso Hamburg*, another tanker deployed for the *Bismarck*, was scuttled by her crew when the cruiser HMS *London* attacked. The *London* and the destroyer *Brilliant* sank the tanker *Egerland* on 5 June. On 12 June, the *Sheffield* sank the tanker *Friedrich Bream*. The light cruiser *Dunedin*, supported by the old carrier *Eagle*'s aircraft, captured the tanker *Lotharingen* on 15 June. The steamer *Babitonga* was scuttled by her crew when they sighted the *London* bearing down on them. On 23 June, the freighter *Alstretor* was also scuttled by her crew when attacked by destroyer *Flotilla 8*. She had supplied the *Admiral Scheer* during the pocket battleship's sortie and subsequently supplied four of the disguised commerce raiders.

On went the hunt. The tanker *Kota Penang*, carrying fuel for surface raiders and U-boats, was sunk on 4 October by the cruisers *Sheffield* and *Kenya*. And on 1 December 1941, the *Dorsetshire* sank the *Python*, a supply ship for the raider *Atlantis* and for U-boats. In total, the Royal Navy sank sixteen supply ships, captured four, and caused twenty-two to be scuttled. The loss of these ships so compromised capital ship operations that, as Dönitz was quick to note, the possibility of their continued use in the Atlantic war was finished by the end of 1941.[32]

But the auxiliary raiders, whose operations were also compromised by the Royal Navy's efforts, did not go quietly. Three were sunk. The *Pinguin*, which sank sixteen merchant ships and captured sixteen more, met her end when intercepted by HMS *Cornwall* off Mombasa, 7 May 1941.[33] The *Kormoran* sank eleven ships but was challenged by the Australian light cruiser HMAS *Sydney* off Western Australia. Both ships were fatally damaged in the ensuing battle. The *Sydney*, hit by shells and a torpedo, retired from the duel and simply disappeared. The *Kormoran*'s crew could not extinguish raging fires caused by the *Sydney*'s shelling, so they abandoned ship and were later taken prisoner.[34] The *Atlantis* sank twenty-two ships before she was hunted down and destroyed by the cruiser *Devonshire* on 22 November 1941. Survivors took to lifeboats or clung to rafts until German and Italian submarines arrived, placed the injured on their decks, and packed each lifeboat with as many as fifty men. The submarines then took the lot in tow and delivered them to a French port, a journey of about 5,000 miles.[35]

Directly attacking German disguised raiders was dangerous. The battle between the *Kormoran* and HMAS *Sydney* proved that. If a raider could sink a regular warship, what horror could it inflict on British AMCs sent to hunt them down? Captain Otto Kähler of the *Thor* knew the answer, having badly damaged two AMCs, the *Alcantara* and the *Carnarvon Castle*. He must have wondered what fate would conjure next when, on 4 April 1941, weeks before the British campaign intensified against the auxiliary cruisers and their supply ships, he entered into a record-setting third battle with an AMC, the 13,245-ton converted liner *Voltaire*, commanded by J.A.P. Blackburn, formerly of HMS *Jervis Bay*. She operated with the South Atlantic Patrol.

Voltaire was ordered from Trinidad on 30 March to search for German supply ships and disguised raiders west of the Cape Verde Islands. Shortly after 6:00 A.M. on 4 April, 900 miles from the islands, Blackburn was alerted to a ship steaming over the horizon to the northeast. He ordered full speed ahead. Unbeknownst to him, the ship was the *Thor*. Captain Kähler spotted *Voltaire* at the same time, turned southwest, and ordered battle stations at 6:21 A.M.

Blackburn requested the oncoming ship to identify herself. Although *Thor* was disguised as a Greek freighter, Kähler did not want the opposing ship, which he thought might be an AMC, to gain any advantage over him. The German battle flag was hoisted and the covers around his 5.9-inch guns dropped. Kähler ordered a shot be put across the British ship's bow. As *Thor* drew closer, Kähler could finally see the guns mounted on the *Voltaire*'s fo'c'sle. Indeed, she was an AMC. He ordered all his port guns to open fire. Shells screamed toward *Voltaire*, destroying the radio and generator rooms.

The *Voltaire*'s gunners returned fire but with the generator gone there was no electricity; consequently, neither the fire control system nor the ammunition hoists worked. Shells and powder bags had to be manhandled up to the guns. The *Voltaire* took hit after hit. Her cabin area burst into flames and soon the decks were ablaze. Like *Jervis Bay*, German shells easily pierced the unarmored ship and, lacking any battle-worthy compartmentalization, the fires swept unimpeded along the passageways.

One of the *Thor*'s guns scored a vital hit when it jammed *Voltaire*'s steering mechanism. No longer controllable, the AMC turned in a wide circle, her crew firing their guns as best they could. But the *Thor*'s gunners also had a problem, albeit of their own making. They had fired 724 rounds, about half their supply. The barrels of the 5.9-inch guns overheated, and the rotation and elevation gears broke down. Kähler, just as he had done earlier in his fights with the *Alcantara* and *Carnarvon Castle*, decided enough was enough. With the battle already two hours old, and since it was obvious that *Thor's* guns would not sink the AMC, he ordered a torpedo fired to finish her off. But at that very moment, Blackburn raised a white flag, deciding his gunners could do no more and that his ship was done for.

Kähler maneuvered the *Thor* close to the stricken ship. The *Voltaire's* lifeboats were either blown to bits or afire, so he launched his own lifeboats. The ensuing rescue effort pulled 197 men from the sea, including Captain Blackburn.

The only damage done by the *Voltaire's* guns to the *Thor* was toppling the wireless mast. Once repaired and with his ship long gone from the battle site, Kähler sent a message to his superiors announcing the sinking. The British picked up the signal. The Canadian AMC HMCS *Prince David* was ordered to follow the *Voltaire's* course and look for any sign of her. The Canadians found only some wreckage floating about—no lifeboats, no bodies, nothing tangible. Within a few days of the battle, Kähler was ordered to bring his ship home. *Thor* docked at Hamburg 30 April 1941.[36] Many months later some of the *Voltaire's* crew were repatriated. Only then did the Admiralty know the full story of the AMC's fate.[37]

Other commerce raiders also returned home. The *Komet* arrived in Hamburg on 30 November 1941. The *Orion*, needing repair, sailed into Bordeaux in August 1942. She was transferred to nonraiding duties until sunk by Allied bombers in May 1945.

Even though the Royal Navy relentlessly hunted down their supply ships, disguised commerce raiders continued to break out into the Atlantic, the last few gasps of a dying strategy. The *Komet* sailed again in October 1942, but British motor torpedo boats were in wait off Dunkirk. She went down in a ball of flames. The *Thor* undertook a second voyage on 30 November 1941, sinking several ships, and arrived in Yokohama, Japan, a year later. She met an ignominious end when a German tanker docked alongside to have her tanks cleaned. She blew up, taking out the *Thor* as well. The *Michel*, sailed in March 1942 and, like the *Thor*, went to the Pacific where she was sunk by the U.S. Navy submarine *Tarpon*. The *Stier* set sail 12 May 1942. In September she engaged the American liberty ship *Stephen Hopkins*. The freighter could only make 9 knots and even though her "big" gun was an obsolete 4-incher on the stern, the Americans dueled the German ship. Eventually both ships, holed and ablaze, went down. As late as February 1943, the raider *Coronel* attempted a breakout but was damaged by RAF fighter-bombers and returned to Kiel never to try again. The day of the auxiliary commerce raiders, the *Handels-Stor-Kreuzer*, was over.

The gradual demise of the surface raiders did not mean that it the U-boats rushed to fill the gap. At the dawn of 1942, Dönitz commanded ninety-one operational submarines. About thirty-three were undergoing repairs, and thirty-six were variously stationed in the Mediterranean, in the Mid-Atlantic off Gibraltar, and off Norway. That left only twenty-two boats for operations in the North Atlantic, and easily half of them were in transit at any given time between their homeport and the battle zone.[38] As the historian Correlli Barnett concluded, that situation was, after two and a half years of war, a "remarkable comment" on the Nazi's misunderstanding of the U-boats' value as a weapon against Atlantic shipping.[39]

In the meantime, the *Bismarck* episode not only led to an eventual withdrawal of Atlantic surface raiders, it also fractured what little remained of the relationship between Raeder and Hitler. The Führer angrily dismissed his admiral's every suggestion and assessment and threatened to scrap all the capital ships. Raeder countered with the idea that the big ships could be concentrated in Norwegian waters where they posed a constant threat to Russia-bound convoys. That would force the British to keep a major part of their big ships at Scapa Flow ready for deployment north. Hitler, afraid the British were going to invade Norway, grudgingly agreed to the organization of a strong fleet in Norwegian waters. But he wanted the *Prinz Eugen, Scharnhorst*, and *Gneisenau*, still at Brest, to join them as reinforcement against an invasion. By what route would the ships return home? Hitler wanted a surprise break back through the English Channel during daylight. Raeder and his staff were flabbergasted. The RAF would bomb the ships and the Royal Navy would descend from Scapa Flow like hungry wolves. No, Raeder countered, it was much safer to bring the ships back via the Denmark Strait. Yet, on 29 December, Hitler ordered the channel dash, telling Raeder that if he continued his negativism all the big ships indeed would be scrapped.[40]

The three ships slipped their moorings the night of 11 February 1942, the British unaware they were gone. Surprise! By dawn, they were entering the channel. British countermeasures, too little, too late, and with interservice coordination collapsing at every juncture, failed to stop the channel run. The ships arrived in German ports on 13 February, the *Scharnhorst* and *Gneisenau* nonetheless damaged by mines.[41]

Perhaps seeking an ally who had Atlantic war experience commanding a big ship, Raeder appointed now Vice Admiral Theodor Krancke as permanent naval representative to Hitler's Supreme Field Headquarters.[42] Hitler's attitude did not change. Certainly he was joyous over the successful channel dash; yet, one cannot but wonder whether his upbeat mood was a response to the ships' arrival or the twinking of Raeder's nose.

By mid-1942, the U-boats were enjoying considerable success, especially against convoys sailing to Russia, as well as resurgence in the North Atlantic. In July, the Russia-bound Convoy PQ-17 was ravaged by torpedo attacks from submarines and a new torpedo bomber wing of the *Luftwaffe*. Seventeen ships went down. In September PQ-18 lost thirteen ships. Opportunities existed for the capital ships stationed in Norway to be involved in both attacks but Hitler kept them in port. Yet, he railed about their inactivity, a classic example of compartmentalized thinking.

In December 1942, it seemed that the big ships would get another chance. Convoy JW-51B, escorted by destroyers, left Loch Ewe, Scotland, on 15 December headed for Murmansk. With Hitler's permission, the heavy cruiser *Admiral Hipper*, the pocket battleship *Lützow* (ex-*Deutschland*), and six destroyers, all commanded by Rear Admiral Oskar Kummetz, were sent to the attack. The *Hipper*, 8-inch guns blazing, would herd the convoy into the 11-inch guns of the *Lützow*. The tactic was simplicity itself, for neither a British cruiser nor a battleship were to be seen.

All started well enough when the *Hipper* damaged a British destroyer. Then the seas kicked up and visibility worsened. Kummetz suddenly found another British destroyer in the murk and moved to attack. Just as abruptly the cruisers HMS *Sheffield* and *Jamaica* steamed through the mist. They opened fire on the Germans, hitting the *Hipper* at least three times, damaging a boiler room and starting fires inside the ship. Kummetz, keeping to Hitler's constant injunction to be prudent, abandoned the whole attack plan and returned to base.

According to the *Fuehrer Conference* minutes of 31 December, Hitler received news of his navy's retreat not from intelligence sources or from Vice Admiral Krancke but from a BBC news broadcast. He went into a rage, furious that the capital ships did not fight the battle given them. He bellowed that the big ships were a waste of men and materiel.[43]

At the following *Fuehrer Conference*, 11 January 1943, Hitler lashed out again at Raeder's desire to maintain capital ships as commerce raiders, arguing that in World War I the High Seas Fleet made little contribution because it "lacked men of action who were determined to fight. . . . [A] large amount of fighting-power lay idle, while the Army was constantly engaged."[44] Now, in World War II, the navy's big ships were idle, this time in Norwegian waters, requiring constant *Luftwaffe* air cover. The *Tirpitz*, sistership of the *Bismarck*, was little more than a target of convenience for the RAF. Worse, the big ships could not even maneuver safely in the Baltic–German home waters because of British mines. Hitler, his tirade reaching its peak, ordered that the capital ships be scrapped and their guns and crews sent to Norway to join the coastal defense.[45]

But Hitler wanted to give the appearance of being on good terms with

Raeder because of the palpable loyalty the Admiral enjoyed throughout the fleet. He invited Raeder to submit a report, as it were a raison d'être, for continued use of the big ships. And what a report! It indicted Hitler for committing the German Navy to war five years earlier than expected, completely trashing Plan Z. Furthermore, capital ships were sent out to raid convoys under Hitler's express orders not to take undo risks, stripping their captains of any initiative. Furthermore, Raeder considered the channel dash not a victory but a retreat from an offensive posture in the Atlantic war.[46]

The report made no difference at all. Hitler remained adamant. Raeder, concluding he could serve no longer, resigned on 30 January. Admiral Dönitz took his place as commander in chief. In March, Hans-Erich Voss, one-time commander of the *Prinz Eugen*, a close friend of Propaganda Minister Josef Goebbels, and much dedicated to the Nazi ideology, replaced Theodor Krancke.

Dönitz remained unquestionably dedicated to building up his submarine force. Hitler gave him an opportunity to push that program when he presented his new commander in chief with a plan to scrap all big ships under construction as well as those afloat except where needed for training, and convert shipyards to the building and repair of U-boats. Dönitz unexpectedly veered from his earlier criticisms of Raeder's surface raider strategy. Given the current circumstances of the naval war, he saw value in having capital ships deployed in Norway either to compel the British to cancel Russia-bound convoys, which they did for a brief time after PQ-18, or attack them if they continued. Thus, on 26 February, doubtless playing to Hitler's vanity, Dönitz convinced his leader to assume personal responsibility for sending the big ships into action. To buttress the strength of the Northern Squadron, Dönitz also secured Hitler's blessing to move the *Scharnhorst* to Altenfjord.[47] Some capital ships escaped the scrapyard, at least temporarily.

The unspoken truce between Dönitz and Hitler foundered in December 1943. At the 19 December conference held at the *Wolfschanzen*, the "Wolf's Lair," near Rastenburg, East Prussia, Dönitz obtained Hitler's reluctant permission to attack the next Russia-bound convoy with surface ships and U-boats.[48] The opportunity came the next day when it was reported that Convoy JW-55B had left Loch Ewe escorted by destroyers, corvettes, and smaller ships. On 24 December, the *Scharnhorst* and a destroyer screen, commanded by Rear Admiral Erich Bey, departed Altenfjord and headed north. Bey's group was ill-served by his leaders at Naval Group North headquarters. German intelligence had intercepted vital British naval signals regarding deployments. But Group North considered the messages too vague and did not pass the information to Bey. The *Luftwaffe*, for its part, backed away from any aerial reconnaissance support, undoubtedly influenced by Herman Göring, who despised the navy. Consequently, Bey did not know that Admiral Sir Bruce Fraser was at sea headed for North Cape at the top of Norway, commanding a force that included the battleship *Duke of York*, the cruiser *Jamaica*, and a destroyer screen. Nor did he know the cruisers *Belfast*, *Sheffield*, and *Norfolk* under Rear Admiral R. L. Burnett were nearby. Bey was running into a trap. At 7:00 A.M., 26 December, he turned the *Scharnhorst* southwest in search of the convoy, his destroyers out front as a screen. So high were the seas and so bad the visibility that any coordination between the *Scharnhorst* and the destroyers was soon lost. The big ship was on its own. Just over two hours later, the *Belfast* and *Sheffield* made visual contact with the battlecruiser. The *Norfolk*, not far behind, opened fire at 9:25 A.M. The *Scharnhorst* was hit twice but turned south and sped away—the prudent maneuver given Hitler's still-standing cautionary orders to his big ships. The British cruisers again made contact at noon. In an exchange of shells, the *Norfolk* lost a forward turret and a fire erupted amidship. Once more, Bey sped away, taking a south-southwest course—unknowingly toward the *Duke of York*.

At 4:17 P.M., Fraser's radar located the *Scharnhorst* at a range of twenty-two miles. At 4:50 P.M., closing to 12,000 yards (not quite seven miles). *Duke of York*'s 14-inch guns opened fire. The *Scharnhorst* was hit again and again. She returned fire but most of her shells fell into the water and the few that reached the *Duke of York* failed to explode. At 6:50 P.M., Fraser ordered four destroyers led by HMS *Scorpion* to launch a torpedo attack. They fired twelve torpedoes. Three or four hit. The *Scharnhorst*, already afire, one turret jammed and another out of action because of a flooded magazine, suffered severe underwater damage and more flooding. *Duke of York* and *Jamaica* further closed the range to under 10,000 yards and pumped shells into the stricken ship. The *Scharnhorst* sustained a probable thirteen hits from the *Duke of York*'s 14-inch guns and another dozen from *Jamaica*'s 6-inch guns.[49]

Like the *Bismarck* before her, *Scharnhorst* refused to go down under the shelling. Fraser ordered his destroyers and cruisers to execute a mass torpedo attack. As many as fifty-five torpedoes were fired during the last ninety minutes of the battle. An estimated eleven hit. At 7:45 P.M., an explosion blew the *Scharnhorst* to bits. Only thirty-six men survived from a crew of nearly 2,000.

This was the last battle between capital ships in the Atlantic war.

CHAPTER 8

THE REASONS WHY

TOWARD AN EVALUATION OF ARMED MERCHANT CRUISERS (AMCs)

Of forty-eight British AMCs, a dozen—one-quarter of the total commissioned—were sunk by the end of 1940, mainly by U-boat attacks. The commander of the Home Fleet at that time, Admiral Sir Charles Forbes, proposed in November that the AMCs be gradually withdrawn and be rearmed with antisubmarine weapons or be taken entirely out of service.[1] Churchill, doubtless still haunted by the *Rawalpindi's* loss in November of 1939, questioned the viability of the AMCs after *Jervis Bay* was destroyed in November 1940. In April 1941 he suggested that a large number of AMCs be released from their warship status and shifted to transport duties.[2] Yet, despite the doubts and recommendations of such powerful men, the AMCs kept sailing into harm's way.

Losses continued to mount through the spring of 1941. Three AMCs were sunk in one month: the commerce raider *Thor*, in an action already described, sank HMS *Voltaire* on 4 April; on 18 April, U-108 torpedoed and sank the *Rajputana*; again on 18 April, U-98 sank HMS *Salopian* during an attack on Convoy SC-30.

But what is often overlooked in evaluating the AMCs is the time, expense, and outright difficulty the Germans incurred trying to sink them. In November 1940, U-99's Captain Otto Kretschmer, frustrated by the buoyancy of the *Patroclus*, which he hit with three torpedoes during a night surface attack, tried to sink her with his 3.5-inch deck gun. The U-boat fired four shots at a range of only 100 yards. Two shells hit, exploding ammunition and setting fires on the promenade deck. But the impudent *Patroclus*, illuminating the scene with star shells, fired back with her 6-inch guns. Kretschmer withdrew to reload his torpedo tubes and avoid the shelling. As old as the *Patroclus*'s guns were, a hit by a 6-inch shell in the U-99's hull or conning tower would jeopardize her ability to submerge. Kretschmer fired a fourth and then a fifth torpedo before *Patroclus* went down. That same night, U-99 fired four torpedoes into the *Laurentic* before she sank.[3] On 1 April 1941, U-47 torpedoed HMS *Worcestershire*. Although badly damaged, the AMC made it back to port.

AMCs engaged German capital raiders only twice. *Rawalpindi* and *Jervis Bay* were two rare feasts for the *Scharnhorst* and *Admiral Scheer*, respectively, amply demonstrating the one-sided nature of such encounters. The two British ships were pulverized, their old 6-inch guns nothing more than defiant gestures against overwhelming odds. However, it took twenty-two minutes for the *Admiral Scheer* to reduce *Jervis Bay* to a wreck. When the raid against Convoy HX-84 ended, the pocket battleship had used 228 rounds of 11-inch ammunition and 564 rounds of 5.9-inch ammunition. This was nearly half her total supply.[4] Given the continuous salvoes fired at *Jervis Bay*, it must be assumed that most of *Scheer*'s ammunition was directed at the AMC, not the convoy's merchant ships. *Jervis Bay* was a stubborn and costly foe.

Stephen Roskill stated that AMCs were inferior to even German disguised commerce raiders, the *Handels-Stor-Kreutzer*, and never triumphed over any of them.[5] In fact, the British AMCs revealed an amazing resiliency when confronting those German ships. In July 1940, the battle between the *Thor* and *Alcantara* lasted for about an hour, the two ships trading broadsides. The fire control system aboard the *Alcantara* was quickly destroyed by the *Thor*'s more accurate gunnery, forcing the British gunners to fire independently and, inevitably, haphazardly. The *Alcantara*, hit repeatedly, was soon rendered immobile. She was *Thor*'s for the taking, but Captain Otto Kähler turned his raider and sped away to avoid any real British cruisers that might be rushing to the scene. *Alcantara* finally made it back to port.[6]

The *Thor* fought the *Carnarvon Castle* in December, another one-hour battle. The British ship was struck eight times: Her funnel and bridge were hit; shells demolished her stern quarter; others smashed into the hull and buckled plates at the water line. Yet, although listing and with fires raging through the passageways, the AMC limped away. Kähler, in effect, let her go, but he used two-thirds of his ammunition trying to sink her.[7] The *Thor*'s third battle with an AMC, the *Voltaire* in April 1941, resulted in sinking the British hip. Although the *Thor's* guns caused severe fires aboard the *Voltaire* within the first three minutes of the engagement, the battle lasted for over an hour. Kähler used half his ammunition to sink the AMC.[8]

The *Thor's* considerable ammunition expenditure was not limited to battles with AMCs. In October 1940, Kähler intercepted the 8,715-ton refrigerator ship *Natia*. The *Thor's* gunners hit the vessel eight times—but fired 175 shells![9] This was a strike ratio of only 4.6 percent. The *Thor* sank the 8,799-ton liner *Britannia* in March 1941. The Germans fired 159 rounds "with few actually hitting their target."[10] If a half-dozen shells hit the passenger ship, that was only about a 3.7 percent score.

This record implies that the *Thor's* gunners were not very good. Comparison with other surface engagements provides some further insight. Kretschmer's deck gunners fired four shots at the *Patroclus* and scored two hits—at a range of only 100 yards. According to Baron Müllenheim-Rechberg, British battleships and cruisers fired 2,878 rounds at the *Bismarck*. About 400 hit the German battleship, a score of about 14 percent. Why all this supposedly bad shooting?

Distance from the target was a factor. A ship at 20,000 yards, or about eleven miles, looked like a thin black sliver against a gray sea. Moreover, regardless of range, ships did not sit still. Speeds and courses altered, and the ships—both those firing and those being shelled—pitched and rolled in the sea. A naval gunner trying to maintain a steady aim under such circumstances would be akin to a mounted rifleman trying to stay on target as his horse galloped over broken ground. In the *Bismarck* battle, HMSs *King George V* and *Rodney*, moving closer and closer to their target, fired their 14- and 16-inch guns on very flat trajectories. It is quite possible that many shells literally skipped over the German battleship much like stones thrown across a pond. Fire control mechanisms varied. Old range finders, such as those installed on British and German auxiliaries, were not as accurate as newer but unavailable models. Even the *King George V* battleships, equipped with up-to-date fire controls, experienced difficulty as sea spray obscured the incorrectly positioned sighting lenses. These variables seem remote in a more modern age of computers, precision radar, thermal imaging, and laser-guided range finders; again, technology in the early years of World War II was of a different order. Perhaps a 14-percent hit ratio was good shooting. One point does seem conclusive: Surface gunnery was not an efficient way to sink a ship.

But surface-fired torpedoes did little better unless the ship doing the firing was almost on top of its target. The *Graf Spee's* torpedoes consistently missed, but so too did those of British destroyers against the *Bismarck*. Only when the *Bismarck* lay helpless and British cruisers closed on her did they

have effective strikes. British aerial torpedoes were often inefi
That was a consequence of two factors: first, the "stringbags" car
rather than 21-inch torpedoes; second, the weather through whic
to launch their torpedoes was often miserable.

In the event, AMCs provoked a dilemma for the British Admi.
cause, regardless of their known shortcomings, the AMCs proved u:
the Royal Navy, filling the cruiser gap as best they could. In Januar
the AMC *Arawa* (formerly *Esperance Bay* and a sistership of *Jervis* .
joined the cruisers *Devonshire* and *Norfolk* in a search for the German rai
Kormoran. That same month, the AMC *Asturias* captured the Vichy Fren'
freighter *Mendoza* near Puerto Rico. The *Chakdina* and *Chantala*, still oper.
ating off the Horn of Africa, reappeared at Berbera, British Somaliland, this
time with the cruiser *Glasgow* and destroyers. Their mission was to support
commando raids against the Italian invaders. On 17 June, *Pretoria Castle* captured the Vichy French freighter *Desirade* east of the Antilles. Early in November, the AMCs *Carnarvon Castle* and *Carthage*, patrolling with the
cruisers *Devonshire* and *Colombo*, captured a five-ship Vichy French convoy
sailing from Madagascar. On 1 December, the *Calvin Castle*, operating in the
South Atlantic, stopped the Brazilian steamer *Itape* and removed twenty-two
Germans. From December 1940 into early May 1941, those AMCs on
Northern Patrol, such as the *Letitia* and *Maloja*, intercepted fifteen German
merchantmen attempting to run the blockade.[11] The AMCs continued service with the Northern Patrol through Spring 1942. They also continued escort duties for many months, primarily with North Africa-bound WS troop
transport convoys.[12]

Three Royal Canadian Navy AMCs provided valuable service. These were
of the Prince class, launched in 1930 for the Canadian Pacific Line. They
were small, at 5,736 tons, and made 22 knots—fast for AMCs. The *Prince
David* and *Prince Robert* mounted four 4-inch guns, the *Prince Robert* also had
four 6-inch guns. Each vessel also was armed with 2-pounders and several
20-mm antiaircraft guns. The *Prince Henry* and the *Prince David* served with
the U.S. Navy in the Aleutian campaign, the latter then returning to Atlantic convoy escort duty.[13]

Notes of sadness often permeate historical narratives of the AMCs, most
certainly the sinkings of the *Rawalpindi* and of *Jervis Bay*. Outgunned and
outmaneuvered, the two hapless ships were doomed. The men aboard *Jervis
Bay* entered the battle against the *Admiral Scheer* sharing a grim realization
that they were a forlorn hope, but they did their duty, knowing there was no
place to hide, knowing that most of them would die that afternoon. They
saved a convoy.

The *Jervis Bay*'s sacrifice introduces a question that has not been satisfactorily answered. What enemy ships were the AMCs on escort duty supposed to fight? The answer could not be submarines because the AMCs did not carry antisubmarine weapons. Nor could the answer be the *Handels-Stor-Kreuzer* because the disguised commerce raiders did not attack convoys. Within those parameters, the sinking of the *Rawalpindi*, which was on patrol, must be viewed as the wrong ship, in the wrong place, at the wrong time. In contrast, *Jervis Bay*, escorting Convoy HX-84, did exactly what was expected of her. Captain Fegen counterattacked the *Scheer*, attracting the attention of her main batteries. That action allowed the convoy to scatter, with most of the ships making it safely back to Halifax and St. John. The escort AMCs were, then, all potential forlorn hopes.

Such a melancholic conclusion is a concomitant to the history of the battle of the Atlantic. What kept all the Atlantic sailors going, whether on AMCs or merchantmen, was loyalty to each other and to their ships, and the hope that the horror would end, and end with victory. Their job was to do their duty, even if it meant dying, and that they did. Over 30,000 civilian merchant sailors lost their lives on that gray sea.[14]

CODA

By the end of 1943, all the British and Canadian AMCs had been withdrawn from duty as cruiser replacements.[15] The British AMC *Bulolo*, for example, a 15-knot, 9,111-ton vessel, and the former French liner and ex-British AMC *Largs*, became headquarters ships in early 1942, their services "brilliantly successful" during Operation Torch, the North African invasion.[16] The *Pretoria Castle*, stripped down to her deck, was rebuilt as a training carrier for the Royal Navy Air Arm.[17] HMS *Cheshire*, although withdrawn from the AMC force to be used as a troop transport, nonetheless was ordered in March 1942 to dust off her 6-inch guns and help hunt down the German blockade runner and mine layer *Doggerbank*. The AMC found the German freighter, but was fooled by her disguise and let her pass without incident.

The Canadian ships also underwent conversion. In March 1943, the *Prince David* and *Prince Henry* were converted to infantry landing ships, disembarking troops in Normandy on D-Day under the Combined Operations Command. In August 1944, both participated in the invasion of southern France. The *Prince Robert* became an antiaircraft ship. With her AMC armament of four 4-inch guns increased to ten, she was sent to the Mediterranean Command. Then, in 1945, she went to the Pacific and was present for the Japanese surrender of Hong Kong.[18] The Prince class demonstrated a versatility and speed that doubtless prolonged their combat worth.

The functions performed by the AMCs were valuable.[19] But was there an alternative to using such generally large, unarmored, and expensive ships? Stephen Roskill, Britain's official historian of the war at sea, stated that no suitable alternatives existed in 1939 and 1940.[20] Now, over sixty years later, and with the wisdom of historical hindsight as an intellectual prop, it is easy to suggest that a different ship did exist for use as AMCs.

At the beginning of the war, the British merchant navy numbered over 2,000 ships. As pure speculation, could not the Admiralty have commandeered forty-eight fast freighters for use as AMCs? The German Navy provided excellent examples of the durability and versatility of such ships, going back to the *Möwe* during World War I. Although only one British AMC was destroyed by a *Handels-Stor-Kreuzer*, the German raiders of World War II always caused more damage to the British vessels. British freighter AMCs would have been less bulky and generally had lower silhouettes than liners and, therefore, presented smaller target areas. With fewer long interior passageways, there would have been less vulnerability to fire. They would have mounted the same 6-inch guns provided the converted liners. Perhaps torpedo tubes could have been installed from obsolete destroyers and cruisers. Some German raiders provided examples: *Kormoran*, *Komet*, *Atlantis*, and *Thor* were all armed with torpedoes. Why not install some on British freighter AMCs? Catapults for small seaplanes, much like the Arado float plane aboard the *Komet*, would have extended the horizons of British AMCs. As events transpired, catapults were mounted on some convoys freighters. They carried a Hawker Hurricane fighter to shoot down the dreaded Focke-Wulf Fw 200 Condors, the long-range German reconnaissance plane used to bomb and to locate convoys for U-boat wolf packs. Unfortunately, once his mission was completed, the Hurricane pilot then had to ditch in the sea or bail out, both risky propositions. A float plane was retrievable.

None of these suggested armaments was useful against submarines. But they would have been potent weapons in the hunt for German commerce raiders. The *Alcantara*, had she been a freighter, would have been well served by a torpedo mounting in her fight against the *Thor*. So, too, a different *Jervis Bay*. A brace of torpedoes launched however inaccurately at the *Admiral Scheer* might have given Captain Krancke second thoughts about continuing his attack against Convoy HX-84. Such prudence would have been dictated less by Krancke's fears than by Hitler's continuous warnings to avoid engagement with enemy warships. A torpedo counterattack would have likely motivated a withdrawal.

Why were such armaments not mounted on the converted liners? The configuration of a liner is quite different from that of a freighter. The liners' greater freeboard made torpedo mounts somewhat impractical. A more limited deck space was filled with 6-inch guns. Moreover, any extra armaments—torpedoes, catapults—would have slowed the conversion process and increased expenses because so much of the upper structure and, perhaps, even the hull would have to be rebuilt to accommodate the weapons.

Speculations aside, alternatives to commissioning passenger liners never materialized in 1939. Rather, looking back at the preceding twenty years to 1919, there emerges an aura of inevitability to their use as warships.

The downward spiral of the Royal Navy's budget, regardless of which political party formed the government, created restraints on the Admiralty's desire to replace and modernize the fleet. The fiscal void was compounded by the impact of the Washington Naval Conference, which eliminated Britain as the world's leading maritime power. Britain's admirals helplessly watched the government, as a codicil to the Washington Naval Conference, weaken British defenses in the Far East by signing the Four Powers Pact with Japan, the United States, and France. This document, in effect, gave Japan leave to do what she wanted in Asia. The much-debated base at Singapore could not contain Japanese aggression, for there never was a squadron of fast battleships and battlecruisers based there. In fact, no warships were ever permanently based at Singapore because the Royal Navy did not have enough to station there. Aerial defenses ran the gamut from inadequate to obsolete. And the army enjoyed the smug conclusion that any attack would come from the sea. But when the Japanese attacked in December 1941, they did not hurl themselves at Singapore's beaches; instead, they came down the length of the Malayan Peninsula in a campaign that not only defeated the British but thoroughly demoralized them.

The 1930 London Naval Conference cut British cruiser strength to fifty ships. This number flew in the face of Admiralty warnings. Admiral of the Fleet and First Sea Lord Sir Charles Madden told the government that fifty was a "starvation" number, and Admiral Jellicoe, governor-general of New Zealand in 1930, thought acceptance of fifty was a "highly dangerous step." Prime Minister Ramsay MacDonald gave the weak reply: "Owing to the political situation our estimate had been brought down to fifty [from the original seventy cruisers wanted by the Admiralty]."[21]

Cruisers were the tip of the British spear. Blunting that weapon reflected the apathy the various governments of Britain had for imperial defense. They compromised again and again for fear of appearing warmongers, afraid of an arms race they could not win, and satisfied with the number of the ships other nations dealt them. Reducing the cruiser force was not, ultimately from the long view, an invention of the London Naval Conference. It was rather the culmination of a decade-long political trepidity coupled with an ability to hear only those who voiced politically acceptable opinions.

As fleet reductions took place, British diplomatic forays created conditions antithetical to a peaceful colonial empire. By agreeing to the Four Powers Pact, Britain became a potential enemy of Japan. Given Japan's expansionism, the two empires could no longer coexist in the same region. In the Locarno Treaty of 1925, Britain took on more international obligations than they could possibly support. The growing chasm between real naval power and political maneuvering was widening, made more so by a penurious Parliament and the Treasury's infamous Ten Year Plan that suffocated any hope of new developments.

Then came Hitler. His cleverly crafted Anglo-German Naval Agreement of 1935 abrogated what was left of the Versailles Treaty limitations on German rearmament. The door to German naval development, already opened a crack by the Weimar Republic's secret submarine program and their lies about the pocket battleships, now swung wide. Hitler walked through the opening, the result of which was Plan Z. But more: The naval agreement paved the way for Hitler's subsequent duplicitous actions and negotiations. How easy to take back the Rhineland in 1936, to march into Austria in 1938, and, like a confidence man, dupe Neville Chamberlain and his colleagues into signing the Munich Pact. Hitler knew his opponents' weaknesses, and concluded that Western democracies were spineless.

Britain's unprepared state in 1939 was the result of poor negotiations and political postures over the two previous decades. Despite a pattern of continuous appeasement—first to the Americans, then the Japanese, then the Germans—one must ask if the interwar British governments were so naive, so gullible, that they could not or would not see the contradictions in which they were trapped. On one hand, they committed Britain to international agreements that overextended a dismantled navy. On the other hand, they expected, as a matter of tradition, that same denuded Royal Navy to be the bulwark of imperial defense. Britain's "talking culture," their belief about what they were, and the reality of what they had become did not coincide.

Those in the Royal Navy and Parliament who pleaded for rearmament were shut down by the pervasive optimism that the League of Nations would work because sensible people talking sensibly would always opt for peace rather than war. The horrors of World War I, a sagging domestic economy during the 1920s that became the Great Depression of the 1930s, and the fear of a militarily resurgent Germany led to the conviction, in the simplest terms, that if Britain gave potential aggressors what they wanted, then Britain would survive in peace.

However great the culpability of Britain's politicians in hastening the Royal Navy's decline, it is certain the admirals did not help their own case. Yes, they wanted modern ships; yes, to no avail they warned the government about Japanese aggression; yes, they voiced grave warnings about accepting the 1930 London Naval Conference cruiser reduction; and yes, they warned about international obligations that the Royal Navy could not possibly meet. But the upper echelons of the Royal Navy saw these issues and problems through prisms ground in the experiences of World War I and the assumptions they developed around those experiences.

The one assumption that arguably enthralled the Admiralty, conditioning their attitudes about any future war, was their devotion to battleships as the primary naval weapon. Once again, the admirals wanted big ships carrying big guns. Just as at the Battle of Jutland, they believed they could draw out the German Navy and destroy it if only they had the capital ships to do the job.

Despite the havoc wrought by German U-boats in World War I, the Admiralty dismissed any possibility of another U-boat menace. ASDIC was the ultimate counterweapon. Confidence in the antisubmarine device was bolstered when the Germans signed the Submarine Protocol. Much like their government masters, the admirals believed the Germans would obey its provisions, especially the article requiring a U-boat to approach a potential victim on the surface. In the early months of World War II that faith seemed justified when Hitler himself impressed on Admiral Dönitz the necessity of complying with the protocol. There was nothing moral in Hitler's position. He wanted Britain and France at the peace table in those early months, and unrestricted U-boat warfare would only alienate the Allies.

The British Admiralty's view of submarines was very different from that of Dönitz, who was devoted to the proposition that U-boats were an offensive weapon that, if used properly and in overwhelming numbers, would choke Britain to death. The British viewed submarines as an adequate means of screening the main fleet and useful for scouting. They did not see the need to increase their force above the fifty-seven boats on hand. Dönitz wanted 300 U-boats.

Essentially the same passive role was crafted for the Naval Air Arm. The eight aircraft carriers available in 1939 were launched between 1916 and 1919.[22] They displaced from 10,000 tons to 26,000 tons. HMS *Eagle*, the largest of them, commissioned in 1918, was armed with nine 6-inch guns, five 4-inch antiaircraft guns, and thirty-six smaller such weapons. Despite its size, it carried only three aircraft flights: one fighter; one torpedo bomber; and one reconnaissance. Depending on the configuration of the flights, the *Eagle* carried between fifteen and twenty-four machines. HMS *Hermes*, launched in 1919 and displacing a modest 10,950 tons, nonetheless carried seven flights.

The basic fighter plane for all carriers was the bi-winged Fairey Flycatcher, in service between 1922 and 1934. It cruised at 134 mph and was armed with two .303-caliber machine guns, one mounted on each side of the fuselage just below the open cockpit. The Gloster Sea Gladiator fighter replaced the Flycatcher in 1934. Speed increased to 250 mph and armament doubled to four .303-caliber machine guns. The machine was still bi-winged but the cockpit featured a closed canopy. The strike capacity of the carriers was not bolstered much by the addition also in 1934 of the Fairey Swordfish. The soon-to-be-famous "Stringbags" proved their worth time and again, but early in the war they could not be classified as truly lethal weapons. They lacked defensive armaments and carried only an 18-inch torpedo. Naval air power remained retrograde into the second year of the war. And why not? During the prewar years and well into 1942, air power was not viewed by the Admiralty as an important, much less plausible, offensive weapon. The Swordfish was used against the *Bismarck* because the Royal Navy had nothing better at the time.

Convoys, regardless of the favorable experiences with them in 1917–1918, remained a centerpiece of constant debate. Lacking a definite policy, the Admiralty ignored convoy requirements for two decades. How much better to put available funds into ships of significance—battleships. Some neglect also must be related to the faith in ASDIC. But equally to blame was the attitude that convoys were defensive and an admission of weakness. Fortunately for Britain, that attitude disappeared early in the war even though many merchantmen continued to sail independently. Unfortunately, the early convoys were inadequately escorted. Thus, Dönitz's wolf-pack tactics coupled with night surface attacks against the convoys resulted in the U-boats' "Happy Time."

FINALE

The AMCs did not fade away because they were ineffective, vulnerable, and expensive to staff and maintain. Had they been needed in any capacity, they would have been retained regardless of their shortcomings. And good men would have served on them whether or not they carried the label "Death Ships." The AMCs were converted to other duties because the war passed them by or, as Roskill noted, they became anachronisms.[23]

The Germans contributed to that passing for, by the end of 1942, Admiral Raeder's Atlantic strategy lay in shambles. *Graf Spee*, *Bismarck*, and *Scharnhorst* were sunk. *Gneisenau* was one step from the junkyard. *Tirpitz* was bottled up in dock by the RAF and Royal Navy. Dönitz later saved the *Lützow* and *Scheer* from the scrap heap by reclassifying them as heavy cruisers, later sending them on bombardment missions. Not one German capital ship threatened the Atlantic. Consequently, the Royal Navy's need for AMCs as escorts, however futile, and as supplements on the Northern Patrol no longer existed.

Effective air coverage over the North Atlantic also helped eliminate the AMCs as escorts. In June 1942, RAF Coastal Command mustered about thirty-seven squadrons. Wellingtons, Blenheims, and American-built Lockheed Hudsons, most prized from Bomber Command, initially provided limited coverage, their total flight ranges varying from 1,000 to 1,200 miles. New Bristol Beaufighters, although not extending the range, provided versatility because they could carry torpedoes, mines, bombs, or, on low-level sorties, their nose-mounted four 20-mm cannons could shred a target. Wider coverage was achieved with the Short Sunderland flying boat that had a range of nearly 1,800 miles. The American Consolidated PBY flying boats stayed aloft for nearly 3,000 miles. But neither flying boat carried much in the way of bombs or depth charges. The American Consolidated Liberator B-24 had a range of 2,100 miles with a full 8,000-pound bomb load. But Coastal Command altered the bomber. Extra fuel tanks were put in one of the bomb bays, extending the range (designated VLR/Very Long Range) well beyond their normal rating. They carried 5,100 pounds of bombs and depth charges.[24] By February 1943, Coastal Command's strength increased to fifty-nine squadrons plus thirty-three flights.[25] Not only were many machines up-to-date models, but some venerable older planes received startling modernizations. Many Fairey Swordfish were shifted to antisubmarine patrols. They were equipped with new radar instruments that made searching for U-boats an easier and more precise task than hide-and-seek, and their lower wings were covered with metal to carry rockets, making them deadly against any surfaced submarines.

The U-boat war tilted back and forth throughout 1942. Then gradually into 1943, perhaps imperceptibly to those engaged, the Royal Navy, together with the Canadians and the Americans, made gains against their underwater nemesis. Flower class corvettes guarded convoys, their short cruising range overcome when tankers for refuelling them were assigned to convoys.[26] The corvettes were reinforced by larger, faster, and more heavily armed sloops, frigates, and destroyer escorts. Small escort carriers built on merchant ship hulls gave convoys constant air coverage and the bombs, depth charges, and rockets carried by their planes played havoc with German submarines.

New antisubmarine technology helped swing the battle of the Atlantic in the Allies' favor.[27] Type 271 radar, for example, detected a surfaced submarine at 5,000 yards and could locate even an extended eight feet of periscope at 1,300 yards. Depth charges improved. Early in the war escort ships attacked a U-boat by rolling depth charges off their sterns or shooting them into the sea abeam of the vessel. This meant the escort overran the target and had to reposition for another attack. New depth charge mortars, so-called "hedgehogs" and "squids," hurled their missiles ahead of the escort. New ASDIC produced more accurate estimations of a target's depth and range. The result was that constant contact and firing position could be maintained.

The Germans tried responding to the Allied technical advances. To counter convoy air screens, U-boats were armed with more antiaircraft guns. Unfortunately, the U-boats had to remain surfaced to use them. The "Schnorkel," one of their more innovative developments, was an air in-take device that enabled submarines to recharge their batteries at periscope depth.

However, the technological gap was too great. During the first twenty-two days of May 1943, thirty-one U-boats were sunk in the North Atlantic, "a frightful total" to Dönitz.[28] On 24 May, he withdrew his submarines to an area southwest of the Azores. Stephen Roskill concluded that the delicate balance of the North Atlantic war had finally tipped away from the Germans. "Our convoy escorts and aircraft won the triumph they had so richly merited."[29]

Nonetheless, the U-boats disappeared for only three months and then came back to the war, their crews as dedicated as ever. Yet Dönitz wrote a despairing entry in the U-boat Command War Diary, dated 1 June 1944: "The U-boat campaign must be continued. . . . We possess no other means with which to tie down so vast an array of forces."[30] The Atlantic would remain a dangerous theater of war but something, after all, had changed. The U-boats became the forlorn hopes of the battle of the Atlantic.

CHAPTER 9

LAST THINGS

THE FATE OF THE *ADMIRAL SCHEER*

The *Admiral Scheer*, worse-for-wear after her long raid, entered the dockyards at Kiel in March 1941.[1] Her main engines, auxiliary motors, and generators were all stripped down, the electrical system was refurbished, and the barrels of her 11-inch guns were relined. Only a skeleton crew, most of those antiaircraft gunners, remained on board while inspectors and workers poked, prodded, took things apart, hauled materials across her deck, and tried to make the ship new again.

Whatever satisfaction Captain Krancke and his crew derived from bringing their ship home safely from such a long and productive operation was rudely shaken by the British.[2] On the night of 7 April, 229 bombers struck Kiel in a five-hour raid to destroy anything they could find. The next night another 160 bombers attacked the town and dockyards. The *Scheer* escaped any damage. In May, yet another raid targeted the battleship *Tirpitz*, which had docked at Kiel following a Baltic workup. The *Scheer* was not damaged.

On 12 June, now Rear Admiral Krancke left the *Scheer*, was soon promoted to vice admiral, and designated the navy's representative to Hitler's headquarters. His successor on the *Scheer* was Captain Meendsen-Bohlken. In July, following basic machine trials, the *Scheer* entered the Baltic for gunnery practice and coordination exercises with the *Luftwaffe*. Was another raiding voyage afoot?

Indeed. Admiral Raeder and his staff were plotting an Atlantic breakout for the *Scheer*.[3] She would leave at the end of August, accompanied by the disguised raider *Thor* and the supply ship *Uckermark*. But one delay followed another. Departure dates slipped into September, then October, November, and December. A final deployment date was fixed for the end of February 1942. Even that date could not be met. The breakout was cancelled.

All was not lost. In late August 1942, the *Scheer* was ordered north to arctic waters around the Kara Sea.[4] On 25 August, the pocket battleship bombarded the Soviet settlement at Cape Zhelaniya on the northern tip of Novaya Island, destroying living quarters, the weather station, and wireless facilities. The *Scheer* then sailed east toward tiny Novy Dikson Island. But the Soviet icebreaker *Sibiryakov* crossed her course. Captain Meendsen-Bohlken tried to disguise the *Scheer's* true identity. The Russians were not fooled. Instead, to protect a small convoy in the vicinity, the *Sibiryakov* opened fire. The *Scheer* responded with a broadside, sending the icebreaker to the bottom. Meendsen-Bohlken ignored survivors and steamed after the convoy, but heavy ice thwarted pursuit. One cannot help but wonder how many of the *Scheer's* crew remembered the *Jervis Bay* during those moments.

The *Scheer* resumed course for Novy Dikson, arriving early in the afternoon of 27 August. Shells from her 11-inch guns tore into the harbor and small town. But the Soviet settlement was well defended with shore batteries, which, together with the armed merchant ships in the harbor, fired back. The *Scheer's* luck abruptly ended as two artillery shells crashed into her. Meendsen-Bohlken moved his ship beyond the Russians' range to check the damage. In a half hour, the Germans returned to the island, heavily bombarded the town and military installations, and damaged two ships in the harbor. The undaunted Soviet gunners scored another hit on the *Scheer*. Meendsen-Bohlken called it quits and steamed west. The *Scheer* arrived in Narvik on 30 August.

The pocket battleship was ordered to Oslo for further training with the *Luftwaffe*.[5] She entered Oslofjord at 10:00 A.M. on 5 September. A RAF bomber returning to Britain reported her position, which was later confirmed by a reconnaissance flight. Around noon on 6 September, four RAF American-built B-17 heavy bombers attacked the *Scheer*. Not one bomb hit the ship. Another raid the next day was equally unsuccessful. On 8 September, the *Scheer* was on her way back to Germany. Scheduled for refit, she sailed first to Swinemunde and then to Wilhelmshaven Navy Yard. On 22 March 1943, sixty-nine U.S. Army Air Force B-17s and fifteen B-24 Liberators raided the naval base to destroy the U-boat construction yards. But there was the *Scheer*. Although 200 tons of bombs were dropped, the *Scheer* escaped damage. She was ordered into the Baltic, out of British and American bomber range. Now commanded by Captain Rothe-Roth, the *Scheer* joined the *Lützow* and the old battleships *Schlesien* and *Schleswig-Holstein* in a training squadron.

That passive role soon changed, for the battleships were needed to bombard the Soviet Army attacking west through Finland and East Prussia.[6] In November 1944, the *Scheer* joined the *Lützow* to support German troops defending the Swobe Peninsula against Soviet advances. Some shells from the two pocket battleships were directed as much as twenty-two miles inland. In turn, they came under heavy Soviet artillery and air attack, but neither ship was hit. The sister ships then covered German evacuation of the peninsula, and sailed for Gotenhafen, arriving on 25 November.

The two pocket battleships continued to support the army during January and February 1945. On 6 March, they sailed west, *Lützow* docking at Swinemunde and the *Scheer* going to Kiel. On the night of 9–10 April, 591 RAF Lancaster bombers raided the naval base. A bomb cluster hit close to the *Scheer*, tearing open her hull. She capsized in the shallow water of the inner basin. There she stayed, keel up.[7] After the war she was buried under dirt and rubble in a landfill operation. Her passing was hardly noticed.

THREE ADMIRALS

Admiral Raeder's resignation catapulted Karl Dönitz into the position of commander in chief, because Hitler, on Raeder's advice (and the last time Hitler paid any attention to anything Raeder had to say), leapfrogged him over several senior officers. Hitler believed a new strategy for the battle of the Atlantic was needed, especially after the *Bismarck* debacle. That was fine with Dönitz, who desperately wanted new thinking in the senior staff. To ensure that, he promoted a number of young officers to top posts. One of them was Theodor Krancke, who was made a full admiral and given command of Naval Group West (France and Belgium) headquartered in Paris.[8]

Alas, Kranke inherited a hopeless job. His force, meager at best, consisted of E-boats (the German equivalent of motor torpedo boats), torpedo boats, several destroyers, minelayers, and a patchwork quilt of coastal vessels. He also commanded naval coast artillery.[9] His ships stood little chance against Allied aerial and naval superiority; any vessel leaving port was immediately spotted by British radar and set upon by destroyers, motor gunboats, or Coastal Command aircraft. Nonetheless, some successes were achieved. Nine E-boats from Cherbourg eluded detection as they crossed the English Channel on the night of 28 April 1944. They fired their torpedoes into an American amphibious landing exercise at Slapton Sands on the Devon coast. Two LSTs (Landing Ship Tank) were sunk and a third damaged at a loss of 638 Americans killed and eighty-nine wounded. The five remaining LSTs, soon joined by two British destroyers, opened fire on the Germans. The fight lasted a half hour but the E-boats escaped.[10]

Krancke wanted to remine the Bay of the Seine between the Cotentin Peninsula to the west and Le Havre to the east. Mines layed earlier in the war had deteriorated. But his own minelayers sat crippled at dockside or, if operational, could not get out of harbor without being attacked. Moreover, Hitler, knowing everything about anything at this stage of the war, put mining priorities northward along the Pas-de-Calais.

Thus, when D-Day came on 6 June, the Allied landings in Normandy—around the western rim of the Bay of the Seine—encountered little difficulty with mines. It is now a truism of the war that Hitler and his sycophants believed the landings would occur along the Pas-de-Calais and that the Normandy operation was merely a feint. But Krancke received radar reports at 3:00 A.M. on 6 June that enemy ships were in the Bay of the Seine and concluded that this was the real thing. He sent a prearranged signal ordering all ships to the invasion area and to predetermined interception points of Allied shipping around southern England. His "fleet" numbered thirty E-boats, four destroyers, and nine torpedo boats.[11]

They were too little and too late. Fifteen E-boats sent out from Cherbourg at 3:09 A.M. turned back because of miserable weather. Others were attacked by Coastal Command Bristol Beaufighters and Wellington medium bombers. On the night of 7–8 June, five E-boats ran into British motor gunboats and two frigates that caused some damage and forced them back to port. The next night, ten E-boats on a mining operation encountered three American destroyers and were forced back to base. That same night Krancke's destroyer Flotilla 8 was intercepted off Cherbourg and sunk. But the E-boats did have some minor successes against landing craft and light vessels such as tugs. Cherbourg, however, was an easy bombing target for the Allies, so the E-boat base was shut down and moved to Le Havre.

There was no hiding. The RAF hit the harbor at Le Havre, during which a 12,000-pound bomb penetrated the concrete cover of the E-boat pen and obliterated it. Forty vessels in the open harbor were sunk.[12]

U-boats ordered out on the morning of 6 June also failed. Sailing from ports on the Bay of Biscay, they were met by an umbrella of patrolling aircraft. Only one of nine boats reached the Isle of Wight but, after sinking one landing craft, it withdrew under heavy attack. Seven more U-boats established a patrol line between Devon and the Scilly Islands off the tip of Cornwall. Four were sunk and the other three, severely damaged, returned to port. Eight more U-boats were sunk within the English Channel. By early July 1944, the Germans lost thirteen U-boats but sank only four Allied ships.[13] Krancke, disheartened after successive failures, ordered the remaining submarines back to base.

So ended Krancke's war. As with many German senior officers, he was not pursued for war crimes. Should he have been? The continued attack upon the *Jervis Bay* when she was obviously helpless, with the crew abandoning ship, was unconscionable. That Krancke was responsible for letting loose all the available firepower at his disposal is unquestioned. But why? The raking fire by *Scheer's* lighter guns did not hasten the sinking. One must conclude that the survivors were correct: The only use such firing had was to increase casualties. This kind of shooting was not an isolated incident. The freighters *Maidan* and *Beaverford* were similarly raked by both the *Scheer's* heavy and light guns as they were sinking. There were no survivors.

Nothing much was heard from Krancke until his memoir *Pocket Battleship*, written with H. J. Brennecke, appeared in 1958 in Germany, Britain, and the United States. But the memoir is somewhat sanitized by the absence of any explanation for the continued firing. And it must be added that continued bombardment was not German Navy policy. Captain Hoffman of the *Scharnhorst*, for example, stopped shelling the *Rawalpindi* and even sent out his lifeboats to assist those abandoning ship.

The argument could be made that the British committed the same depredations as the *Scheer* in sinking the *Bismarck*. Closing the range, the British battleships and cruisers kept firing into the German ship even after it was reduced to a hulk. What was different? At least one survivor from each ship. Paymaster Sargeant from *Jervis Bay* and Müllenheim-Rechberg from the *Bismarck*, felt the enemy was using them for target practice. Nonetheless, *Jervis Bay* was never a real danger to the *Scheer*. Her old 6-inch guns never fired a shell close to the pocket battleship. The only possible serious damage *Jervis Bay* could have caused the *Scheer* was by ramming her, but there is no clear evidence that that is what Captain Fegen intended. In contrast, the *Bismarck* was the most powerful ship on the Atlantic. That she might have been towed to port if left afloat, that she might have been repaired (unlikely, but who knew?), and the boost to German morale if the *Bismarck* survived the battle no matter in what condition, represented risks the Royal Navy was not willing to take. Lurking in the background, however, is the ghost of the *Hood*, blown to bits by the *Bismarck*. That the British pummeled the *Bismarck* out of revenge, regardless of any other reasons, cannot be easily dismissed.

Whether or not Krancke should have done something to rescue the survivors of *Jervis Bay* is more difficult to assess. Captain Hoffman began to rescue the *Rawalpindi* survivors but hastily departed when HMS *Newcastle* approached. Some of the *Bismarck's* survivors were picked up but many more were left in the sea when a U-boat warning was sounded and the British left in haste. Most *Handels-Stor-Kreuzer* captains rescued survivors of the ships they sank or had the crews transferred before sinking the ship. Even Krancke took prisoners from individual ships that he attacked, such as the *Mopan* and the *Tribesman*. But he attacked a whole convoy in November 1940. He had a job to do, however reprehensible, and he had no time to stop for survivors of *Jervis Bay* nor from any of the merchant ships he subsequently destroyed. But the practical considerations of convoy attack cannot be used to justify the indiscriminate firing on *Jervis Bay*, *Beaverford*, and *Maidan*. Should Krancke have answered for what he ordered? Yes—in a perfect world.

In contrast, neither Erich Raeder nor Karl Dönitz was allowed to fade from the war. They experienced a more definitive end. Raeder, upon his resignation as commander in chief, retired to the Berlin suburb of Babelsberg to regain his health, which had deteriorated because of extended exhaustion. He wanted to smell the flowers and make notes for a book he wanted to write. Officers from the three services visited him with briefings about the war's progress; yet, he "scrupulously abstained from any political activities whatsoever."[14] Similar words punctuate his memoirs.

Then came 20 July 1944. The botched attempt by various officers to assassinate Hitler on that day had unexpected repercussions for Raeder. An acquaintance told him he was suspected of being a member of the conspiracy, a rumor Raeder attributed to those "unfriendly" toward him in the entourages of Hermann Göring and Heinrich Himmler. Raeder had to act fast to deflect any suspicion. Thus, on 22 July, he flew to Hitler's headquarters in East Prussia. He had lunch with the Führer, who then gave him a personal tour of the blast site. The two men parted cordially and Raeder heard nothing more about being a conspirator.

Early 1945 found Raeder in poor health. On 7 May, the day Germany surrendered, he was in hospital. Ten days later he experienced a heart attack. A week later, the Soviets arrested him as a prisoner of war and put him in Lichtenberg Prison. On 8 July, Raeder and his wife were flown to Moscow, where they stayed for three months. The Soviets then returned him to Babelsberg under house arrest.

In November he was transferred to Nuremberg for trial before the International Military Tribunal. He was charged with preparing the German Navy for a war of aggression, and a more specific charge of waging a war of aggression against Norway.[15]

Dönitz's path was different. In early April 1945, Hermann Göring was under arrest for his ill-timed and ill-conceived plan to assume supreme power in Germany. Hitler had seen through his plot. Dönitz was quite shaken by the obvious lack of central authority exemplified in the growing competition to succeed or usurp Hitler. He vowed to carry on as the navy's commander in chief in the face of political disintegration. Thus, German Navy units would continue to lend support to the army's retreat from the east and try to keep open evacuation corridors for as long as possible. When that was no longer feasible, he would surrender himself and the fleet.[16]

On 30 April 1945, Dönitz received an unexpected cipher from Martin Bormann, the Nazi Party secretary. The accusation was made that *Reichsfuhrer* Heinrich Himmler had met with Count Bernadotte, the Swedish council in Lubeck. Himmler wanted to communicate through Bernadotte to General Dwight Eisenhower, supreme Allied commander in the west, that he was willing to surrender Germany to American forces. Bormann, described by Wiliam L. Shirer as murky and worm-like, further stated, "The Führer orders you to proceed at once, and mercilessly, against all traitors."[17]

How Dönitz was to accomplish this was not mentioned. Himmler had at his disposal the entire SS. Dönitz lacked any forces. Yet, virtually alone, he met Himmler and confronted him with the accusation. Acting as if he were already head of state, Himmler calmly lied to Dönitz, denying what Bormann had written.

Late that evening, Dönitz received another message from Bormann, informing him that Hitler had appointed Dönitz his successor. What Bormann did not say was that Hitler already had committed suicide in the Berlin bunker. Certainly the message came as a surprise because Dönitz had not seen Hitler since 20 July 1944. Yet, he accepted the mantle because he thought it his duty.

Dönitz spoke by radio to the German people and vowed to continue the fight in the east to prevent Soviet enslavement of the German people. He would continue to fight the British and Americans, as well, so long as they supported the Soviet advance. Shirer called his speech a "silly distortion," because German forces were already surrendering in great masses on both fronts.[18] There would not be a continued fight because there was nothing left with which to resist. Dönitz knew it.

Indeed, the Third Reich had come to an end. Dönitz interpreted his appointment as head of state to mean that he was to end the war. The realization that Hitler meant him to continue the war was something he discovered only at the Nuremberg trials.[19]

He remained head of state until 15 May, the date Eisenhower removed him from office. A week later he was arrested as a prisoner of war and accused, along with Raeder, of being a war criminal in naval warfare.

Admiral Raeder was convicted of crimes against peace and war crimes against Norway. Dönitz was convicted of similar charges. Raeder, over seventy years of age, was given a life sentence. However, because of poor health, he was released in 1955. He died five years later. Dönitz received a ten-year sentence, served the full term, and was released in 1956. He died in 1980.

Both men served their nation and fought their war. Yet, one must wonder to what extent their apolitical stances were in fact rationalizations by which to hide themselves from the more horrific aspects of Nazi rule. Both men protested they knew nothing about the death camps and other Nazi depredations until after the war. But they knew of much violence perpetrated by the Nazis before the war: the murders of Ernst Rohm and other Brown Shirts; the "Night of Broken Glass," that violent assault on Jews; the book burnings; the arrests of Jews and political dissidents. What boggles the mind is that Raeder and Dönitz, amid this environment of violence and intimidation, gave themselves to the German Navy with single-minded devotion, cloaked by the excuse that they served the legally constituted government of Germany. As fatuous as the question may seem, did they not realize what kind of government they were serving?

Admiral Friedrich Ruge believed that Raeder, for fourteen long years, actually protected the German Navy from political extremism.[20] This may be too kind for, as Dan van der Vat concluded, Hitler did not need to suborn the navy because Raeder—and one must add Dönitz—marched under the Swastika, enabling the navy to carry on as if nothing had happened in 1933.[21] Consequently, it seems utterly dissembling that, having placed surface raiders and U-boats on station in the North Sea and Atlantic before September 1939, the two admirals then claimed Britain's declaration of war shocked them. The only other explanation is that Raeder and Dönitz repeated their mantra "We are nonpolitical" so often that they came to believe it themselves. But war is not a board game and warships are not set pieces. Yet, seeing the navy very much in those terms, they went along with the Hitlerian machine. Their sailors died for it.

HMS *JERVIS BAY*: REMEMBERING

At 52° 45' north, 32° 13' west, HMS *Rodney* arrived on a gray November day at the position where HMS *Jervis Bay* met her destruction. The sea had left nothing, sweeping away in its neutrality any vestige of the battle. A bos'un's whistle broke the silence. A small group of *Rodney*'s crew (all others were at action stations) gathered at the rail near the forward turret, said a prayer, and dropped a wreath upon the sea. Earlier, Captain J.A.P. Blackburn, late of *Jervis Bay* and then of the AMC *Voltaire*, was escorting an HX convoy to England. But he received a wireless message that *Jervis Bay* had been destroyed by a German raider whose present location was not known. Blackburn's convoy was ordered back to Halifax. His course brought the *Voltaire* to the position where *Jervis Bay* had battled the *Scheer*. He slowed his ship as a firing party lined the rail. The crew had made a wreath from Remembrance

Day poppies. Blackburn read the burial service, the wreath went onto the sea, and the riflemen fired a salute.[22] That was all any seaman could have done. But the watery salutes did not mean that *Jervis Bay* was forgotten as the sea rolled on, the events upon it becoming larger and more engulfing.

A little later in November 1940 Captain Edward Stephen Fogarty Fegen was posthumously awarded Britain's highest decoration for bravery in face of the enemy: the Victoria Cross.

In August 1941 a ceremony took place at Ross Memorial Park, St. John, New Brunswick, Canada. A memorial, an obelisk about twelve feet high, was unveiled, honoring Captain Fegen, HMS *Jervis Bay*, and all who sailed aboard her. Among those attending was Paymaster Sub-Lieutenant John Gordon Sergeant, who placed a wreath at the base of the monument. A bronze plaque reads:

> In Honoured Memory of
> Captain E.S. Fogarty Fegen V.C. Officers and
> Men of HMS Jervis Bay
> Who Gave Their Lives In Gallant Action
> Against Overwhelming Odds With
> A German Raider In The North Atlantic
> November 5 1940 In Order That
> 36 Ships Under Their Care Might Be Saved

On 5 November 2000, about 200 people gathered at the renamed *Jervis Bay*-Ross Memorial Park to commemorate the sixtieth anniversary of the AMC's sinking. Included were survivor Robert Squires and some thirty relatives—sons, daughters, grandchildren, nieces, and nephews—of the crew. Michael Chappell donated to the little museum his father's discharge book—the record of the ships on which he had served. Michael, age seven in 1940, first knew of his father's ship being sunk when he heard a radio news broadcast. He told his mother who did not believe him; a subsequent broadcast confirmed the loss. In about three days she received an Admiralty telegram stating that her husband, Commander (E) James Chappell, was missing at sea. Some three months later she was sent his discharge book stamped DECEASED. It was the only final notification from the Admiralty.

The Canadians have proven steady guardians of memory. The No. 53 *Jervis Bay* Branch, Royal Canadian Legion, has devoted much effort to preserving and developing the memorial and, with the cooperation of New Brunswick Community College, a web site has been established through which information about *Jervis Bay* is available (see Bibliography). There is even a *Jervis Bay* (Memorial) Pipe Band.

Other memorials to the ship and her crew have been established. There is a small monument in Bermuda. On 6 August 1950, a memorial service was held in the Church of S. George, Royal Naval Barracks, Chatham, and a plaque was unveiled dedicated to *Jervis Bay* and her crew. This was a special observance on a hill overlooking Chatham in the Naval Memorial. The names of those Royal Navy men who lost their lives in World War I are inscribed on bronze plaques at the base of the monument. The names of those who died in World War II, including the officers and ratings of *Jervis Bay*, are found on bronze panels mounted on a circular wall. Two more general monuments are in London. One is the War Memorial Trinity Gardens, and the other is the Tower Hill Memorial, dedicated to the merchant seamen who died as volunteers (RNR) or Article 124 combatants aboard Royal Navy auxiliary vessels. Among them are plaques for all those merchant seamen who went down with the *Jervis Bay*. Perhaps the most recent memorial to the *Jervis Bay* is in the National Arboretum, donated by the Shaw-Saville Society.

The mass media have not been far behind. In 1941, the Canadian Broadcasting Corporation recorded the actor Sir Cedric Hardwicke reciting Gene Fowler's poem "*Jervis Bay* Goes Down." In 1962, the Canadian Department of National Defense produced a film *The Jervis Bay Incident*, in which two panelists discuss the battle. In the 1990s, the Canadian Broadcasting Corporation produced a television series titled "The Days Before Yesterday," which included a segment on *Jervis Bay*. In England, the British Broadcasting Corporation first did a radio dramatization followed a few years later by a television production of the sinking as part of their "Battle of the Atlantic" series.

Another remembrance must be noted. Beginning in 1947, available survivors met annually at London's Marylebone Station restaurant on the Saturday closest to 5 November. They toasted Captain Fegen and their absent comrades, and drank another to "our grand and happy ship,"[23] while a ship's bell was rung at the exact time of the sinking. The bell is now in the messroom of the modern MV *Jervis Bay* and is rung on the anniversary of the sinking.

So what can be added to all the monuments, stories, poems, memories, and dramatizations that have ennobled those who sailed on *Jervis Bay*? The choice made here was to write a book that put the battle in its historical setting, the better to understand not only what happened, but why it happened. Having done that, how does one close? All the glory words have been used and are too easily repeated. Perhaps those of the survivor Samuel Patience, spoken when he was interviewed by BBC-TV, will suffice to capture the true spirit of what happened on 5 November 1940: "Our job was to protect that convoy and that's what we did."

· APPENDIX A ·

SELECTED CONVOY CODE DESIGNATIONS

HG   Gibraltar to United Kingdom

HX   Halifax, Nova Scotia, to United Kingdom

JW   Loch Ewe to Russia

OB   Liverpool to Halifax

ON   United Kingdom to North America

OS   Liverpool to Freetown

PQ   United Kingdom to Northern Russia via Iceland

SC   Sydney, Nova Scotia, to United Kingdom

SL(S) Freetown, Sierra Leone, to United Kingdom

WS   United Kingdom to North Africa via Cape of Good Hope (mostly troop
      convoys)

Sources: Stephen Roskill, *The War at Sea*, vol. 2, Appendix F, pp. 453–56; and Arnold Hague, *The Allied Convoy System, 1939–1945*, pp. 109–14.

LIST OF MERCHANT SHIPS IN CONVOY HX-84

Name of Ship	Registry Other Than UK	Type Other Than Freighters
Andalusian		
Anna Bulgari	Greece	
Athel Empress		tanker
Athel Templar		tanker
Beverford		
Briarwood		
Castilian		
Cetus	Norway	
Cordelia		tanker
Cornish City (ship of Convoy Commodore)		
Danea IT		
Dan-y-Bryn		
Delhi	Swedish	
Delphinula		tanker
Emile Francqui	Belgium	
Empire Penguin		
Erodona		tanker
Fresno City		
Hjalmar Wessel	Norway	

James J. Macguire		tanker
Kenbane Head		
Lancaster Castle		
Maidan		
Oil Reliance		tanker
Pacific Enterprise		
Persier	Belgium	
Puck	Poland	
Rangitiki		transport
San Demetrio		tanker
Solfonn	Norway	tanker
Sovac		tanker
St. Gobain	Sweden	tanker
Stureholm	Sweden	
Trefusis		
Trewellard		
Varoy	Norway	
Vingaland	Sweden	

Source: George Pollock, *The Jervis Bay*, p. 97. The Polish freighter *Morska Wola* had been part of the original convoy but developed engine trouble and dropped out on 1 November.

List of *Jervis Bay* Crewmen Lost in the Battle

Abbott, John Royal Navy Volunteer Reserve coder age 20

Alldridge, Harry Royal Navy petty officer age 32

Anderson, James Royal Navy Reserve seaman age 27

Avery, Wilson RN able seaman age 22

Bain, James RNR seaman age 27

Bain, John RNR seaman age 27

Baker, Leonard RNVR able seaman age 22

Baldwin, John RN able seaman

Ball, Frederick RN able seaman age 38

Banks, George RN able seaman

Barham, William Merchant Navy fireman age 30

Barry, Joseph RNR lieutenant age 38

Bartle, Arnold RNR lieutenant age 29

Beal, Frederick RN chief petty officer of sick bay

Beland, Alfred RN able seaman

Bigg, Dudley RNR lieutenant, engineering age 43

Blanchard, Joseph Royal Canadian Navy Reserve stoker age 29

Blyth, John RN leading seaman age 39

Bowles, Herbert RN able seaman age 41

Boyce, James Merchant Navy pantryman age 48

Boyland, Victor RNVR able seaman age 23

Bradley, Walter Merchant Navy carpenter age 44

Bremmer, David RNR seaman age 29

Bremmer, William RNR seaman age 32

Brewis, Peter RNVR able seaman

Bruce, William Merchant Navy carpenter's mate age 20

Carr, Alfred Merchant Navy assistant steward age 40

Carson, Morley Royal Canadian Volunteer Reserve signalman age 20

Chappell, James RNR commander (E) chief engineer age 45

Charlton, George RNVR signalman

Cheesman, Sidney RN able seaman age 35

Clark, Lionel Merchant Navy assistant cook age 23

Clark, Walter RN petty officer age 46

Clarke, Patrick RN petty officer age 27

Cole, Francis RN able seaman

Collins, Reginald RN able seaman age 38

Colloff, John Merchant Navy chief cook age 36

Condon, Joseph RNVR able seaman age 24

Cooke, Joseph Merchant Navy pantryman age 40

Costello, Thomas (aka John Sullivan) Merchant Navy greaser age 55

Crane, Charles Merchant Navy carpenter's mate age 24

Crouch, Robert Merchant Navy assistant steward

Curry, Richard RN ordinary signalman age 19

Danby, William RCNVR signalman age 20

Daniels, Joseph RNVR able seaman

Davenport, Harry Merchant Navy scullion age 34

Davey, Bertram Merchant Navy captain's steward age 37

Day, Alfred Merchant Navy fireman age 34

Demeza, Arthur Merchant Navy writer age 25

Dennis, Patrick RN able seaman age 36

Desborough, Arthur Merchant Navy carpenter's mate age 25

Driscoll, Arthur RNR lieutenant commander age 36

Dunbar, Stephen Merchant Navy baker age 58

Durham, Charles RN sick bay attendant age 45

Ellender, Francis RN engine room machinist

LIST OF *JERVIS BAY* CREWMEN LOST IN THE BATTLE

Esmond, Henry Merchant Navy watchkeeping officer age 25

Evans, John Merchant Navy writer age 46

Evans, Tyrrell RNVR lieutenant commander surgeon age 43

Farmer, Reginald Merchant Navy greaser age 49

Farthing, Maurice RNVR able seaman age 20

Fegen, Edward Stephen Fogarty (VC) RN captain age 49

Ferguson, Henry able seaman age 23

Finch, George RN able seaman

Findlater, Thomas RN chief petty officer age 40

Galloway, Frank Merchant Navy greaser age 41

Gibson, John RNVR chief petty officer age 33

Gospage, David Merchant Navy fireman age 34

Green, George RNVR acting sub-lieutenant age 23

Greenley, William RNR seaman

Griss, Wilfred Merchant Navy assistant storekeeper age 24

Gulless, Alexander RNVR able seaman

Hall, Robert RNR sub-lieutenant, engineering age 26

Hart, Reginald Merchant Navy fireman age 29

Hart, William Merchant Navy greaser age 31

Hawn, David RCNVR leading seaman age 23

Heard, Hubert RNR seaman age 29

Hennessy, Martin Merchant Navy assistant cook age 52

Hill, Walter RNR lieutenant age 50

Hinstridge, Harold Merchant Navy second cook age 43

Houghton, Walter RNVR able seaman age 19

Howes, Eric Merchant Navy assistant steward age 31

Hudson, Jack RN able seaman

Innes, John RNR seaman age 33

Ireland, Arthur Merchant Navy junior engineer age 27

Jarvis, William RN chief petty officer age 49

Jeffcott, John RNVR able seaman age 27

Johnson, Alexander RCNR stoker age 37

Jones, Charles Merchant Navy watchkeeping officer age 25

Kelly, Cornelius Merchant Navy assistant baker age 26

Kershaw, James RN master at arms age 42

Kilgour, Robert Merchant Navy second electrician age 23

Lane, David Merchant Navy fireman age 22

Lang, Herbert Merchant Navy carpenter's mate age 30

Latch, Cyril RNR midshipman

Lattimore, Norman RNVR able seaman

Lecomber, Thomas Merchant Navy fireman

Leddra, Morris RNR lieutenant commmander, engineering age 53

Lee, William Merchant Navy saloon steward age 44

Lethby, George RNVR able seaman

Liddle, Robert RNVR able seaman

Lloyd, Joseph Merchant Navy donkeyman age 38

Lowe, Ralph RNVR signalman age 21

Mabbott, Leslie Merchant Navy assistant steward age 29

Macdonald, Alexander RCNVR stoker age 31

Macdonald, William Merchant Navy junior watchkeeping officer age 31

Mackay, William RNCVR engine room machinist age 38

Major, Harry RN able seaman age 32

Mallon, Frank RNVR able seaman

Mardell, William Merchant Navy cooper age 40

Margetts, William RN petty officer age 31

Martin, Henry Merchant Navy assistant baker age 21

Martin, James Merchant Navy plumber age 26

Matcham, Henry RN petty officer

Matheson, William Merchant Navy third electrician age 25

May, Thomas RNR leading seaman

McNamara, Michael RN able seaman age 34

McRae, Harry RCNVR engine room machinist age 45

Miles, Samuel RN able seaman age 36

Miller, Lawrence Merchant Navy watchkeeping officer age 22

Miller, Wiliam RNR seaman age 27

Milroy, Gordon Merchant Navy first electrician age 25

Mitchell, Arthur Merchant Navy assistant steward age 39

Moore, Dennis RN chief yeoman signals age 41

Moore, Henry RCNVR engine room machinist age 35

Morgan, Jeffrey RNVR able seaman age 20

LIST OF *JERVIS BAY* CREWMEN LOST IN THE BATTLE

Morrison, Keith RNR lieutenant commander age 38

Munro-Cormack, John RNR seaman age 27

Newton, William RNR lieutenant, engineering age 58

Ogilvy, David Merchant Navy watchkeeping officer

O'Kane, James Merchant Navy greaser

Owen, Sidney Merchant Navy cook age 31

Owens, Richard RNR midshipman

Parent, Joseph Merchant Navy fireman age 26

Parker, Charles RNVR able seaman

Parker, George Merchant Navy engine room storekeeper age 59

Pattinson, Hugh RNVR acting sub-lieutenant age 22

Peskett, Harry Merchant Navy storekeeper

Peters, Sidney Merchant Navy chief butcher age 39

Porter, William Merchant Navy carpenter's mate age 28

Price, Albert RCNVR engine room machinist age 23

Rainsbury, Thomas RNVR able seaman

Randall, Reginald Merchant Navy fireman age 24

Read, Bob RN leading seaman age 32

Reeve, John Merchant Navy writer age 36

Reid, James Merchant Navy boatswain age 41

Rice, Oswin RN able seaman age 31

Robins, William Merchant Navy assistant steward age 27

Rockhill, Henry RNVR able seaman

Roe, George RNR lieutenant commander navigator age 33

Rooney, John Merchant Navy fireman age 38

Rooney, Thomas Merchant Navy fireman age 43

Ross, Patrick RCNVR signalman age 20

Saville, Stanley Merchant Navy fireman age 36

Searles, John Merchant Navy greaser age 38

Sheppard, Gordon RN ordinary seaman

Simmons, Ernest Merchant Navy chief steward age 38

Sinton, George Merchant Navy assistant steward age 40

Skinner, Albert RN leading seaman age 40

Smith, Donald RNVR able seaman age 21

Spencer, Stanley RN able seaman age 32

Stamp, James RN ordinary seaman

Stannard, Edward RN gunner age 30

Stansbury, Cecil RN ordinary seaman age 28

Staples, Frederick Merchant Navy carpenter's mate age 29

Stevenson, John Merchant Navy junior engineer age 21

Story, Thomas RN able seaman age 36

Stott, Anthony RNR lieutenant age 24

Taylor, Harold RCNVR able seaman age 21

Thiselton, Walter RNR midshipman

Tolfree, Arthur RN able seaman age 35

Toop, William RN leading seaman

Turnbull, Frank RNVR able seaman age 20

Voaden, Frederick RNVR able seaman age 21

Waldron, William Merchant Navy assistant steward

Walker, Benjamin RN leading seaman age 35

Ward, Albert RN petty officer

Ward, Alfred Merchant Navy lamp trimmer

Warren, Albert Merchant Navy boilermaker age 40

Waters, William Merchant Navy assistant steward

Watts, Reginald RN able seaman age 37

Webster, Alexander RNR seaman age 31

Weightman, Robert Merchant Navy second steward age 33

White, Ernest RNR lieutenant commander age 59

Williams, Eric RNVR able seaman age 26

Williamson, Hugh Merchant Navy first radio officer age 42

Wood, George RN lieutenant commander age 38

Wood, Roy RCNR stoker age 26

Woodridge, Geoffery RN able seaman age 36

Woollett, Albert Merchant Navy third cook age 32

Young, Harry Merchant Navy painter age 24

Sources: Edited from HMS "Jervis Bay": Convoy HX-84 5 November 1940: Casualties, Highland Archive; St. John Heritage Resources; also Michael Chappell, who provided names missing from the original list based on information provided by the Commonwealth War Graves Commission. The ages of some men were not available.

LIST OF *JERVIS BAY* SURVIVORS

OFFICERS

Butler, Ronald A. G. Royal Navy Reserve Midshipman
Byman-Corstiaens, Guy F. Merchant Navy sub-lieutenant
Currie, John Hewitt Merchant Navy 3rd radio officer
Moss, Harold Gordon RNR lieutenant
Robertson, Arthur John RNR lieutenant
Sergeant, John Gordon RNR paymaster sub-lieutenant
Shackleton, Richard Merchant Navy 2nd radio officer
Urquhart, Randolph W. Merchant Navy sub-lieutenant
Wood, Norman E. RNR lieutenant

RATINGS: INJURED

Bain, Donald RNR seaman
Egglestone, John Christopher Royal Fleet Reserve able seaman
Patience, Samuel S. RNR seaman
Taylor, Arthur William Hostilities Only ordinary seaman
Wood, James Harold RNR leading seaman

RATINGS: UNINJURED

Appleyard, Arthur Robert RFR able seaman

Armstrong, Robert Royal Canadian Naval Reserve stoker (later reclassified as injured)

Barker, John Royal Navy Volunteer Reserve able seaman

Barnett, William Merchant Navy assistant steward

Beaman, George RCNR stoker

Billinge, Fredercik W. G. RFR able seaman

Bonney, Harry Lionel RFR leading seaman

Castle, Charles Royal Navy petty officer

Christie, Donald Merchant Navy assistant steward

Cooper, William RNVR able seaman

Crowson, George Merchant Navy stoker

Darnbrough, Walter L. RCNVR able seaman (later reclassified as injured)

Davison, Thomas RNR able seaman/quartermaster

Doull, George RNR seaman

Dove, Charles Merchant Navy assistant steward

Draper, Bernard RFR able seaman

Drury, Dennia Merchant Navy stoker

Dunbar, David RNR seaman

Durrand, John S. RNR seaman

Durrand, Robert RNR seaman

Ellmes, Shedrack C. Merchant Navy stoker

Funge Christie Royal Canadian Navy stoker

Gibb, RFR Leading seaman

Greene, Dalton RCNVR engine room assistant

Grubb, Victor S. RNVR able seaman

Gunn, Robert RNR seaman

Handley, Alfred RFR able seaman

Hanlon, John T. W. RFR leading seaman

Lane, Henry James Hostilities Only able seaman

Lis, Frank Sidney RNR seaman

MacQueen, William Merchant Navy storekeeper

Marginson, Kenneth RCNVR engine room assistant

McConnell, John Merchant Navy stoker

LIST OF *JERVIS BAY* SURVIVORS

Moonie, Alee RNR seaman

Mordaunt, Charles Merchant Navy assistant steward

Morrill, Thomas Arthur RFR able seaman

Morrow, Edward Merchant Navy scullion

Nicholls, Horace J. RFR able seaman

Oag, William RNR seaman

Ormston, Sidney W. Merchant Navy assistant butcher

Payne, Percy Charles Merchant Navy assistant steward

Rushall, Francis B. RFR leading seaman

Reid, James RNR seaman

Rushall, Francis B. RFR leading seaman

Smith, John Thomas RCNVR stoker

Spiller, Charles H. J. RFR able seaman

Squires, George Malcolm HO ordinary seaman

Squires, Robert A. RNR seaman

Stevens, Warren D. RCNR stoker

Tillery, Louis HO ordinary seaman

Wallis, Walter R. RNR petty officer

Whiting, Hugh Douglas Pensioner petty officer

Source: Edited from RG 24, Series D-10, vol. 11105, File 53-1-9, "Merchant Cruisers—HMS *Jervis Bay*, 1940–43." Courtesy of the Library and Archives of Canada.

NOTES

CHAPTER 1

1. Carl Swanson, *Predators and Prizes: American Privateering and Imperial Warfare, 1739–1748* (Columbia: University of South Carolina Press, 1991), pp. 29–34.

2. For a complete narrative, see Fleming MacLiesh and Martin Krieger, *The Privateers* (New York: Random House, 1962).

3. Swanson, *Predators and Prizes*, pp. 54–56 and Table 3.2.

4. Ibid., pp. 57 and 62, and Table 3.7.

5. Ibid., pp. 205–19.

6. For a complete narrative see Melvin Jackson, *Privateers in Charleston, 1793–1796* (Washington, DC: Smithsonian, 1969).

7. See Reginald Horsman, *The War of 1812* (New York: Knopf, 1969) and C. S. Forester, *The Age of Fighting Sail: The Story of the Naval War of 1812* (Garden City, NY: Doubleday, 1956). For a British perspective, see Gomer Williams, *The Liverpool Privateers* (London: Heinemann, 1897).

8. This figure is disputed by Forester, *The Age of Fighting Sail*, pp. 87–88, who contends that many of the so-called privateers were actually blockade runners carrying contraband cargo, the profits from which usually exceeded those from privateering.

9. Horsman, *1812*, p. 66; London *Times*, 20 March 1813.

10. George Little, "Privateering," in Jon E. Lewis, ed., *Life before the Mast* (London: Constable, 2000), pp. 401–2.

11. Edmund Taylor, *The Fall of the Dynasties* (Garden City, NY: Doubleday, 1963), p. 230.

12. Martin Gilbert, *The First World War* (New York: Holt, 1994), p. 127.

13. Ibid., p. 256.

14. Dan van der Vat, *Gentlemen of War: The Amazing Story of Captain Karl von Müller and the SMS Emden* (New York: Morrow, 1983), p. 27.

15. This narrative is drawn from Tony Bridgland, *Sea Killers in Disguise: The Story of the Q Ships and Decoy Ships in the First World War* (Annapolis, MD: Naval Institute Press, 1999), pp. 148–264. For primary sources on the Möwe, see RM 5/v. 2237–40, *Möwe, SM Hilfskreuzer; Schriftwechsel und Zeitungen*.

16. Reginald Bacon and F. E. McMurtie, *Modern Naval Strategy* (London: Frederick Muller, 1940), pp. 144–45.

17. Bridgland, *Sea Killers in Disguise*, pp. 245–64; also Lowell Thomas, *Count Luckner: The Sea Devil* (Garden City, NY: Doubleday, 1927).

18. See Bridgland, *Sea Killers in Disguise*, pp. 1–147.

CHAPTER 2

1. Correlli Barnett, *Engage the Enemy More Closely: The Royal Navy in the Second World War* (New York: Norton, 1991), pp. 1–3.

2. Stephen Roskill, *Naval Policy between the Wars*, vol. 1, *The Period of Anglo-American Antagonism*, 1919–1929 (London: Collins, 1968).

3. Erich Raeder, *Grand Admiral*, trans. H. W. Drexel (New York: Da Capo, reprint 2001), p. 105.

4. Ibid., p. 113.

5. Winston Churchill, *The Second World War*, vol. 1, *The Gathering Storm* (Boston: Houghton Mifflin, 1948), pp. 7–10.

6. Karl Dönitz, *Memoirs: Ten Years and Twenty Days*, trans. R. H. Stevens (New York: Da Capo, reprint 1997), p. 5.

7. Raeder, *Grand Admiral*, p. 154.

8. Edwyn Gray, *Hitler's Battleships* (Annapolis, MD: Naval Institute Press, 1999), p. 14.

9. Raeder, *Grand Admiral*, p. 113.

10. Dönitz, *Memoirs*, pp. 52–53 and 476–78.

11. William L. Shirer, *The Rise and Fall of the Third Reich* (New York: Simon and Schuster, 1960), pp. 219–22.

12. Raeder, *Grand Admiral*, p. 170.

13. Ibid.

14. Ibid., pp. 167–68.

15. Shirer, *Rise and Fall*, p. 289.

16. Dönitz, *Memoirs*, p. 12.

17. Shirer, *Rise and Fall*, pp. 287–89.

18. Churchill, *The Second World War*, vol. 1, p. 140.

19. Raeder, *Grand Admiral*, pp. 180–81.

20. Churchill, *The Second World War*, vol. 1, p. 140.

21. Dönitz, *Memoirs*, p. 12.

22. Ibid., pp. 37–39; Raeder, *Grand Admiral*, pp. 272–73.

NOTES

23. Raeder, *Grand Admiral*, p. 272.

24. Friedrich Ruge, *Der Seekrieg: The German Navy's Story, 1939–1945*, trans. M. G. Saunders (Annapolis, MD: Naval Institute Press, 1957), p. 39.

25. Raeder, *Grand Admiral*, p. 273.

26. Ruge, *Der Seekrieg*, p. 38.

27. Ibid., p. 39.

28. John Keegan, *The Second World War* (New York: Viking, 1990), p. 60.

29. Shirer, *Rise and Fall*, p. 471.

30. Ibid.

CHAPTER 3

1. Correlli Barnett, *The Collapse of British Power* (New York: Morrow, 1972), pp. 425–28.

2. Quoted in ibid., p. 61.

3. Correlli Barnett, *Engage the Enemy More Closely: The Royal Navy in the Second World War* (New York: Norton, 1991), p. 19.

4. Stephen Roskill, *Naval Policy between the Wars*, vol. 1, *The Period of Anglo-American Antagonism, 1919–1929* (London: Collins, 1968), p. 215. See also Barnett, *Collapse of British Power*, pp. 277–78.

5. Barnett, *Engage the Enemy*, pp. 19–20.

6. Quoted in Roskill, *Naval Policy*, vol. 1, p. 115.

7. Stephen Roskill, *Churchill and the Admirals* (New York: Morrow, 1978), p. 74.

8. Roskill, *Naval Policy*, vol. 1, pp. 275–82.

9. Ibid.

10. Ibid., p. 279.

11. Quoted in Roskill, *Churchill and the Admirals*, p. 79; also Barnett, *Collapse of British Power*, p. 275.

12. Ibid., 276.

13. For surveys of interwar negotiations see Barnett, *Collapse of British Power*, pp. 237–577, and Roskill, *Naval Policy*, vol. 1, pp. 300–353. For an American viewpoint, see Alexander de Conde, *A History of American Foreign Policy* (New York: Scribner's, 1963), pp. 495–502.

14. Barnett, *Collapse of British Power*, pp. 277–78, and Roskill, *Churchill and the Admirals*, p. 73.

15. Barnett, *Engage the Enemy*, pp. 28, 42, 43; see also de Conde, *American Foreign Policy*, pp. 512–13.

16. Barnett, *Collapse of British Power*, p. 232, and *Engage the Enemy*, pp. 13–14, 35.

17. Barnett, *Engage the Enemy*, p. 24.

18. Barnett, *Collapse of British Power*, p. 297.

19. Barnett, *Engage the Enemy*, pp. 24–25.

20. Ibid., pp. 27–28; see also CAB 27/246, "Report to the Committee of Imperial Defense Sub-Committee on Preparations for War for the League of Nations Disarmament Conference."

21. Barnett, *Engage the Enemy*, p. 29; see also COS 292, "Chiefs-of-Staff Report, January 1932."

22. Barnett, *Engage the Enemy*, p. 30; see also COS 310, "Annual Review, 1933"; and A.J.P. Taylor, *The Origins of the Second World War* (New York: Atheneum, 1962), pp. 23–25.

23. Quoted in Barnett, *Engage the Enemy*, p. 32.

24. Ibid., p. 37.

25. Ibid.

26. Roskill, *Naval Policy*, vol. 1, pp. 345–47; see also Reginald Bacon and F. E. Mc-Murtie, *Modern Naval Strategy* (London: Frederick Muller, 1940), pp. 148–49.

27. Roskill, *Naval Policy*, vol. 1, p. 536.

28. Ibid. Italics in the original.

29. Taylor, *Origins of the Second World War*, p. 26.

30. Ibid., p. 48.

31. Winston Churchill, *The Second World War*, vol. 1, *The Gathering Storm* (Boston: Houghton Mifflin, 1950), p. 220.

32. Leonard Mosley, *On Borrowed Time: How World War II Began* (New York: Random House, 1969), p. 11.

33. Quoted in Churchill, *The Second World War*, vol. 1, pp. 262–63.

34. See Taylor, *Origins of the Second World War*, pp. 151–86, and William L. Shirer, *The Rise and Fall of the Third Reich* (New York: Simon and Schuster, 1960), pp. 357–427.

35. Taylor, *Origins of the Second World War*, p. 161.

36. Ibid., p. 189.

37. Garnett Wolseley, *A Soldier's Life* (New York: Scribner's, 1903), vol. 1, p. 98. For a list of the Royal Navy's regular warships in service, near commissioning, or under construction by September 1939, see Stephen Roskill, *The War at Sea, 1939–1945*, vol. 1, *The Defensive* (London: HMSO, 1954), Appendix D, pp. 577–82.

CHAPTER 4

1. Quoted in A.J.P. Taylor, *The Origins of the Second World War* (New York: Atheneum, 1962), p. 195. See also Leonard Mosley, *On Borrowed Time: How World War II Began* (New York: Random House, 1969), pp. 205–12; also William L. Shirer, *The Rise and Fall of the Third Reich* (New York: Simon and Schuster, 1960), pp. 455–512.

2. Mosley, *On Borrowed Time*, p. 205.

3. Quoted in Shirer, *Rise and Fall*, p. 468. See also *Fuehrer Conferences on Naval Affairs, 1939–1945* (Annapolis, MD: Naval Institute Press, 1990), p. 29.

4. Quoted in Shirer, *Rise and Fall*, p. 187.

5. Numbers differ by author because each had a different perspective and access to different information. See Erich Raeder, *Grand Admiral*, trans. H. W. Drexel (New York: Da Capo, reprint 2001), pp. 280–81; Karl Dönitz, *Memoirs: Ten Years and Twenty Days*, trans. R. H. Stevens (New York: Da Capo, reprint 1997), p. 46; Karl Dönitz, memorandum of 1 September 1939, in *Fuehrer Conferences*, p. 3; and

NOTES

Friedrich Ruge, *Der Seekrieg: The German Navy's Story*, 1939–1945, trans. M. G. Saunders (Annapolis, MD: Naval Institute Press, 1957), p. 46.

6. Raeder, *Grand Admiral*, p. 278.

7. Ibid., pp. 280–81.

8. Dönitz, *Memoirs*, p. 47.

9. *Fuehrer Conferences*, pp. 39–40. As late as 2 June 1940, Hitler stated that England would "soon be ready for peace." See Franz Halder, *The Halder War Diary*, *1939–1942*, Charles Burdick and H. A. Jacobsen, eds. (Novato, CA: Presidio Press, 1988). See also John Lukacs, *Five Days in London: May 1940* (New Haven, CT: Yale University Press, 2001), p. 193 and note 8, wherein Lukacs thought the statement might have been a rationalization for stopping further advances against Dunkirk.

10. Dönitz, *Memoirs*, p. 54. Italics added.

11. Shirer, *Rise and Fall*, pp. 636–38, and Dönitz, *Memoirs*, pp. 65–66. See also *Fuehrer Conferences*, p. 39.

12. Shirer, *Rise and Fall*, p. 638, and Raeder, *Grand Admiral*, p. 293.

13. Winston Churchill, *The Second World War*, vol. 1, *The Gathering Storm* (Boston: Houghton Mifflin, 1948), p. 424.

14. *Fuehrer Conferences*, pp. 39–40.

15. *North Atlantic Run: The Royal Canadian Navy and the Battle of the Convoys* (Toronto, Canada: Toronto University Press, 1985), p. 15.

16. Peter Kemp, *Decision at Sea: The Convoy Escorts* (New York: Elsevier-Dutton, 1978), p. 10.

17. Stephen Roskill, *The War at Sea*, vol. 1, *The Defensive* (London: HMSO, 1954), p. 179.

18. Donald Macintyre, *The Naval War against Hitler* (New York: Scribner's, 1971), p. 54. See also Correlli Barnett, *Engage the Enemy More Closely: The Royal Navy in the Second World War* (New York: Norton, 1991), p. 66, and Kemp, *Decision at Sea*, p. 15.

19. Barnett, *Engage the Enemy*, pp. 66–68.

20. Roskill, *The War at Sea*, vol. 1, pp. 67 and 271, and Appendix E, pp. 583–87 for a global distribution of the cruiser force.

21. Barnett, *Engage the Enemy*, pp. 166–67. See also Martin Gilbert, ed., *The Churchill War Papers*, vol. 1 (New York: Norton, 1993), p. 1223.

22. Churchill, *The Second World War*, vol. 1, pp. 497–98. No book has been written about the *Rawalpindi*, but among short narratives are Bernard Edwards, *Salvo: Classical Naval Gun Actions* (London: Brookhampton, 1999), pp. 84–94, and Edwyn Gray, *Hitler's Battleships* (Annapolis, MD: Naval Institute Press, 1999), pp. 44–46.

23. Roskill, *The War at Sea*, vol. 1, p. 384.

24. *Churchill War Papers*, vol. 1, pp. 283–84, 384, 676–77.

25. Stephen Roskill, *Churchill and the Admirals* (New York: Morrow, 1978), p. 90.

26. Churchill, *The Second World War*, vol. 1, pp. 513–14.

27. Raeder, *Grand Admiral*, p. 290.

28. There is a considerable bibliography on the *Graf Spee*. Among the latest is Eric J. Grove, *The Price of Disobedience* (Annapolis, MD: Naval Institute Press, 2001). For Churchill's reaction to the battle see *Churchill Papers*, vol. 1, pp. 535–37.

29. Churchill, *The Second World War*, vol. 1, p. 517.

30. Roskill, *The War at Sea*, vol. 1, p. 384.

31. *Fuehrer Conferences*, pp. 68–69.

32. T. K. Derry, *The Campaign in Norway: History of the Second World War* (London: HMSO, reprint 1953).

33. Lukacs, *Five Days in London*, pp. 14–16. Lukacs noted that the French considered surrendering within a short time. The War Committee met in Paris on 25 May, during which General Maxime Weygand stated, "France had committed the immense mistake to enter into the war without the material or the military doctrine that were needed. It is probable that [France] will have to pay dearly for this criminal thoughtlessness." Quoted by Lukacs, pp. 87–88.

34. See L. F. Ellis, *The War in France and Flanders, 1939–1940: History of the Second World War* (London: HMSO, reprint 1953); also Peter Fleming, *Operation Sea Lion* (New York: Simon and Schuster, 1957); Raeder, *Grand Admiral*, pp. 328–31.

35. *Fuehrer Conferences*, pp. 117–18.

36. Dönitz, *Memoirs*, pp. 109–13.

37. Ibid. See also Roskill, *The War at Sea*, vol. 1, p. 350.

38. Roskill, *The War at Sea*, vol. 1, p. 265.

39. From Kretschmer's war diary, quoted in Dönitz, *Memoirs*, pp. 171–73.

40. Ibid., p. 173.

41. Among the several books about these ships are James P. Duffy, *Hitler's Secret Pirate Fleet* (Westport, CT: Praeger, 2001); August K. Muggenthaler, *German Raiders of World War II* (Englewood Cliffs, NJ: Prentice-Hall, 1977); Kenneth Langmaid, *The Sea Raiders* (London: Jarrolds, 1956); Paul Schalenbach, *German Raiders* (Annapolis, MD: Naval Institute Press, 1979). Studies of individual ships include H. J. Brennecke, *Cruise of the Raider HK-33 [Pinguin]* (New York: Crowell, 1954), and Edwin Hoyt, *Raider 16 [Atlantis]* (New York: World, 1970). See also Raeder, *Grand Admiral*, pp. 347–49, and ADM 234/324, "Disguised Raiders, 1940–41."

42. Duffy, *Hitler's Secret Pirate Fleet*, pp. 78–80.

43. Ibid., pp. 86–87; also Roskill, *The War at Sea*, vol. 1, p. 285.

44. Dönitz, *Memoirs*, pp. 116–17.

CHAPTER 5

1. Edwyn Gray, *Hitler's Battleships* (Annapolis, MD: Naval Institute Press, 1999), p. 32.

2. Ibid.

3. Theodor Krancke and H. J. Brennecke, *Pocket Battleship: The Story of the Admiral Scheer* (London: Kimber, 1958), p. 10.

4. Friedrich Ruge, *Der Seekrieg: The German Navy's Story, 1939–1945*, trans. M. G. Saunders (Annapolis, MD: Naval Institute Press, 1957), p. 83.

5. Krancke and Brennecke, *Pocket Battleship*, pp. 11–15.

6. M. J. Whitley, *German Capital Ships of World War Two* (London: Arms and Armour, 1989), p. 129.

7. Ibid. See also Dan van der Vat, *The Atlantic Campaign: World War II's Struggle at Sea* (New York: Harper's, 1988), p. 157.

8. George Pollock, *The Jervis Bay* (London: Kimber, 1958), p. 21.

9. Signal from Royal Canadian Navy Admiralty to *Jervis Bay*, 13 June 1940, RG 24, Series D-1-a, vol. 5670, File 78-88-1, "Imperial Warships, HMS Jervis Bay—General, 1941–42." Hereinafter "Imperial Warships—HMS Jervis Bay."

10. Pollock, *Jervis Bay*, pp. 47–49.

11. Ibid., p. 21, and ADM 196/54, p. 8, "Edward Stephen Fogarty Fegen."

12. Stephen Cashmore, "HMS Jervis Bay, Armed Merchant Cruiser," pp. 1–7 (Highland Archives at www.internet promotions.co.uk/archives/caithness/jervisbay .ltd).

13. Terry Hughes and John Costello, *The Battle of the Atlantic* (New York: Dial, 1977), p. 80; also Stephen Roskill, *The War at Sea*, vol. 1, *The Defensive* (London: HMSO, 1954), Appendix C, p. 576.

14. Pollock, *Jervis Bay*, p. 71.

15. Ibid., p. 75.

16. For an extensive explanation, see Winston Churchill, *The Second World War*, vol. 1, *The Gathering Storm* (Boston: Houghton Mifflin, 1948), Appendix A, pp. 708–10. See also RG 24, Series D-1-a, vol. 5670, File, 78-88-8, "Imperial Warships—HMS Jervis Bay—Repairs, 1940–41."

17. Churchill, *The Second World War*, vol. 1, Appendix K, p. 716.

18. Ibid., Appendix H, p. 710.

19. "Imperial Warships—HMS Jervis Bay—Complement, 1941."

20. For more on convoys see Arnold Hague, *The Allied Convoy System, 1939–1945* (Annapolis, MD: Naval Institute Press, 2000), pp. 19, 20–28, 124; also Samuel Morison, *History of United States Naval Operations in World War II*, vol. 1, *The Battle of the Atlantic* (Boston: Little, Brown, reprint 1961), pp. 17–19 and 39–43.

21. Pollock, *Jervis Bay*, p. 52.

22. Krancke and Brennecke, *Pocket Battleship*, pp. 23–28.

23. Ibid., p. 30.

24. Ibid., p. 31.

25. Ibid., p. 37.

26. The most extensive battle narratives are found in ibid., pp. 38–62, and Pollock, *Jervis Bay*, pp. 108–54. Among shorter sources are Whitley, *German Capital Ships*, pp. 129–31; Gray, *Hitler's Battleships*, pp. 84–87; and Hughes and Costello, *Battle of the Atlantic*, pp. 116–18. Archival sources include RM 92/5228, *Kriegstagebuch "Admiral Scheer"*; Monograph Files, German Monographs (Record Group 38) Office of Naval Intelligence, Report by Commander Ben Wyatt, USN, Naval Attache, Madrid, "Description of Raid on Convoy and Tactics Employed by Vessels of the Convoy," 11 December 1940; and RG 24, Series D-10, vol. 11105, File 53-1-9, "Merchant Cruisers—HMS Jervis Bay, 1940–43."

27. *Kriegstagebuch "Admiral Scheer,"* p. 19. Cf., Krancke and Brennecke, *Pocket Battleship*, p. 45; also Gray, *Hitler's Battleships*, p. 85.

28. Captain Waite of the tanker *San Demetrio* so identified the ship, but Able

Seaman E. Flesler of the *Trewellard* was later shown silhouettes of various warships and thought the raider looked like the French battleship *Dunkerque*. See "Merchant Cruisers—HMS Jervis Bay," Enclosure 7.

29. Pollock, *Jervis Bay*, pp. 117–21.

30. *The War Illustrated*, 29 November 1940, p. 563.

31. Based on independent reports of Captain Waite and L. Daniel, master of the *Trewellard*, in "Merchant Cruisers—HMS Jervis Bay," Enclosures 1 and 2. The debate over who fired the first shot continues.

32. Krancke and Brennecke, *Pocket Battleship*, p. 46.

33. Ibid., p. 47.

34. Both interviews were recorded for radio broadcast by the Canadian Broadcasting Corporation and are preserved in the Canadian National Archives as Audio Tape 401113-1. They are at the very end of the second side. See also Pollock, *Jervis Bay*, p. 151.

35. Ibid., p. 134.

36. Krancke and Brennecke, *Pocket Battleship*, p. 50.

37. Audio Tape, 401113-1, and Pollock, *Jervis Bay*, p. 144.

38. The description of what transpired is a summary based on ibid., pp. 142–43.

39. Quoted in ibid., p. 153.

40. Ibid., p. 161, and Audio Tape 401113-1.

41. *The War Illustrated*, p. 563.

42. "Merchant Cruisers—HMS Jervis Bay," Enclosures 1, 2.

43. Ibid., Enclosure 8.

44. Krancke and Brennecke, *Pocket Battleship*, claim the *San Demetrio* was the first target. Captain Waite and Captain Daniel independently reported that the *Rangatiki* was the first target. See "Merchant Cruisers—HMS Jervis Bay," Enclosures 1, 2.

45. Pollock, *Jervis Bay*, pp. 190–91.

46. "Merchant Cruisers—HMS Jervis Bay," Enclosure 1. Cf., Krancke and Brennecke, *Pocket Battleship*, p. 59. See also Table of Targets in *Kriegstagebuch "Admiral Scheer,"* which names three ships among which only *Jervis Bay* was firmly identified. The table in *Pocket Battleship*, pp. 59–60, is based on postwar information but is only relatively accurate when checked against navy interviews in Halifax. See "Merchant Cruisers—HMS Jervis Bay," passim.

47. "Merchant Cruisers—HMS Jervis Bay," Enclosure 1.

48. Ibid., Enclosure 4.

49. Ben Wyatt, Intelligence Report, "Description of Raid on Convoy."

50. Narrative based on Captain Waite's report in "Merchant Cruisers—HMS Jervis Bay," Enclosure 2, and F. Tennyson Jesse, *The Saga of the San Demetrio* (London: HMSO, 1942).

51. Krancke and Brennecke, *Pocket Battleship*, p. 52.

52. Ibid., p. 59.

53. Ibid., pp. 56–57.

54. Ibid., pp. 58–59.

55. See Jesse, *San Demetrio*, passim.

NOTES

56. "Armed Merchant Cruisers—HMS Jervis Bay," Enclosures 2 and 5.

57. Ibid., Enclosure 1.

58. Ibid., Enclosures 1, 4, and 5.

59. RG 24, Series P-10, vol. 11105, File 53-1-9, "Merchant Cruisers—HMS Jervis Bay, Report to the Admiralty, London, from Chief Officer, Halifax, 19 November 1940."

60. Ibid., and Olander's day journal entry (*Journalutdrag*) for 12 November 1940, in which he states that twenty men were rescued from a lifeboat, fifteen rescued in two trips by his own crew (presumably to two rafts), and what must have been another thirty-three "from three remaining rafts," for a total of sixty-eight. The three men buried at sea were Acting Sub-Lieutenant Hugh Pattison, Second Cook Harold Hinstridge, and Seaman Alexander Webster. A copy of this document was provided by Michael Chappelle.

61. Pollock, *Jervis Bay*, p. 199.

62. Ibid., pp. 188–90.

63. Both messages courtesy of Michael Chappelle.

64. Audio tape 401113-1.

CHAPTER 6

1. Stephen Roskill, *The War at Sea*, vol. 1, *The Defensive* (London: HMSO, 1954), p. 289.

2. Ibid.

3. Ibid.

4. Theodor Krancke and H. J. Brennecke, *Pocket Battleship: The Story of the Admiral Scheer* (London: Kimber, 1958), p. 63.

5. M. J. Whitley, *German Capital Ships of World War Two* (London: Arms and Armour, 1989), p. 130. See also George Pollock, *The Jervis Bay* (London: Kimber, 1958), p. 195.

6. The following narrative of the *Scheer's* further raiding is drawn from Krancke and Brennecke, *Pocket Battleship*, pp. 65 et seq. For a good summary statement see Whitley, *German Capital Ships*, pp. 131–36.

7. Roskill, *The War at Sea*, vol. 1, p. 290.

8. Ibid., wherein Roskill states the *Duquesa* was allowed by Krancke to send the R-R-R signal to draw hunter groups from northern waters so that the *Hipper* could breakout into the Atlantic. But Krancke makes no mention of this scheme. See *Pocket Battleship*, pp. 115–21. For further adventures of the *Duguesa* see James P. Duffy, *Hitler's Secret Pirate fleet* (Westport, CT: Praeger, 2001), pp. 88–155.

9. James P. Duffy, *Hitler's Secret Pirate Fleet*, pp. 26–27.

CHAPTER 7

1. Martin Gilbert, ed., *The Churchill War Papers* (New York: Norton, 1993), vol. 1, p. 434.

2. Stephen Roskill, *The War at Sea*, vol. 1, *The Defensive* (London: HMSO, 1954), p. 376.

3. Ibid., p. 378; also Edwyn Gray, *Hitler's Battleships*. (Annapolis, MD: Naval Institute Press, 1999), pp. 99–101.

4. Roskill, *War at Sea*, vol. 1, p. 393; Gray, *Hitler's Battleships*, pp. 105–9; Robert Jackson, *The German Navy in World War II* (London: Brown Books, 1999), pp. 83–91. See also Richard Garrett, *Scharnhorst and Gneisenau: The Elusive Sisters* (London: David and Charles, 1978).

5. Karl Dönitz, *Memoirs: Ten Years and Twenty Days*, trans. R. H. Stevens (New York: Da Capo, reprint 1997), p. 165.

6. Ibid. For his early assessment of the U-boat fleet see RM 87/2, *Führer der Uboote West Dönitz, Kriegstagebuch—unterlagen 28.3.39–31.7.40.*

7. Dönitz, *Memoirs*, p. 166. Italics in the original.

8. *Churchill War Papers*, vol. 1, pp. 100–101.

9. The full text of the Operational Order is in Baron Burkard von Müllenheim-Rechberg, *Battleship Bismark: A Survivor's Story*, trans. Jack Sweetman (Annapolis, MD: Naval Institute Press, 1980), pp. 253–59. A General Order follows on pp. 260–63.

10. Gray, *Hitler's Battleships*, p. 111.

11. There are many works related to the *Bismarck* sinking. Among these are Ludovic Kennedy, *Pursuit: The Chase and Sinking of the Bismarck* (London: Collins, 1974); Russell Grenfell, *The Bismarck Episode* (London: Faber and Faber, 1948); and Müllenheim-Rechberg, *Battleship Bismarck*. Among shorter and sometimes more difficult to find narrations are Roskill, *War at Sea*, vol. 1, pp. 354–418; Captain Assman, Chief of Fleet Division, Department of Naval Operations, "The Operations of the Bismarck Task Force against Merchant Shipping in the Atlantic," in *Fuehrer Conferences on Naval Affairs, 1939–1945* (Annapolis, MD: Naval Institute Press, 1990), pp. 200–218; and ARM 234/322, "Battle Summary 5: The Chase and Sinking of the German Battleship *Bismarck*, 2327 May 1941."

12. Müllenheim-Rechberg, *Battleship Bismarck*, pp. 75–76, and 84.

13. Ibid., pp. 89 and 93.

14. Roskill, *War at Sea*, vol. 1, p. 396; Correlli Barnett, *Engage the Enemy More Closely: The Royal Navy in the Second World War* (New York: Norton, 1991), p. 284.

15. Barnett, *Engage the Enemy*, pp. 289–90; Roskill, *War at Sea*, vol. 1, Map 30 facing p. 397.

16. Müllenheim-Rechberg, *Battleship Bismarck*, pp. 116–17.

17. Barnett, *Engage the Enemy*, p. 300.

18. Müllenheim-Rechberg, *Battleship Bismarck*, p. 118.

19. Ibid., p. 134.

20. Ibid., pp. 136–44.

21. Quoted in ibid., p. 141.

22. Ibid., p. 142.

23. ARM 234/322. Also Roskill, *War at Sea*, vol. 1, pp. 410–11; Barnett, *Engage the Enemy*, pp. 303–4.

24. Müllenheim-Rechberg, *Battleship Bismarck*, pp. 167–75. Late on 26 May, several British destroyers attempted a torpedo run from 4,000 yards but *Bismarck's* excellent night radar gunnery and turbulent seas thwarted the attack and precluded anything more daring. See Grenfell, *Bismarck Episode*, p. 39, and Barnett, *Engage the Enemy*, p. 309.

25. Müllenheim-Rechberg, *Battleship Bismarck*, p. 39; Barnett, *Engage the Enemy*, p. 309.

26. Müllenheim-Rechberg, *Battleship Bismarck*, p. 243.

27. Ibid., p. 206. See Grenfell, *Bismarck Episode*, pp. 172–87.

28. Erich Raeder, *Grand Admiral*, trans. H. W. Drexel (New York: Da Capo, reprint 2001), p. 258.

29. Ibid.

30. Dönitz, *Memoirs*, p. 163.

31. Roskill, *War at Sea*, vol. 1, Table 24, p. 44, and Appendix N, pp. 606–8. Also Barnett, *Engage the Enemy*, pp. 315–16.

32. Dönitz, *Memoirs*, p. 170.

33. James P. Duffy, *Hitler's Secret Pirate Fleet* (Westport, CT: Praeger, 2001), pp. 105–24.

34. Ibid., pp. 143–64.

35. Ibid., pp. 1–34.

36. Ibid., pp. 27–93. See also RM 100/75, *Vernichtunq brit.Hilfskreuzer "Voltaire"— Gefechtsbericht*, 4.4.41. For more about the cruise see RM 100/70, *Kriegstagebuch "Thor"* (Hilfskreuzer 4, *Schiff* 10)—*unterlagen*, 15.3.1940–31.5.1941.

37. Roskill, *War at Sea*, vol. 1, pp. 383–84.

38. Dönitz, *Memoirs*, p. 197.

39. Barnett, *Engage the Enemy*, p. 441.

40. Gray, *Hitler's Battleships*, p. 129.

41. Ibid., pp. 131–40; also Terrence Robertson, *Channel Dash* (New York: Dutton, 1958).

42. *Fuehrer Conferences*, p. ix. See also Walter Warlimont, *Inside Hitler's Headquarters*, trans. R. H. Barry (New York: Praeger, 1964), pp. 232–33.

43. *Fuehrer Conferences*, p. 306.

44. Ibid., pp. 306–7.

45. Ibid.

46. Raeder, *Grand Admiral*, pp. 372–75.

47. Dönitz, *Memoirs*, p. 372.

48. *Fuehrer Conferences*, p. 374. Also Gray, *Hitler's Battleships*, pp. 170–76, and Dönitz, *Memoirs*, pp. 374–85.

49. Barnett, *Engage the Enemy*, p. 744, and Gray, *Hitler's Battleships*, p. 175.

CHAPTER 8

1. Stephen Roskill, *The War at Sea, 1939–1945*, vol. 1, *The Defensive* (London: HMSO, 1954), pp. 265–67.

NOTES

2. Martin Gilbert, ed., *The Churchill War Papers*, vol. 3 (London: Heinemann, 2000), p. 495.

3. Karl Dönitz, *Memoirs: Ten Years and Twenty Pays*, trans. R. H. Stevens (New York: Da Capo, reprint 1997), pp. 172–73.

4. RM 92/5228, *Kriegstagebuch "Admiral Scheer,"* pp. 21–22. Also George Pollock, *The Jervis Bay* (London: Kimber, 1958), p. 195.

5. Roskill, *War at Sea*, vol. 1, p. 260; and Stephen Roskill, *The War at Sea, 1939–1945*, vol. 3, *The Offensive* (London: HMSO, 1960), p. 62.

6. James P. Duffy, *Hitler's Secret Pirate Fleet* (Westport, CT: Praeger, 2001), pp. 82–83.

7. Ibid., p. 87.

8. Ibid., p. 93.

9. Ibid., p. 84.

10. Ibid., p. 89.

11. Roskill, *War at Sea*, vol. 1, p. 265.

12. Roskill, *War at Sea*, vol. 3, p. 176.

13. Ken Macpherson and John Burgess, *The Ships of Canada's Naval Forces, 1910–1981* (Toronto: Collins, 1981), pp. 32, 33, and 156. There are many files about the *Prince David*. Among the most pertinent are RG 24, vol. 4016, Files 1057-106-11G and 1057-106-11G, "Guns and gunnery, 1941–1943," 24, vol. 6814, File 8700-412/1, "Movements, 1940–1945," and RG 24, vol. 11665, File 700-2-39, "Passage in Escort Vessels and AMCs."

14. Robert Jackson, *The German Navy in World War II* (London: Brown Books, 1999), p. 19.

15. Roskill, *War at Sea*, vol. 3, p. 62.

16. Correlli Barnett, *Engage the Enemy More Closely: The Royal Navy in the Second World War* (New York: Norton, 1991), p. 546.

17. *Jane's Fighting Ships of World War II* (New York: Crescent, reprint 1989), p. 38.

18. Macpherson and Burgess, *Ships of Canada's Naval Forces*, p. 156.

19. Roskill, *War at Sea*, vol. 3, p. 63.

20. Ibid.

21. Barnett, *Engage the Enemy*, p. 290.

22. *Jane's Fighting Ships*, pp. 33–37.

23. Roskill, *War at Sea*, vol. 3, p. 62.

24. Ibid., p. 110. For specifications see *Jane's Fighting Aircraft of World War II* (New York: Crescent, reprint 1992), and Christopher Chant, *Encyclopedia of World Aircraft* (New York: Mallard, 1990).

25. Roskill, *War at Sea*, vol. 3, p. 363, Table 29, and Arnold Hague, *The Allied Convoy System, 1939–1945* (Annapolis, MD: Naval Institute Press, 2000), pp. 73–76.

26. Roskill, *War at Sea*, vol. 3, p. 107.

27. For fuller statements see Hague, *Allied Convoy System*, pp. 59–104, and Terry Hughes and John Costello, *The Battle of the Atlantic* (New York: Dial, 1977), pp. 171 and 307–8.

28. Dönitz, *Memoirs*, p. 340.

29. Roskill, *War at Sea*, vol. 3, p. 377.

30. Dönitz, *Memoirs*, p. 420.

CHAPTER 9

1. Edwyn Gray, *Hitler's Battleships* (Annapolis, MD: Naval Institute Press, 1999), p. 105, and M. J. Whitley, *German Capital Ships of World War Two* (London: Arms and Armour, 1989), p. 172.

2. Gray, *Hitler's Battleships*, pp. 105–6.

3. Whitley, *German Capital Ships*, p. 176.

4. Ibid., pp. 186–87, and Gray, *Hitler's Battleships*, pp. 154–55.

5. Whitley, *German Capital Ships*, p. 176, and Gray, *Hitler's Battleships*, p. 126.

6. Whitley, *German Capital Ships*, pp. 209–10, and Gray, *Hitler's Battleships*, p. 183.

7. Whitley, *German Capital Ships*, p. 211, and Gray, *Hitler's Battleships*, pp. 183–84.

8. Karl Dönitz, *Memoirs: Ten Years and Twenty Days*, trans. R. H. Stevens (New York: Da Capo, reprint 1997), p. 368.

9. Ibid., pp. 391 and 394.

10. Correlli Barnett, *Engage the Enemy More Closely: The Royal Navy in the Second World War* (New York: Norton, 1991), p. 798. See also Samuel Morison, *History of United States Naval Operations in World War II*, vol. 11, The Invasion of France and Germany (Boston: Little, Brown, reprint 1961), p. 66.

11. Dönitz, *Memoirs*, p. 395, and Morison, *Naval Operations*, vol. 11, p. 156.

12. Barnett, *Engage the Enemy*, pp. 830–31, and Morison, *Naval Operations*, vol. 11, p. 174.

13. Barnett, *Engage the Enemy*, pp. 831–32, and Morison, *Naval Operations*, vol. 11, pp. 324–25.

14. Erich Raeder, *Grand Admiral*, trans. H. W. Drexel (New York: Da Capo, reprint 2001), p. 375.

15. Ibid., p. 387.

16. The following narrrative is based on Dönitz, *Memoirs*, pp. 440–73.

17. William L. Shirer, *The Rise and Fall of the Third Reich* (New York: Simon and Schuster, 1960), p. 1132.

18. Ibid., p. 1138.

19. Dönitz, *Memoirs*, pp. 444–46.

20. Friedrich Ruge, *Der Seekrieg: The German Navy's Story, 1939–1945*, trans. M. G. Saunders (Annapolis, MD: Naval Institute Press, 1957), p. 27.

21. Dan van der Vat, *The Atlantic Campaign: World War II's Great Struggle at Sea* (New York: Harper's, 1988), pp. 311–12.

22. George Pollock, *The Jervis Bay* (London: Kimber, 1958), pp. 202–3.

23. Ibid., p. 7.

GLOSSARY

able seaman—an experienced seaman who can perform routine duties.

armed merchant cruiser—usually a passenger ship converted to use as a warship, mostly for patrol and/or escort duty.

barque (bark)—a sailing ship with three or four masts, square-rigged on all but the aft mast which mounted a gaff-rigged sail.

barquentine (barkentine)—much the same as a barque but usually smaller with auxiliary sails rigged between the masts.

battlecruiser—a warship with the speed of a cruiser and the guns (such as 15-inch) of a battleship. More lightly armored than the latter; e.g., HMS *Hood*.

battleship—the most heavily armored warship; carrying guns from 14-inch to 16-inch, multiple secondary guns from 4.1-inch to 6-inch, and many antiaircraft weapons. Displacements ranged from 32,000 to 50,000 tons.

beam—the side of a ship or its width; also, abeam—to the side.

boat deck—a deck level, usually on a passenger ship, where lifeboats are stored, often behind the funnel(s).

Bofors gun—1-, 2-, or 4-barrelled 40-mm antiaircraft gun, originally Swedish-made but licensed to several nations. Replaced the earlier pom-pom guns in the Royal Navy.

bow—the front or leading edge of a vessel.

bridge—the operational center of a ship, i.e., navigation, steering; transverse decking and housing built midship for those functions.

brig—a two-masted, square-rigged sailing vessel.

Coastal Command—a wing of the Royal Air Force that protected the waters around the British Isles, e.g., reconnaissance, antisubmarine patrols, and bombing missions against German installations along coastal France.

GLOSSARY

collier—a ship designed to carry coal.

corvette—a class of small escort ships mounting antisubmarine gear and light weaponry.

cruiser—long-range, high-speed warships of two types: (1) light cruisers, displacing 5,000–10,000 tons, mounting 6-inch guns; (2) heavy cruisers, displacing up to 10,000 tons, mounting 8-inch guns. Both carried additional lighter armaments.

davit—small curved cranes used to raise or lower lifeboats, pivoting in-board for storage, out-board for lowering.

degaussing—reducing a ship's magnetic field by placing electrified cables around the hull.

destroyer—in World War II, a fast ship displacing from 900 to 2,600 tons, mounting from four to ten guns ranging in caliber from 4-inch to 5-inch, together with torpedo tubes, numerous light antiaircraft guns, and antisubmarine gear. Uses: escort capital ships, convoys, fleet screening, reconnaissance, bombardment of shore installations.

dual-purpose gun—capable of firing at other ships or overhead aircraft.

ENIGMA—German code machine, looking like a typewriter. Operated with rotating cylinders so that the depression of one key sent an alternate letter that would not be repeated. Cylinders and their settings were regularly changed. See ULTRA.

fall—the rope of a block and tackle that raises or lowers small boats such as lifeboats. *See* davit.

fire control—the directing of gunfire, i.e., target selection, range, trajectory; the equipment used to calculate these.

first lord of the Admiralty—British cabinet appointment; syn.: secretary of the navy.

first sea lord—commander in chief of the Royal Navy.

flotilla—a group of naval ships usually of the same type, e.g., destroyer flotilla. The exact number of ships varies widely.

fo'c's'le (forecastle), also fo'c'sle—foremost section of the weather deck, often stepped up, just above and behind the bow. On older ships, the crew's sleeping quarters.

force (of wind)—measure of wind velocity by the Beaufort Scale, ranging from force 0 (calm) to force 12 and over for hurricanes.

freeboard—the part of a ship's hull above the waterline.

frigate—(1) the cruiser of sailing ships, characterized by long-range and speed, with guns on the weather deck and often on another deck below. Various riggings. (2) a modern escort ship, slightly smaller and more lightly armed than a destroyer; similar to a sloop.

gunwale or gun'el—the upper edge of a hull.

Handels-Stor-Kreuzer **(HSK)**—literally, a German merchant cruiser, usually a freighter, with disguised 5.9-inch guns, smaller weapons, perhaps torpedo tubes and/or mines. Also classified as auxiliary cruisers or disguised raiders.

Hilfskreuzer—armed merchant cruiser.

"Hoch der Kaiser"—(idiom) "Up the Kaiser" or "F—— the Kaiser." A phrase used toward the end of World War I.

GLOSSARY

HO—hostilities only. Royal Navy designation for conscripts or volunteers after 1939 who served only for the duration of the war.

Hotchkiss gun—a light machine gun firing rifle ammunition (.303 caliber).

Jacob's ladder—a rope or chain or wood-slatted ladder suspended over a ship's side.

knot—a nautical mile or 6,080.20 feet; the speed of a ship measured by how many knots covered in an hour.

Kriegsmarine—the name given the German Navy by Hitler in 1935; lit., war navy.

Kriegstagebuch—war diary; an official record kept by a commander.

laid down—the beginning of the building of a ship; laying the keel.

leading seaman—an experienced seaman capable of directing others.

letters of marque and reprisal—a government license issued to private investors for arming and provisioning a ship with which to capture and auction enemy commerce.

liberty ship—an American cargo ship of World War II. Prefabricated and mass produced, they displaced 10,000 tons. Reciprocating engines produced a speed of 9 knots.

lugger—any small multimasted sailing vessel.

ordinary seaman—an inexperienced seaman.

packet—a small ship used to carry light cargo, mail, and passengers on a regular route.

painter—a rope line used to secure a light craft to a larger vessel; or to secure several light craft together as a line of lifeboats.

panzer—armored.

panzerschiff—armored ship; syn.: with pocket battleship.

petty officer—a noncommissioned officer in the navy or merchant navy, much like a sergeant in the army.

pom-pom gun—British 4-barrelled 2-pounder (40-mm) antiaircraft gun.

poop—a small structure on the aft section of a ship; also poop deck.

Port—direction—the left side of a ship when facing forward.

Pounder—archaic—the weight of a projectile fired from a smooth bore cannon; mod.—British artillery designation, e.g., 2-pounder/40-mm; 6-pounder/57-mm.

privateer—a privately owned armed ship, sailing under government license for the purpose of capturing enemy shipping and profiting from the sale of both ship and cargo. See letters of marque and reprisal.

prize crew—the crew placed aboard a captured ship by a privateer or, during both world wars, by a regular warship or commerce raider.

Q-boat/ship—various types of vessels from trawlers to freighters that carried hidden weapons and were used to combat U-boats, mostly in World War I.

rating—Royal Navy enlisted personnel.

Reichsmarine—name of the German Navy under the Weimar Republic, 1918–1933.

RFR—Royal Fleet Reserve—A class of Royal Navy reservists. With the commissioning of merchant cruisers, those with army artillery background were sought.

salvo—the simultaneous or successive firing of a ship's guns, usually the main batteries.

schooner—two-to-four-masted sailing vessel with fore-and-aft sails (in line from bow to stern; contrast to square-rigged) on all masts.

scullion—kitchen worker.

scuttle—(1) when a crew purposely sinks its own ship; (2) an opening in a deck or in the side of a ship that is covered by a door, hatch, or lid; (3) sometimes portholes.

sea anchor—a drag dropped from the stern of a boat to keep the bow headed into the wind.

Sitzkrieg—literally, the sit-down war; referring to the nonaggression along the western front October 1939–May 1940.

sloop—(1) archaic—any vessel mounting fewer than twenty-four guns on a single deck; (2) a single-masted sailing vessel rigged with one mainsail and jibs forward; (3) mod.—a long-range escort vessel, slightly smaller and more lightly armed than a destroyer and similar to a modern frigate.

SS—*Schutzstaffel*—Hitler's bodyguard and later private army commanded by Heinrich Himmler; a.k.a. Black Shirts.

Starboard—direction—the right side of a vessel when facing forward.

Stern—the aft or rear part of a vessel.

Stoker—archaic—one who shovels coal into a steamship's furnaces; mod.—regulates oil flow into furnaces; syn.: with fireman.

U-boat—German submarine; abbreviation for *Unterseeboot.*

ULTRA—The British organization at the code and cypher school, Bletchley Park, developed to decript German ENIGMA messages. Their computer "Colossus" was built to produce complete and often instantaneous decipherments of German messages.

Wehrmacht—the regular German Army.

Windjammer—(1) a steel-hulled, three-masted sailing ship, the British answer to the American clipper ship; (2) any large square-rigged sailing ship.

SELECTED BIBLIOGRAPHY

WEB SITES

Cashmore, Steven. "HMS Jervis Bay" Armed Merchant Cruiser [Highland Archives]
www.internet-promotions.co.uk/archives/caithness/jervisbay.htm
Jervis Bay-Ross Memorial Park: www.saintjohn.nbcc.nb.ca/jervisbay/00nov5.htm

ARCHIVAL SOURCES

Freiburg, Bundesarchiv: RM 5/vols. 2237-2240, "Möwe," S.M. *Hilfskreuzer*; *Schriftwechsel und Zeitungen*; RM 87/2, *Führer der Uboote West Dönitz*, *Kriegrstagebuch—Unterlagen* 23.8.1939–31.7.1940, *Lagebetrachtungen, Einsatz, und Standorte der boote*; RM 92/5228, *Kriegstagebuch "Admiral Scheer"*; RM 100/70, *Kriegstagebuch "Thor"* (*Hilfskreuzer* 4, *Schiff* 10) 5.3.1940–31.5.1941; RM 100/75, *Vernichtung brit. Hilfskreuzer "Voltaire"—Gefetsbericht*, 4.4.41.

Kew, Richmond, Public Records Office: ADM 196/54, p. 8, "E. S. Fogarty Fegen"; ADM 199/725, "HMS *Rawalpindi*, Report of Proceedings, 23 November 1939"; ADM 234/322, "Battle Summary 5: The Chase and Sinking of the German Battleship *Bismarck*, 23–27 May 1941"; ADM 234/324, "Disguised Raiders, 1940–41"; CAB 27/476, "Report to the Committee of Imperial Defense Sub-Committee on Preparation for the League Disarmament Conference"; COS 310, "Annual Review, 1933"; COS 392, "Staff Report, January 1932."

Ottawa, Library and Archives of Canada: RG 24, Series D-1-a, vol. 5670: File 78-88-1, "Imperial Warships—HMS *Jervis Bay* general, 1941–1942"; File 78-88-6 "Imperial Warships—HMS *Jervis Bay*—Complement, 1941"; File 78-88-8, Imperial

Warships—HMS *Jervis Bay*—Repairs, 1940–41"; File 78-88-13, Imperial War-ships—HMS *Jervis Bay*—Compensation for Loss of Effects"; RG 24, Series D-10, vol. 11105, File 53-1-9 [commander in chief, Canadian Northwest Atlantic] "Armed Merchant Cruisers—Jervis Bay, 1940"; RG 24, vol. 4016, File 1057-106-11G and 1057-106-11GE, "*Prince David*: Guns and Gunnery-43"; vol. 6717, File 8000-412, "HMS *Prince David*, General Information, 1946–48"; vols. 7749–7750, "Armed Merchant Cruiser and Landing Ship (Infantry) *Prince David*, 10 December 1940–2 March 1945"; vol. 11665, File 700-2-39, Passage in Escort Vessels and AMCs, Outward, 1941"; Audio Tape 401113-1, Canadian Broadcasting Corporation, "Interview of *Jervis Bay* Survivors."

Washington, DC, U.S. National Archives: Office of Naval Intelligence [USN], Monograph Files, German Monographs (Record Group 38), Intelligence Re-port by Commander Ben H. Wyatt, Naval Attaché, Madrid, 11 December 1940, "Description of Raid on Convoy [HX-84] and Tactics Employed by Ves-sels of the Convoy."

NEWSPAPERS

London	*Illustrated London News*	1940
	The War Illustrated	1940
	Times	1930–1940
Manchester	*The Guardian*	1930–1940
Magazines	*Life*	1939–1940
	Time	1939–1940

BOOKS

Bacon, Reginald and F. E. McMurtie. *Modern Naval Strategy*. London: Frederick Muller, 1940.

Barnett, Correlli. *The Collapse of British Power*. New York: Morrow, 1972.

———. *Engage the Enemy More Closely: The Royal Navy in the Second World War*. New York: Norton, 1991.

Behrens, C.B.A. *Merchant Shipping and the Demands of War*. London: Longmans, Green, 1955.

Bekker, Cajus. *Defeat at Sea*. New York: Holt, 1955.

———. *Hitler's Naval War*. London: Macdonald, 1974.

Bennett, Geoffrey. *Battle of the River Plate*. London: Irwin Allen, 1972.

Brennecke, H. J. *Cruise of the Raider HK-33 [Pinguin]*. New York: Crowell, 1954.

Bridgland, Tony. *Sea Killers in Disguise: The Story of the Q Ships and Decoy Ships in the First World War*. Annapolis, MD: Naval Institute Press, 1999.

Chant, Christopher. *Encyclopedia of World Aircraft*. New York: Mallard, 1990.

Churchill, Winston. *The Second World War*. Vols. 1 and 2. Boston: Houghton Mif-flin, 1948, 1949.

SELECTED BIBLIOGRAPHY

De Conde, Alexander. *A History of American Foreign Policy.* New York: Scribner's, 1963.

Derry, T. K. *The Campaign in Norway: History of the Second World War.* London: HMSO, reprint 1953.

Dönitz, Karl. *Memoirs: Ten Years and Twenty Days.* Trans. R. H. Stevens. New York: Da Capo, reprint 1997.

Dorr, Manfred. *Die Ritterkreuztrager der Uberwassser-streitkrefte der Kriegsmarine.* Vol. 1. Osnabruck: Biblio Verlag, 1995.

Duffy, James P. *Hitler's Secret Pirate Fleet.* Westport, CT: Praeger, 2001.

Ellis, L. F. *The War in France and Flanders, 1939–1940: History of the Second World War.* London: HMSO, reprint 1953.

Fleming, Peter. *Operation Sea Lion.* New York: Simon and Schuster, 1957.

Forester, C. S. *The Age of Fighting Sail: The Story of the Naval War of 1812.* Garden City, NY: Doubleday, 1956.

Fuehrer Conferences on Naval Affairs, 1939–1945. Annapolis, MD: Naval Institute Press, 1990.

Garrett, Richard. *Scharnhorst and Gneisenau: The Elusive Sisters.* London: David and Charles, 1978.

Gibson, Charles. *The Ship with Five Names.* London: Abelard-Schuman, 1965.

Gilbert, Martin. *The First World War.* New York: Holt, 1994.

———, ed. *The Churchill War Papers.* Vol. 1. New York: Norton, 1993.

———, ed. *The Churchill War Papers.* Vol. 3. London: Heinemann, 2000.

Gray, Edwyn. *Hitler's Battleships.* Annapolis, MD: Naval Institute Press, 1999.

Grenfell, Russell. *The Bismarck Episode.* London: Faber and Faber, 1948.

Grove, Eric J. *The Price of Disobedience.* Annapolis, MD: Naval Institute Press, 2001.

Hague, Arnold. *The Allied Convoy System, 1939–1945.* Annapolis, MD: Naval Institute Press, 2000.

Halder, Franz. *The Halder War Diary, 1939–1942.* Eds. Charles Burdick and H. A. Jacobsen. Novato, CA: Presidio Press, 1988.

Hawkins, Nigel. *Starvation Blockades: The Naval Blockades of World War I.* Annapolis, MD: Naval Institute Press, 2003.

Horsman, Reginald. *The War of 1812.* New York: Knopf, 1969.

Hoyt, Edwin. *The Phantom Raider [Möwe].* New York: Crowell, 1969.

———. *Raider-16 [Atlantis].* New York: World, 1970.

Hughes, Terry, and John Costello. *The Battle of the Atlantic.* New York: Dial, 1977.

Jackson, Melvin. *Privateers in Charleston, 1793–1796.* Washington, DC: Smithsonian, 1969.

Jackson, Robert. *The German Navy in World War II.* London: Brown Books, 1999.

Jane's Fighting Aircraft of World War II. New York: Crescent, reprint 1992.

Jane's Fighting Ships of World War II. New York: Crescent, reprint 1989.

Jesse, F. Tennyson. *The Saga of the San Demetrio.* London: HMSO, 1942.

Keegan, John. *The Second World War.* New York: Viking, 1990.

Kemp, Peter. *The Escape of the Scharnhorst and Gneisenau.* London: Irwin Allen, 1975.

———. *Decision at Sea: The Convoy Escorts.* New York: Elsevier-Dutton, 1978.

SELECTED BIBLIOGRAPHY

Kennedy, Ludovic. *Pursuit: The Chase and Sinking of the Bismarck*. London: Collins, 1974.

Kennedy, Paul M. *The Rise and Fall of British Naval Mastery*. London: Alien Lane, 1976.

Koop, Gerhard. *Pocket Battleships of the Deutschland Class*. Annapolis, MD: Naval Institute Press, 2000.

Kraig, Walter, et al. *Battle Report: The Atlantic War*. New York: Farrar and Rinehart, 1946.

Krancke, Theodor, and H. J. Brennecke. *Pocket Battleship: The Story of the Admiral Scheer*. London: Kimber, 1958.

Law, D. *The Royal Navy in World War II*. London: Greenhill, 1988.

Little, George. "Privateering," in Jon E. Lewis, ed., *Life before the Mast*. London: Constable and Robinson, 2000, pp. 395–415.

Lukacs, John. *Five Days in London: May 1940*. New Haven: Yale University Press, 1999.

Macintyre, Donald. *The Naval War against Hitler*. New York: Scribner's, 1971.

MacLiesh, Fleming, and M. Krieger. *The Privateers*. New York: Random House, 1962.

MacPherson, Ken, and John Burgess. *The Ships of Canada's Naval Forces, 1910–1981*. Toronto: Collins, 1981.

Martienssen, Anthony. *Hitler and His Admirals*. New York: Dutton, 1949.

Millington-Drake, E., ed. *The Drama of the Graf Spee and the Battle of the River Plate: A Documentary Anthology*. London: Peter Davies, 1964.

Milner, Marc. *North Atlantic Run: The Royal Canadian Navy and the Battle of the Convoys*. Toronto, Canada: University of Toronto Press, 1985.

Morison, Samuel. *History of United States Naval Operations in World War II*. Vols. 1, 10, and 11. Boston: Little, Brown, reprint 1961.

Mosley, Leonard. *On Borrowed Time: How World War II Began*. New York: Random House, 1969.

Muggenthaler, August K. *German Raiders of World War II*. Englewood Cliffs, NJ: Prentice-Hall, 1977.

Müllenheim-Rechberg, Burkard Baron von. *Battleship Bismarck: A Survivor's Story*. Trans. Jack Sweetman. Annapolis, MD: Naval Institute Press, 1980.

Peden, G.C. *British Rearmament and the Treasury*. Edinburgh, Scotland: Scottish Academic Press, 1979.

Pollock, George. *The Jervis Bay*. London: Kimber, 1958.

Poolman, Kenneth. *Armed Merchant Cruisers: Their Epic Story*. London: Leo Cooper/Seckert and Warburg, 1985.

Powell, Michael. *Graf Spee*. London: Hodder and Stoughton, 1956.

Raeder, Erich. *Grand Admiral*. Trans. H. W. Drexel. New York: Da Capo, reprint 2001. Previously titled: *My Life*, 1960.

Ranft, Bryan, ed. *Technical Change and Naval Policy, 1860–1939*. London: Hodder and Stoughton, 1977.

Robertson, Terrence. *Channel Dash*. New York: Dutton, 1958.

Rohmer, J., and G. Hummelchen. *Chronology of the War at Sea*. Vol. 1, 1939–1942. Trans. D. Masters. New York: Arco, 1972.

Roskill, Stephen. *The War at Sea, 1939–1945*. 3 vols. London: HMSO, 1954, 1956, 1960.

———. *Naval Policy between the Wars*. Vol. 1. London: Collins, 1968.

———. *Churchill and the Admirals*. New York: Morrow, 1978.

Ruge, Friedrich. *Der Seekrieg: The German Navy's Story, 1939–1945*. Trans. M. G. Saunders. Annapolis, MD: Naval Institute Press, 1957.

Schalenbach, Paul. *German Raiders*. Annapolis, MD: Naval Institute Press, 1979.

Shirer, William L. *The Rise and Fall of the Third Reich*. New York: Simon and Schuster, 1960.

Swanson, Carl. *Predators and Prizes: American Privateering and Imperial Warfare, 1739–1748*. Columbia: University of South Carolina Press, 1991.

Taylor, A.J.P. *The Origins of the Second World War*. New York: Atheneum, 1962.

Taylor, Edmund. *The Fall of the Dynasties*. Garden City, NY: Doubleday, 1963.

Thomas, Lowell. *Count Luckner: The Sea Devil*. Garden City, NY: Doubleday, 1927.

van der Vat, Dan. *Gentlemen of War: The Amazing Story of Captain Karl von Müller and the SMS Emden*. New York: Morrow, 1983.

———. *The Atlantic Campaign: World War II's Great Struggle at Sea*. New York: Harper's, 1988.

Warlimont, Walter. *Inside Hitler's Headquarters*. Trans. R. H. Barry. New York: Praeger, 1964.

Whitley, M. J. *German Capital Ships of World War Two*. London: Arms and Armour, 1989.

Williams, Gomer. *The Liverpool Privateers*. London: Heinemann, 1897.

INDEX

About the Author

BRUCE ALLEN WATSON is Professor Emeritus of Art History and History at Diablo Valley College. He is the author of seven books, including *Exit Rommel: The Tunisian Campaign* (Praeger, 1999) and *Sieges: A Comparative Study* (Praeger, 1993).